Germans against Hitler

TERENCE PRITTIE

with a foreword by Hugh Trevor-Roper

Germans

against

Hitler

with photographs

An Atlantic Monthly Press Book

LITTLE, BROWN AND COMPANY · Boston · Toronto

The author wishes to thank the following for permission to use excerpts from copy-
righted material:

Excerpts from *20 July* by Constantine FitzGibbon, copyright © 1956, by Constantine
FitzGibbon, are reprinted by permission of the publisher, W. W. Norton & Company,
Inc., New York, New York. First published in the United States in 1956.

Excerpts from *The Rise and Fall of the Third Reich* by William L. Shirer, copyright ©
1959, 1960 by William L. Shirer, are reprinted by permission of the publisher, Simon
and Schuster, Inc., New York.

Extracts from *The Nemesis of Power,* by Sir John Wheeler-Bennett, 1964 edition,
are reprinted by permission of the publisher, St. Martin's Press, Inc., New York, and
Macmillan & Co., Ltd., London.

The photographs of Beck, Leber, Goerdeler, Stauffenberg and Bonhoeffer appeared
in *Das Gewissen steht auf* by Annedore Leber, published by Verlag Annedore Leber,
who kindly gave permission for their use in this book.

To those brave German men and women who gave their lives to the cause of freedom and humanity, and also to those survivors who have helped me to write this book.

contents

illustrations

Germans against Hitler

foreword

When Hitler was appointed Chancellor of Germany in January 1933 he had a career of violence behind him and he had promised, explicitly, that his rule would be tyrannical and vindictive: 'heads will roll in the sand'. It might be hoped, and optimists did hope, that these threats were mere bluster and that, once in power, the gangster would turn to constructive politics. But the omens were not good, and in 1934, after the old German parties had meekly dissolved themselves in his favour, Hitler gave conclusive evidence that his rule was not merely violent but criminal. In order to disembarrass himself of inconvenient allies, the legal Chancellor of Germany, disposing of the whole police and judicial system of the country, had several hundreds of his fellow-citizens murdered without evidence, charge or trial. And, to the astonishment of the civilized world, German society not only acquiesced in this brutal slaughter, unparalleled since the Massacre of St. Bartholomew; it applauded. The President thanked the Chancellor, though a previous Chancellor, appointed by him, was among the victims. The Vice-Chancellor, whose two assistants had been murdered, continued to serve their murderer. The German Army obediently swore an illegal oath of personal allegiance to its bloodstained master. And the German people, on the next opportunity, emphatically confirmed his régime.

The Blood-Bath of June 30, 1934, set the tone for Hitler's rule. It showed that it was not only a dictatorship, but a criminal dictatorship. It also showed that German society, at all levels, accepted such a dictatorship. For ten years of repression, aggression, violence, murder and war, no visible conspiracy or revolt threatened it. This in itself is unparalleled in history. Only on July 20, 1944, when the defeat of Germany was already in sight, did a group of officers attempt to assassinate Hitler. They failed; and Hitler, having wreaked a terrible revenge on his enemies at home, exposed his country to final defeat and perhaps permanent partition by its enemies abroad.

This extraordinary lack of German opposition to Hitler inevitably aroused the astonishment, even the contempt, of foreigners. Why did nobody, as it seemed, stand up against the dictatorship until it was plainly about to be defeated in war? In their contempt, Allied observers did less than justice to the 'men of 20th July' who, it then seemed, having fought for Hitler as long as there seemed a chance of victory, were now turning against him only to escape the fulness of defeat. And this contempt was not lessened when the Allies entered Germany and heard from every double-dyed Nazi official whom they arrested that he was really 'a member of the Resistance'. The German Resistance, it seemed, having been non-existent so long as there was something to resist, sprang to life when it was no longer necessary, as a dishonest alibi.

Such contempt for the German Resistance was natural in 1945. But now that twenty years have passed, we can adopt a more critical view, and find that it must also be a more generous view. Time has winnowed the false resisters from the true, and the very magnitude of their task, while it explains their failure, illustrates the heroism of the few men and women who seriously sought to oppose Nazism and to create an alternative to it. For that alternative had to be not merely an alternative government, or even an alternative system of government but a new morality. In a healthy society, a poisonous growth can be cut out; but when a whole society is diseased, the cure must be more radical. It must also start from a narrower basis: a basis which must lie not in this or that class or party, but in the individual.

For any study of the German Resistance must start with this admission. Attempts have been made to represent certain sections of the German population, certain organized bodies, as anti-Nazi. These attempts are vain. The Catholic Church has its individual heroes and martyrs, but as an institution its record is of early and eager compliance. The Protestant Churches, if they can look back to a great individual defiance, the defiance of the human conscience

—*hier stehe ich, ich kann nicht anders*—have a record also of collective subservience to the state. The Centre Party, the party of Stresemann and Bruening, now re-formed as the party of Adenauer and Erhard, voted for Hitler's dictatorial powers and then committed an ignominious suicide. The Socialists, if they resisted with their votes, accepted the same ultimate fate. The Communist Party, which produced some of the toughest organizers of resistance, was, for two vital years, the most shameless of Hitler's accomplices.

All these collective compliances can be explained. We can refer to the defeat of 1918, the inflation of 1923, the depression of 1929, the lack of a positive democratic tradition in Germany. All these had undermined any firm liberal convictions; and to men without such convictions, or to aggregates of men who are bound together rather by gross general interests than by refined scruples, Hitler offered more than they could resist. To every class of Germans he offered something: markets, employment, land, status, self-assurance, revenge. Only individuals could bring themselves to say that these benefits were being offered at too high a price. Unfortunately, in politics, individuals cannot operate effectively unless they can mobilize class-interests. Hitler himself was an individual. He had mobilized the German classes for his programme. He had mobilized their interests, and also their weaknesses. How could other individuals outbid him when they could only appeal to moral principles which had been so successfully undermined?

The failure of such an attempt might seem pre-determined. Fortunately, even in Germany, there were some individuals who were resolved, nevertheless, to make the attempt. 'The desire to oppose Hitler', says Mr. Prittie, 'was built up out of every sort of instinct, ingrained belief, emotion or even prejudice'. There were conservatives and radicals, Catholics and Protestants, soldiers and civilians. Some of them were activists who believed that positive revolution or assassination was essential to change the government of Germany. The greatest, most striking, most captivating of them was Claus von Stauffenberg, at once the brain and the hand of the conspiracy of July 20, 1944. Others believed that assassination was not enough, or might even be wrong. They believed that no mere change of government would cure the evils which, in Germany, had produced Hitler and, what was even more shameful, the compliance with Hitler. They believed that, whatever happened in politics, the Christian virtues must be revived in society, a new *élite* created on a new, moral basis, and plans laid for the future. In 1945, as we looked back on the ruinous years of war, these men—the Kreisau group of Helmuth von Moltke, the Catholic and Protestant martyrs —seemed ineffective. Today we can see that they were no less necessary than the activists. In the end, modern Germany owes even more to them.

For in fact, as nobody could have guessed in 1945, the memory of the German Resistance has triumphed over the memory of Nazism. In spite of defeat and the neuroses of defeat, the neo-Nazism which was so often prophesied in 1945 has not appeared. The post-1945 generation in Germany, unlike the post-1918 generation, does not listen to the shrill voice of resentment and revenge. On the contrary, it turns with respect to those few who, however vainly, opposed Hitler. The attempt of the old Nazis to brand the 'men of 20th July' as traitors failed. They have been recognized as the truer patriots. The young Germans of today believe that the generation of their fathers failed them. They look with respect not to the conformists but to the non-conformists of the Nazi age.

This book is an account of those non-conformists and of their work and ideas. Mr. Prittie was for many years the correspondent of the *Guardian* in Germany. He knows post-war Germany as few other men do, and has studied it, and written about it, both critically and sympathetically. His criticism, which has involved him in occasional trouble (the inevitable reward of an independent mind), is a guarantee that his sympathy is well based. In this book it is eloquently expressed. And it is expressed in a good cause. I can think of no Germans who so well deserve to be remembered as some of these genuine members of the Resistance who not only refused, at a terrible cost, to bow before the grim, apparently invincible Leviathan of the twentieth century, but also gave to their successors a redeeming example: Tresckow and Stauffenberg, Moltke and Leber, the Catholic priests Alfred Delp and Provost Lichtenberg, the Protestant bishops Wurm and Meiser, the Protestant pastor Paul Schneider, and the young idealists of the 'White Rose'.

Hugh Trevor-Roper

one

Opposing Hitler

'Who shoots at the midday sun, though he be sure that he shall never hit the mark; yet as sure he is he shall shoot higher than who aims but at a bush.'

SIR PHILIP SIDNEY, *Eclogues*

WHY is so little known outside Germany of the German Opposition to Hitler? One reason may be that a great many people outside Germany believed Hitler's propaganda, and therefore believed the 99 per cent 'Yes-vote' figures put out by Dr. Josef Goebbels, Hitler's Minister of Propaganda, whenever a Nazi-organized referendum was held. To believe these figures was to assume the virtually unanimous support of Hitler by the German people.

Another reason is more indirect. So much has been written about the resistance movements in European countries occupied by the Germans that the very idea of resistance to Hitler has become identified with those countries—Poland, Holland, Belgium, Norway, Jugoslavia and, above all, France. How should one equate whatever opposition existed in Germany with European resistance movements which produced brilliant guerilla actions and even pitched battles? French, Belgian and other heroes abounded. But could there be German heroes too?

There have been very few books dealing with the German Opposition to Hitler in the English language. There have been a great many in German, but their fault has often been that they have given no clear picture of the scope, the composition and the aims of the German Opposition. It has almost been as if their authors have feared to make even the attempt to put the German Opposition into its historical context.

15

In America and Britain, to name only two countries outside Germany, inveterate critics of the German people—like the Beaverbrook Press in Britain and the Prevent World War III group in America—have lost no opportunity of playing down the part of the German Opposition. Their attitude has been that only a very few Germans—most of them disgruntled Generals—tried in any way to oppose Hitler, and that they did so only when it became plain that Germany was losing the war. Opposition, in fact, was restricted to the 1944 bomb plot, and that plot began to be hatched only after the shattering German defeat at Stalingrad at Christmas, 1942.

This, for instance, was the view of a restrained critic in Britain of Hitler's German opponents. In a book review written for one of Britain's daily newspapers he offered this opinion: 'However much we admire von Stauffenberg [whose bomb nearly killed Hitler on July 20, 1944], we should remember that he, like the others, fought hard for Hitler, until his madness was evident to all, and until it was obvious that he was bent on the destruction of the German Army as well as of the German people.'

Lord Birkenhead's diction is urbane but obscure. Did Stauffenberg fight for Hitler? History will probably decide that he fought for his country. Did he wait until Hitler's 'madness was evident to all'? On the contrary, he sought to destroy Hitler at a time when the mass of the German people, willy-nilly, continued to follow their Fuehrer. Was it 'obvious' that Hitler was 'bent on the destruction of the German Army' in July 1944? Nothing of the sort; Hitler was ready to risk German lives recklessly and in the superstitious belief in his own 'star', but he still hoped to win the war and leave the German Army as the military arbiter of the Old World. Did the German Opposition to Hitler, in any case, consist only of a 'few generals', and did they begin to oppose him only in 1944? The answer to both questions is 'No'.

Views like those that I have quoted suggested to me that the efforts of Hitler's German opponents—either to tumble him from power, or to help his victims, or just to defend their beliefs—should be set down baldly and factually, and without bias or emotion. They should also be put into some kind of historical perspective—not least because the difficulties of resisting a dictator are so great. This point seems to elude most of those ready critics who are obsessed by the fact that Hitler was eventually to die by his own hand, and only after Nazi Germany had reduced European civilization to chaos. And the after-effects of opposition to Hitler have been considerable inside Germany; Fabian von Schlabrendorff, one of Hitler's most daring and persistent enemies, believes that it will be 'like the Reformation, a subject of furious debate for hundreds of years'.

There are other reasons, of course, for writing about Hitler's German opponents—for I prefer this way of describing them to the loose, generic and largely misleading term of 'resistance movement'. One cogent reason is that far too much stress has been laid by foreign commentators on the 'failure' of Hitler's opponents. In his *Course of German History* A. J. P. Taylor, for instance, claims that 'good' Germans are really only people who 'obtrude into every discussion of the German question, their "goodness" being synonymous with their ineffectiveness'. Taylor adds that the historian 'cannot deal with the politically impotent except in so far as their dead weight is thrown into the scale by more agile and positive forces'. One wonders what SS. Matthew, Mark, Luke and John were wasting their time over; or were they the 'more agile and positive forces' which could redeem Christ's manifest political impotence?

It seems to me that this is a one-sided view of history. For ideas have an intrinsic value, which should not be subjected to arbitrary definition. Their long-term significance cannot always be assessed at the time that they were produced. This is true of the ideas of Hitler's German opponents.

Largely in a condemnatory vein was an article written by R. T. Clark in the *Manchester Guardian* of May 30, 1947, on the subject of Hitler's German opponents. It was entitled 'An Ineffectual Counter-Revolution'. In it Clark made some useful points—the generals who played the biggest part in active and constructive opposition to Hitler were interested first and foremost in saving the German Army, and through the German Army their country as a whole; and they and other enemies of Hitler were 'lamed' by the British and French policy of appeasing the Nazis. Clark was right, too, when he wrote that the Nazi regime could be overset by conspiracy but not by revolution. This was a point underlined time and again by, among others, Dr. George Bell, the Anglican Bishop of Chichester, who came into close contact during the war with Hitler's opponents. His phrase was: 'There was opposition to Hitler, of one kind and another, from 1933 onwards. But there is little scope for an armed revolution in a police state.'

But Clark, too, did not want to accord due credit to Hitler's opponents. He said that it was 'characteristic' that the civilians among them relied on the soldiers to carry out the main conspiracy —which came to a head in July 1944. Is that fair? It was not so much characteristic as inevitable; the conspiracy, in order to be successful, required detailed planning for the period *after* Hitler had been disposed of. It required physical power into the bargain. Only the armed forces could have implemented concrete plans; only they might have been able to prevent a furious, catastrophic civil war.

Clark, again, expressed surprise that the generals were hesitating to act against Hitler in 1943 and 1944. Was it really at all surprising that they did so hesitate? Their country was fighting a battle to the death against a large part of the Western world and the massive armies of the Soviet Union. The average general—the average German, for that matter—believed that Germany's defeat by the Soviet Union would mean the virtual extinction of the Reich. In the event they were perfectly right, and in the circumstances it was not surprising that they hesitated. It was far more surprising that they finally acted against the head of the German State, in contravention of their sworn oath of fealty to him, and with the Communist foe at their gates.

Clark saw the Opposition to Hitler as 'an upper-class revolution' (a curious description in that he himself admitted that a revolution was not even feasible against a perfectly functioning dictatorship). Well, the 'upper classes' certainly played a big part in what took place. But this has been generally true of any successful major movement in Western Europe, directed against constituted authority. Cromwell and his generals were members of the landowning gentry in England; but Wat Tyler's Peasant Revolt failed. Even among the French revolutionary leaders were the Marquis de Lafayette, the Marquis de Mirabeau, the Abbé Sièyés, Talleyrand, the ex-Bishop of Autun, and Phillipe Egalité, the Duke of Orléans.

The so-called 'upper class' has a way of leading. This is a habit produced by education, self-confidence, personality and the ability to command. The leaders among Hitler's opponents were largely men of this kind, but they included as well men of more 'humble' origin, socialists and workers, Communists, students and simple clergymen. In this Opposition were the seeds of a truly national movement, but there was never a chance that such a movement could come to fruition in a few years. History was moving, during the twelve-year Nazi era which was intended by Hitler to be prolonged into a '1,000-year Reich', at a hand-gallop. Hitler's opponents had to act before their country was overwhelmed by its enemies. A popular and national movement never had a chance to mature.

In a strictly material sense, of course, Hitler's German opponents failed. After the climax of the July 1944 conspiracy a great deal of the resistance to the Nazis crumbled away. After July 1944, for instance, no German general seems to have thought in other terms than of fighting on until the war should end (a minor exception was the resourceful General von Choltitz, who refused to carry out a scorched-early policy in Paris and, in defiance of Hitler's orders, surrendered the city in order to avoid needless carnage). Hitler's conservative opponents were morally and mentally crushed by the failure to kill him. All of their leaders were either captured or murdered by the Nazis. An 'élite cadre' was swept away.

Here and there, after July 1944, socialist and Communist 'cells' of resistance were maintained. Here and there, the individual member of one or other of the Christian Churches continued to speak his mind. But the defeat in 1944 of Hitler's opponents—who were tortured, tried and hounded to death in their hundreds—was superficially as total as the defeat of their country less than one year later. There was one outstanding difference. Hitler's opponents, even from their cells and from the dock, continued to assert the sense and purity of their intentions, whereas in 1945 the great mass of the German people descended into a black pit of abasement, self-reproach, shame and despair.

Too much should not be made of material failure. Twice at least Hitler's most active opponents came within an ace of killing him, and on half a dozen other occasions they were robbed by fortuitous circumstances of the chance of doing so. Moreover, those who participated in the July 1944 culmination of opposition believed that it was their duty to act, irrespective of whether their action was successful. Germany's good name had somehow to be won back.

19

This was why the leader of the 1944 conspiracy, Stauffenberg, said: 'It must be done, *coute que coute*'. His leading Social Democratic supporter, Julius Leber, when asked what the chances were of over-throwing Hitler, replied: 'I don't know, and it doesn't make any difference. I have only one head to lose. I know of no better cause than this for which to risk it.'

And Major-General von Tresckow, a few hours after the 1944 conspiracy had failed, had this to say: 'Now everyone will turn upon us and cover us with abuse. But my conviction remains unshaken—we have done the right thing. Hitler is not only the arch-enemy of Germany, he is the arch-enemy of the whole world. In a few hours' time I shall stand before God, answering for my actions and my omissions. I think I shall be able to uphold with a clear conscience all that I have done in the fight against Hitler. . . . The worth of a man is certain only if he is prepared to sacrifice his life for his convictions.'

Too much, I say, should not be made of material failure. In the final version of the statement of Hitler's opponents—which was to have been broadcast to the German nation of July 20, 1944, had the conspirators succeeded in seizing the radio stations in Berlin—occurred this passage:

'Let us once again tread the path of justice, decency and mutual respect! In this spirit each of us will do his duty. Let us follow earnestly and in everything we do the commands of God which are engraved on our conscience, even when they seem hard to us; let us do everything to heal wounded souls and alleviate suffering. Only then can we create the basis for a sure future for our people within a family of nations filled with confidence, sound work and peaceful feelings.'

The phrase to remember here is 'the basis for a sure future for our people'. The opponents of Hitler, whatever the nuances of their views and plans, did want a genuinely 'sure future' for Germany. This, ultimately, was the root, the heart, the very essence of their struggle.

It may seem to readers of this book that in the pages which follow there are too many oblique or direct references—in connection with the men and women who opposed Hitler—to Christ's sufferings on the Cross. No reference of such a kind has been made in a spirit of inconsequence, let alone of blasphemy. There is no direct parallel between the sufferings of our Lord and those of any human being. Yet references of this sort may not be altogether out of place. The Germans who opposed Hitler had, very often, little hope of earthly profit or recognition. What they did was done at the dictates of their consciences. They were labelled when they died as traitors to their country. Christ, for that matter, was labelled by such of his contemporaries who did not believe in him merely as an astonishingly pigheaded minor prophet who set himself up as a Messiah and offended the Roman overlords of Palestine. The Germans who opposed Hitler shared at least one characteristic with Christ's earliest followers— the readiness to sacrifice their lives.

They sacrificed them—quite plainly—for the ideal of freedom (the only exception, in Western eyes, is the Communist Opposition to Hitler) and for the good of their country and their fellow-men. How far this is true, and how far-reaching opposition to Hitler really was, will be explained in this book. It does not set out to be a history and it has not been written by a historian. But if it can tell a true story, and fit the German Opposition into the huge, often murky and frightening canvas of German history, the author will be well satisfied.

two

The Mood of Germany in 1933

'Our enemies have gained the upper hand in Germany. The so-called national parties, the fanatics of Germanism, are strutting about in their overbearing conceit, as ridiculous as they are coarse. They dream that their turn at playing the leading role in world history has arrived and that they will gather all the lost German tribes from east and west to the fold of German nationalism.'

HEINRICH HEINE *in a letter to a friend in the middle of the nineteenth century*

A GREAT many historians have already examined the origins of Nazism and the reasons that the Nazis were able to seize power in 1933. These reasons have been set out in scores of books, many of them by Germans who have been less interested in analysing historical causes than in explaining the innocence of the great bulk of the German people. Nobody has been able to state with any certainty what was the most potent single reason for the Nazis' success, and this will remain for ever a subject of debate. Germans have generally been inclined to attribute it to circumstances, non-Germans to the curiosities of the German character and of Germany's development as a nation after 1870. A great many Germans, again, regard the Nazi era as an isolated episode in German history. Non-Germans have, on the whole, tended to see it as the final stage in the tempestuous growth of German nationalism, on which was superimposed a pre-1914 mood of national arrogance and a post-1919 mood of national frustration.

Nobody, at any rate, will deny that economic factors had much to do with the growth of Nazism. In the 1920s the sudden staggering inflation of the German currency wiped out the small man's savings and badly shook his already uncertain allegiance to the Weimar Republic. There followed the world economic crisis. By 1932 an estimated 15,000,000 Germans, or over 20 per cent of the population, were living on or below the breadline, drawing unemployment pay of fifty-one marks (then £3 5s.) a month, supplemented by small, irregular earnings. This was materially the rock-bottom point, until then, of the last 150 years of German history. The German worker could often no longer afford even the price of a glass of beer, and the German worker was probably even more demoralized by lack of work.

Before this period of bleak economic want there had been five years of intermittent civil and frontier warfare (1918–23), followed by a slow but steady decline of confidence in the political efficacy of the Weimar Republic which was set up when the Kaiser, Wilhelm II, fled into Holland at the end of World War I. This decline of public confidence led in turn to the fragmentation (*Zersplitterung*) of political parties and to the same sort of political impotence which displayed itself in the France of 1945–55. By their quarrels, indecision and inability to compromise with one another the 'orthodox' parties of the centre and 'moderate' right and left rendered the formation of stable administrations increasingly difficult. This led in turn to the growth of the parties of the extreme right and left wings, the Nazis and the Communists. The decaying apple of the Weimar Republic was left without a core. Political disintegration opened the road for Hitler.

There were other less evident but equally destructive influences at work during the fifteen-year life of the Weimar Republic. One was the disastrous decline of German liberalism. It is questionable whether the majority of Germans—and this has been proved true again since 1945—ever understood what liberalism was about. They seemed to have assumed in the past that it was a moderately useful, certainly not inexpendable, adjunct to man's theoretical political thought. It did not occur to them that it was a way of life, a code of behaviour and an attitude towards one's fellow-men. The so-called liberals of the post-1945 Free Democratic Party in Western Germany have often declared quite openly that liberalism was helpful in forming German thought in the nineteenth century but that the turn of the century ended any need for its further development in the hearts of the people. Nearly twenty years after the end of World

War II it is possible to say that Germans are only just beginning to appreciate the value of a liberal way of thought and life and to realize that this concept has still not rooted itself in the minds and behaviour of the vast majority of the German community.

In his recently published and admirable book *The Mind of Germany* Hans Kohn has explained how the almost total absence of the liberal outlook in Germany produced right-wing nationalists and left-wing Marxists who were anti-liberal and anti-Western, and who developed their own trend towards political nihilism. There were right-wingers like Hans Zehrer (since the war the editor of the leading German daily newspaper *Die Welt*) and Ernst von Salomon, who wrote in 1930: 'If there is a power whose destruction it is our task to accomplish by any means, it is the West and the German class that has allowed itself to be alienated by it.'

There were philosophers like Ernst Juenger, who glorified total war as an expression of the life-force of the immensely virile Teutonic race. Juenger was intent on preparing the German people for a new war, and in the late 1920s and early 1930s was writing this sort of rubbish: 'When the last men of a ship sunk in battle go down with a hurrah and flying flags, then a radiant transfiguration spreads over the waves, as infinite and eternal as the sea itself. And even if they went down for a cause which children ridicule, we must weep and be proud at the same time'; or: 'The face which looks from under the steel helmet . . . has changed. . . . It has become more metallic, its surface . . . galvanized, the bones stand out clearly, the features are sparse and tense. The gaze is calm and fixed, trained to observe things which can only be perceived in a state of fast movement. . . . We see here develop a kind of élite regiment, a new backbone.'

Oswald Spengler's *Decay of the West* exercised an even more baneful influence than anything written by picaresque literateurs like Salomon or by war-worshippers like Juenger. Spengler preached the virtues of 'hardness, a bold scepticism, a class of socialist mastermen'. He believed in a 'new Prussian socialism', in traditionalism allied to a ruthless spirit of progress, in the harshness of life and the necessity of struggle. He thought that the West was doomed by the immutable force of history which only seers like himself could sense and interpret. A similar intellectual arrogance, bordering on insanity, dominated the thinking of many otherwise rational Germans of the

24

1915–45 period. Spengler's concepts of power, doom and an un-regenerate life-force must have made a considerable contribution to Hitler's belief in himself as the agent of the Apocalypse. Even Thomas Mann, venerated today by Germans and non-Germans alike, produced such gems of inanity as: 'The German soul is opposed to the pacifist ideal of civilization, for is not peace an element of civil corruption?'

Basically more operative than the theories of Spengler and Juenger was the ever more ingrained German veneration of the power of the State. During the nineteenth-century quest for German national unity the belief strengthened—particularly in Prussia—that the individual should, in serving the State, be prepared to sacrifice his ideas as well as his selfish interests. Bismarck's 'blood and iron' slogan was a genuine expression of his political belief, but Bismarck was in addition profoundly contemptuous of public opinion and of the constitution. In order to unite Germany, the Prussian State had to be strong. Bismarck's corollary—partly inspired by his fanatical hatred of liberalism—was that the State, in a unified Germany, must remain dominant and the sole repository of political power.

The power of the State found its crowning symbol in the person of the 'All-Highest', the Kaiser (or German Emperor). In one of his wilder letters Kaiser Wilhelm II explained in 1898 that 'there is only *one real Kaiser* in the world, and that is the *German Kaiser*, not through his personality or his special qualifications, but through the right of the millenary tradition; and his Chancellor has to *obey*!' The collapse of the German Imperial regime in 1918 was a deep psychological shock to many Germans. For them the Weimar Re-public was never an adequate substitute. Nazism, on the other hand, gave them the chance of rededicating themselves to the State.

What made these various negative German tendencies—the extinction of the liberal outlook, the surrender of the individual to the State, the serious attention given to arrogant, offensive, pseudo-patriotic claptrap—so crystallize in the 1930s as to impel the German nation along its road to ruin? I believe that this crystallization was due most of all to the nation-wide belief that the Treaty of Versailles was a brutal and unfair piece of trickery perpetrated on a German people which was temporarily deprived of the ability to resist. Versailles was bitterly resented by all Germans—by socialists, workers and intellectuals as well as by nationalistic conservatives and the officer caste. It was as much resented by Hitler's opponents as by the Nazis, and virtually all Germans supposed that the Treaty had been imposed on a fighting race which had not really lost the war.

Shortly after the end of World War I a British general, Sir Neill Malcolm, asked Field Marshal Erich Ludendorff, Germany's best general in 1914–18: 'Are you trying to tell me you were stabbed in the back?' And Ludendorff, allegedly, answered in a state of high excitement: 'That's it! I was—stabbed in the back!' This was the official birth of the 'stab in the back' legend, but even before this, on December 11, 1918, the first President of the Weimar Republic, Friedrich Ebert, welcomed the returning German troops at the Brandenburg Gate in Berlin with the words: 'I salute you, who return unvanquished from the field of battle.' This legend of German invincibility did much to make Versailles totally unacceptable to the German people.

How harsh a treaty was Versailles? Article 231 of it asserted Germany's exclusive war-guilt. This war-guilt, it was held, justified clauses of the Treaty which, looking back, appear to have been tough and not always logical. Germany lost all of her colonies under the Treaty and some territory in Europe which—like the Saar, Danzig and Upper Silesia—was predominantly or almost wholly German in character. These territorial changes were not consonant with the victorius Allies' assertion of the right of self-determination.

The President of the United States, Woodrow Wilson, strayed into mental confusion while searching for an 'ideal' solution—on the one hand he said that there should be no punitive reparations, while on the other he laid down that Germany must repair the damage of war. The reparations agreed upon were too great to be discharged, but their actual imposition left an abiding sense of grievance on the German mind. 'The Germans', A. J. P. Taylor wrote in his *The Origins of the Second World War*, 'began with the more or less rational belief that they were being ruined by reparations. They soon proceeded to the less rational belief that they were being ruined by the Peace Treaty as a whole.'

In addition, the restriction of Germany's military potential—however justified it may have been—was regarded as an insult to the nation. The armed forces were restricted to a total strength of

100,000 men, the German Navy was handed over to the Allies, and the Rhineland was occupied, while a demilitarized strip thirty miles wide was left to the east of it. All this was intolerable to a people which had talked itself into believing that it had never lost the war. It was especially intolerable to the officer caste.

Nor should it be forgotten that plenty of non-Germans in the West thought Versailles was a harsh treaty. The British economist J. M. (later Lord) Keynes attacked the Treaty trenchantly in his book *The Economic Consequences of the Peace*. Nearly twenty years later the British Ambassador in Berlin, Sir Nevile Henderson, was writing: 'I believed that there was no real prospect of stability either in Germany or in Europe generally until the grievances arising out of the Versailles Treaty had been rectified so far as the Germans were concerned.'

Henderson added: 'The basic fault of the Versailles Treaty was that it failed to accord to Germans the same right of self-determination which it granted to Poles, Czechs, Jugoslavs.' Henderson thought that the conversion of German Danzig into a Free City, and the creation of the Polish Corridor which cut off East Prussia from the rest of Germany, were serious mistakes which had to be corrected. Is it surprising that Germans should have thought the same or that so level-headed and intellectually able a man as General Hans von Seeckt, the organizer of the Reichswehr, should have said: 'The chains of Versailles, which curtailed Germany's freedom of action, must not be allowed to bind her spirit'?

The flaws in the Treaty blinded most Germans to the reality of their own country's contribution towards causing World War I. Indeed, one of the chief German complaints about the Treaty was that it specifically pinned war-guiltiness on the German people. With singular opaqueness, Germans refused to consider that they had any responsibility at all for war breaking out. Thus the Catholic Centre Party politician, Matthias Erzberger, maintained that the 1914 German invasion of small, friendly, neutral, neighbouring Belgium was fully justified by military exigencies, and as an act of 'self-defence'. Erzberger, as the Kaiser's adviser on propaganda, was set to work on plans for the annexation of roughly half of Europe—in the event of the expected German military victory. This is the sort of thing which German historians—a bad and unreliable breed—have consistently chosen to forget. A great section of the German people forgot once again in 1945.

Erzberger, ironically, was assassinated by a right-wing nationalist for allegedly assisting to implement the hated Treaty. So were the Foreign Minister of the first post-war years, Walter Rathenau, and others who wanted lasting friendship with the West. Few Germans envisaged the possibility that their country might have transgressed in 1914—they were far more intent on proving that somebody else, the Russians, the Austrians, the French or even the Serbs, might have transgressed more. In the same way Germans shrugged off the war-crimes committed by their troops in World War I, and put down stories of them to enemy propaganda of the crudest kind.

Well, the German armed forces massacred 211 Belgian civilians in Andenne, 384 in Tamines and 612 in Dinant. Much more would have been heard of these massacres but for the Belgian capacity to play down the excesses of foreign armies which have been marching through their country since the dawn of history. In 1918 Germans were unable to accept any portion of war-guilt, although revelling in an ecstasy of self-pity. Thirty years afterwards many Germans were still insisting that they were forsaken, miserable and bankrupt from 1918 to 1933. Totally forgotten were the Locarno Pact with the Western Powers, Germany's admission into the League of Nations and the massive American loans which enabled the economy to right itself. Totally forgotten were the facts that the bulk of the reparations bill was never paid, that the world economic crisis neither began nor ended with Germany and that Germany was no worse affected by it than were her neighbours.

A. J. P. Taylor has written, convincingly, of Hitler: 'In one sphere alone he changed nothing. His foreign policy was that of his predecessors, of the professional diplomats of the foreign ministry, and indeed of virtually all Germans. Hitler too wanted to free Germany from the restrictions of the peace treaty; to restore a great German army; and then to make Germany the greatest power in Europe from her natural weight.' Most Germans would have agreed implicitly with these objectives, and this may have been the biggest reason of all why most Germans were prepared to tolerate the Nazi regime, even if they did not support it openly. For the Nazi regime could, in their eyes, become the instrument—even if a rough-and-ready one—of Germany's 'rebirth', involving the restoration of the nation's morale, prestige and self-confidence, and the mobilizing anew of national strength.

It may seem that the significance of the Versailles Treaty has been unduly laboured in these pages. Yet national hatred of the Treaty was, I believe, by far the biggest factor in ensuring that effective opposition to Hitler was so hard to organize in Germany either before or after he came to power. This national hatred of Versailles extended through every section of society, down to the man-in-the-street, who perhaps more than in any other country in Western Europe has been chronically unwilling to express a political opinion of his own.

Anyone who lived long enough in the Germany of 1933 to 1939 was quickly made aware of the national mood. Some months spent in Southern Germany in 1933 first gave me this awareness. The phrases on so many lips were: '*Der Fuehrer hat gesagt*' ('The Leader has said'), and '*Der Adolf meint* . . .' ('Adolf thinks that . . .'). Then the grievances would come pouring out. Why did Britain not give the Germans their colonies back? Why did France not restore the Saar (which was under League of Nations control until the 1934 plebiscite)? Why, above all, were Germany's eastern frontiers not 'corrected'? The award of Upper Silesia to Poland had inflicted heavy losses on the large landowners in the area, who were exclusively German and whose possession of its immensely rich coalmines made them into some of the richest men in Central Europe. This was a flaming 'local' issue in the rest of proud Prussia.

The loss of Danzig and, to a very minor extent, of Memel was keenly felt, but their administration by the League of Nations left open a possible loophole for their eventual return to Germany through negotiation. The creation of the Polish Corridor to the Baltic, on the other hand, was regarded as an affront by every German to whom one spoke. It was wounding to national pride and appeared to be geographically nonsensical. And long before Hitler came to power Germans had regarded it as axiomatic that the Poles were a 'backward' and, by inference, an 'inferior' race. The Germans' belief in themselves as a 'master race' was partly founded on the theory that good roads, bourgeois comforts and '*Ordnung*' ended on their eastern frontier, and that beyond lay mud, muddle and sub-civilization.

Hitler was, I believe, supported and followed far less as the potential architect of a new Germany than as the proclaimed avenger of the infamous Treaty. This was why he was accepted at the outset by conservatives and soldiers who wanted strong government and who had lost all faith in the makeshift, 'semi-dictatorial' administrations of von Papen and von Schleicher, who ruled by decree and lacked any semblance of popular backing. Hitler was accepted, too, by liberals, intellectuals and churchmen whose principles mattered less to them than the national honour, and by a younger generation whose surging vitality and latent enthusiasm cried out to be canalized in the service of their Fatherland. The German concept of *'Ehre'* (honour), like the French of *'gloire'*, was the enemy of rational analysis.

Hitler was seen as the only possible alternative to the Weimar Republic, which doomed itself in the eyes of the people by pursuing an *Erfuellungspolitik*, or policy of fulfilling the clause of the Treaty of Versailles. This, surely, was why the results of the various Nazi 'elections' and referendums, even if they were undoubtedly partially falsified, gave Hitler such resounding votes of public confidence. In his life of Carl Goerdeler the historian Gerhard Ritter summed up the situation in 1933: 'The crisis of the Weimar Republic was a crisis of confidence. Hitler knew how to use not only the economic discontent but also the impatience of the nation. . . .' Impatience with what? With unemployment, misgovernment and political uncertainty, but much more, and always, with the Treaty of Versailles.

It was not surprising that opposition to Nazism seemed to have been totally eliminated in 1933. There were subsidiary reasons for this. One was the disposition of Germans, even those with brains, intellect and experience, to underrate the Nazis. It was fashionable in some quarters to make fun of Hitler's *Mein Kampf*, and it was unusual for anyone to plough the whole way through its turgid pages. The substitute bible of the Nazis, Alfred Rosenberg's *Myth of the Twentieth Century*, was dismissed as the ramblings of a mystic and racial crank. Germans who were critical of the Nazis, but who thought in these terms, argued that the Nazis would have only a short period of power. Even the Reich President, Field Marshal Paul von Hindenburg, declared in January 1933 that 'If Hitler wants to have power, he can be Minister of Posts. I will never make him

Reich Chancellor.' Members of the landowning aristocracy and the civil service wrote off Hitler as an undesirable, rabble-rousing *parvenu*; the leading soldiers tended to look on him as a joke and gave him the nickname of 'the Bohemian Corporal'.

In the second place the Nazis were at great pains to ingratiate themselves with 'people who mattered'. On February 2, 1933, Hitler had a meeting with the highest-ranking officers of the Army and Navy at the home of General Kurt von Hammerstein (the General, almost alone among those present, at once formed the impression that Hitler was a menace and became one of his most convinced opponents). Hitler gave an assurance that the armed forces would not be 'demeaned' by being used to put down civil disturbances. They would be free to press ahead with their own expansionary re-armament plans, and the end of that road would be the creation of a big army for a strong Germany and the expunging of the Treaty of Versailles.

In July 1933 the Nazis passed a law abolishing the jurisdiction of civil courts over members of the armed forces. The generals were delighted, and it is revealing to find that a man like Admiral Wilhelm Canaris, who later worked closely with Hitler's opponents, saw no reason at this stage for opposing the Nazis. The reasons were plain: Canaris had not forgotten the 1918 naval mutinies and the rise of the militant Spartacist Communist organization. He wanted the restoration of strong government, the building up of a bigger navy and, needless to say, the revision of Versailles.

In addition, the Nazis won over the most powerful German industrialists to their cause. Men like Emil Kirdorf and Fritz Thyssen, two of the biggest tycoons in the Ruhr, were in close touch with the Nazis in the 1920s. In January 1932 Hitler addressed a meeting of several hundred industrialists and bankers in the 'Industry Club' of Duesseldorf, the gathering-place of the industrial élite (it became that once again after 1945). He promised them a sound currency and a policy of economic expansion, made possible by a strong central-ized government in place of weak and ineffectual democratic ad-ministration, and the winning of greater 'living space' as the basis of a bigger internal market.

In Duesseldorf Hitler was rapturously applauded. He had similar successes at meetings of prominent industrialists in Bad Godesberg and Hamburg; and in Berlin on February 20, 1933, Hermann Goering extracted promises of immense financial support from a smaller group of industrial leaders which included the steel and engineering king, Gustav Krupp, and Georg von Schnitzler, the director of the I. G. Farben chemical trust.

After such manœuvres Nazism could be regarded as tolerably 'respectable'. Its true nature was, indeed, hidden as far as possible behind a flamboyant façade of patriotic fervour. In his *Rise and Fall of the Third Reich* William Shirer has written: 'The Nazi terror in the early years affected the lives of relatively few Germans, and a newly arrived observer was somewhat surprised to see that the people of this country did not seem to feel that they were being . . . held down by a brutal dictatorship. On the contrary they supported it with genuine enthusiasm.'

From personal observation this judgement can instantly be confirmed. Indeed, the arrival of the Nazis in power seemed to have restored normal order and something at least slightly more akin to sound government than what had been offered during the declining years of Weimar. The street fights which had gone on for years between the Nazi Storm Troopers, the Communist *Rot-Armisten* and the Social Democratic *Reichsbanner*, came to an abrupt end. The unrepresentative Papen and Schleicher administrations were replaced by a Nazi government which at least commanded the votes of 43 per cent of the electorate.

A final argument for acquiescing in the Nazi regime was that there appeared to be no clear and feasible alternative to it. Just before the Nazis came to power an American journalist, H. R. Knickerbocker, wrote a book, *Germany—Nazi or Communist?*, which may have somewhat over-simplified this aspect of the Nazi seizure of power. Knickerbocker believed that democracy had failed in Germany and he could visualize only some kind of authoritarian government taking over. In the November 1932 elections the Communists increased their seats in the Reichstag (the German Parliament) from 89 to 100, and were within reasonable reach of overhauling the Social Democrats (121 seats) and becoming the second strongest party.

Knickerbocker was deeply impressed by the wretched living standards in the working-class quarters of Berlin and other big cities, and by the vigour and militancy of the Communist Party. The

Communists, moreover, were alone among German political parties in having a powerful backer abroad, the Soviet Union. They always had the additional, if remote, prospect of forming a 'Popular Front' with the Social Democrats; and who would have doubted, had this happened—as it did in France a year or two later—that these proletarian lean kine would have swallowed up their plumper, more apathetic brethren?

The Communist bogey seemed to be an excellent reason for tolerating the Nazis. To the average German, Communism was a foreign product and un-German. Regimented patriotism seemed distinctly preferable to red revolution. Opposition to the Nazis, because of this ingrained feeling, was largely incidental and fortuitous. Thus the financial wizard Hjalmar Schacht quarrelled with Hitler primarily over economic policies. With reason, he was troubled by Hitler's plan to create more and more medium-term credit in order to finance rearmament. General Ludwig Beck, later to be a pillar of the military Opposition to Hitler, first turned against the Nazis because of the inherent risks of prematurely provoking war in Hitler's treatment of Central European problems. Beck's main concern seems to have been with military problems rather than with the evils of dictatorship.

Admiral Canaris was alienated by Nazi bureaucracy and by bungling over military counter-intelligence. Leading German conservatives fell foul of the Nazis because of their objections to the flying of the Nazi swastika flag (one of them was Dr. Konrad Adenauer, Lord Mayor of Cologne at the time, and later to be Chancellor of the Federal German Republic). The civil service and the police quite simply resented undue Nazi interference in their affairs. The workers grumbled sometimes, but then they had been grumbling ever since 1917.

Sometimes the reason for individual opposition to the Nazis could be mildly bizarre. In the Black Forest town of Freiburg in 1933 I knew a retired schoolmaster who remained, in his early sixties, deeply and even passionately attached to the game of tennis. This, surely, should not have brought him into conflict with the Nazis. But it did. The ex-schoolmaster was convinced that the Nazis sought to demean his favourite sport as being too soft and selfish for virile, team-minded German youth. There may have been something in this. At all events the ex-schoolmaster began to make disparaging remarks about the Nazis. In due course they banned Freiburg's leading tennis-player from taking part in tournaments because he had one Jewish parent. This brought wilder and more vitriolic remarks from the ex-schoolmaster, which were duly reported back to Nazi officials.

He was warned twice, was then arrested and sent to a lunatic asylum. There he died and he may well have been insane at the end. But the tragic thing about the futile 'resistance' of this single inconspicuous man was that he was perfectly sane at the outset of it. This story of individual impotence must have been repeated hundreds of times during the early years of Nazi rule, although one need not suppose that only tennis-fans were concerned. And such acts of incidental opposition had practically no impact on the rest of the community, and none whatever on the Nazis themselves.

How many Germans, then, believed in 1933 that active opposition to the Nazis was necessary, and should perhaps be pushed to extreme lengths? The conservatives were almost all relying on the new regime to make Germany strong again and wipe out all memory of Versailles. The middle class was heart and soul for the Nazis, for their *Ruhe und Ordnung* (quiet and order) and for an imposing, power-minded administration which would help them to forget their own bitterness and ingrained inferiority complex.

The workers were chiefly concerned with their standard of living and could hardly fail to be impressed by the speed with which Hitler began to fulfil his promises (unemployment was brought down from 6,000,000 at the end of 1932 to under 1,000,000 at the end of 1937, and a quarter of a million new homes a year were being built from 1933 onwards). The Christian Churches were looking for a *modus vivendi* with the Nazis, for peaceful coexistence which was far preferable to their haunted day-dreams of the 'Bolshevik Anti-Christ'.

The Social Democrats, or what remained of them after their party was officially dissolved and the entire apparatus of party organization swept away, continued to oppose Nazism as far as they could. So, too, did the Communists—although many of them came over to the Nazis after 1933 in the assumption that it was less painful to exchange one form of authoritarianism for another than to try to revive the corpse of Weimar.

For the rest, a few isolated individuals began to plan against the Nazis and to collect small groups of like-minded people around them. Such a one was Fabian von Schlabrendorff, a young lawyer who later risked his life repeatedly in his efforts to destroy Hitler and who recognized the dangers of Nazism long before Hitler came to power. Such a one was the landowner Ewald von Kleist-Schmenzin, who refused to give the 'Hitler salute'—right arm flung up at an angle of forty-five degrees—or to let the swastika flag be flown from the steeple of the church on his Prussian estate. Another was the diplomat Albrecht von Kessel, who, thinking back to those early days of the Nazi era, conceded in 1963: 'A few of us set out as soon as they came to power to oppose the Nazis. But our opposition was altogether too gentlemanly, too refined. We should have realized that there was only one thing to do, to kill Hitler, and we should have tried to do that as soon as possible.'

To kill Hitler—that would have been an improbable thought in 1933, when huge processions of wildly enthusiastic Germans wound through the streets of every city, chanting the Horst-Wessel marching song until tears ran down the cheeks of the watching thousands; when squads of burly brown-shirted Storm Troopers patrolled the roads, ready to pounce on the smallest offender; when the Nazi system of spying, informing and denouncing was being extended into all places of work and into most private homes. In reality the great mass of the German people set out to adapt themselves to circumstances which seemed to have changed mainly for the better.

In this process of adaptation varying moods and attitudes were built up which had little to do with a spirit of revolt. There were many Nazis and, at the outset, comparatively few anti-Nazis. There were, as well, 'nominal Nazis' and 'non-Nazis'. The 'nominal Nazis' went along with the Party in all of their outward appearances and activities, very often joined it as members, and only confessed their doubts about it in private. Typical of such nominal Nazis was a civil servant with whom I discussed the problems of behaviour, during the Nazi era, long after the end of it. He had been surprised when asked to join the Party late in 1933. He had never made any secret of his lack of interest in politics and could not imagine why the Party should need him.

Indeed, he was not told the answer to this riddle, but was assured that he need attend only one big political meeting 'as a formality'. Otherwise he would merely have to pay his party dues. Nor was he able, long afterwards, to work out why he had been needed. Yet the reason was obvious. He was a model civil servant, honest, reliable, hard-working and much liked and respected by his fellow civil servants. Excellent psychologists as they were, the Nazis wanted him precisely because he was popular.

Parallel to this case, but on a different plane, was that of Dr. Gerhard Schroeder, Federal Minister of the Interior in two post-war Adenauer cabinets and Federal Foreign Minister since 1962. Schroeder found himself enrolled in the Party as a rising young lawyer and the sort of robust physical specimen which the Nazis favoured. He saw nothing wrong in joining. But he drew the line at membership of the brown-shirted S.A., and its Berlin branch gave up the idea of enrolling him on the grounds that he 'showed a lack of positive interest'. Schroeder later left the Party; married to a half-Jewish wife and himself a practising Evangelical Christian, he came to loathe it. For the Party this was a loss, for he would have been the best kind of recruiting poster.

More intriguing than Schroeder's was the case of Weiss-Ferdl, the Munich cabaret entertainer. Even up to 1936 Weiss-Ferdl pursued his habit of ending the evening's programme at the 'Platzl' music-hall with an anti-Nazi joke. One evening he told his audience: 'Do you know, I saw the biggest Mercedes car in Bavaria the other day in the Ludwigstrasse, and it didn't have a Nazi in it?' For this sally Weiss-Ferdl was sent to prison for a few days, as a 'mild' warning.

On the first evening after he came out the 'Platzl' audience waited with bated breath for the end of the programme. Weiss-Ferdl did not fail them. 'Do you know,' he told them, 'I was wrong about that Mercedes car, after all—there was a Nazi sitting in it all the time.' In order to save face, the Nazis ignored this second joke at their expense. But a year or two later Weiss-Ferdl became a member of the Party—and a 'nominal' Nazi too.

'Non-Nazis', according to Fabian von Schlabrendorff, were an obstacle to constructive opposition to the Nazis. They were content to 'sit-out' the Nazi era. They carried out orders, obeyed the laws and avoided any sort of showdown with the authorities. Often they went so far as to discourage all criticism of the regime—in the belief that merely listening to criticism might make them culpable in the eyes of the Nazis. This was especially true of the large non-Nazi section of German officialdom.

Schlabrendorff thought that most non-Nazis tried to make the minimum concessions which were unavoidable, but to remain morally unaffected. The author of *The German Opposition to Hitler,* Hans Rothfels, even considered that 'showing no evidence of Nazi activity' was in itself a kind of resistance. This suggestion is open to doubt. For tacit acceptance of the regime gave the Nazis confidence to push ahead with their policies. It was a source of encouragement. To be a non-Nazi became, in time, tantamount to co-operation with the regime in everything but the formulation of its plans. And in that the Nazis did not need their help; they intended to deal with planning themselves.

The non-Nazis, by their passivity and sheer numbers—perhaps two-thirds of the adult population of 60,000,000—were partly responsible for the slow growth of opposition to Hitler during the early years of the Nazi era. They underwrote the diffident conformism of the German people. They deadened the effects of the occasional gesture of defiance against the Nazis. In June 1934 Franz von Papen, the Reich Vice-Chancellor and himself a non-Nazi, made a striking speech at the University of Marburg. He warned against political radicalism, mob-law and anti-social propaganda. A few days later Papen was arrested and three of his close friends and assistants were murdered. The stultifying effect of non-Nazi disinterest robbed this single bold action of real impact.

Gestures of defiance were made by others. One of them was Ernst Niekisch, a left-winger and 'parlour Bolshevik' who produced subtly anti-Nazi articles in the Press and distributed openly anti-Nazi brochures. Niekisch kept up this activity until 1938, when he was sent to a concentration camp. Rudolf Pechel, who produced veiled criticisms of the regime in his *Deutsche Rundschau,* contrived to remain a free man until 1942. Another critic of the Nazis was Theodor Steltzer, who circulated a memorandum condemning Nazi policies, was arrested and charged with treason, and then temporarily released. Men like these did not think in terms of organized opposition to the regime, but they were courageous enough to speak their minds. It is unfortunate that their efforts were simply never heard of abroad and have been largely forgotten in Germany itself. The reason is clear: their impact on a predominantly Nazi-cum-non-Nazi (but not anti-Nazi) population was very small.

During those early years of the Nazi era there was created something which the Germans themselves called '*der deutsche Blick*' (the German look). It consisted of a long, shifty stare around, in order to make certain that no one was listening when one wanted to speak one's mind. A great many Germans became increasingly oppressed by the knowledge that they were being watched, and by the increasingly lively fear which this caused. The *deutsche Blick* became a great deal more prevalent after the Roehm Blood-Bath of June 30, 1934, when several hundred people—some of them veterans of the radical wing of the brown-shirted S.A.—were murdered by Hitler's orders. At least sixty-one of them were high-ranking members of the S.A. and the total death-roll has been variously estimated at from 400 to 1,000. Hitler claimed to have acted because Roehm was plotting his downfall and would have used the S.A. to engineer it.

Even Nazi Party members could not be so sure of themselves after this. But Pechel's suggestion that the Blood-Bath was a shocking setback to the incipient Opposition to Hitler may not be justified. If it were a setback it was only in the indirect sense that the brutalities of the Blood-Bath discouraged opposition in general. But the Blood-Bath was at least a salutary lesson; the French Ambassador in Berlin, André François-Poncet, found the right phrase for it when he said that 'The 30 January was the victory of the Boche over the Germans. But the 30 June was the victory of sadists over pederasts.' Hitler's utterly ruthless suppression of opposition within his own Party should have convinced everyone outside it of the true nature of the regime. It is one of the most striking failures of the non-Nazis that they accepted the Blood-Bath as the lesser of two evils—they preferred Hitler's compromise with society to further socialistic experimentation.

June 1934 represented a turning-point in Nazi rule. Until then it had been cloaked with a spurious legality. Up to then it was not unreasonable for the average German to assume that the Nazis should at least be given a chance of governing, and to hope that their violence and uncouthness would be modified after a period of power and responsibility. The Blood-Bath should have swept away these illusory hopes. Yet not only did the bulk of the German people close their eyes to what had happened, but the Army actively connived at the massacre of Captain Roehm and his lieutenants, and of those others among Hitler's opponents who were dealt with by the black-shirted S.S. élite at what Hitler found an appropriate moment for settling old scores. In order to stave off temporary chaos, the Army courted ultimate catastrophe for Germany.

The Blood-Bath represented a turning-point for the Army itself. On August 2, 1934, all members of the armed forces were instructed to take an oath of personal loyalty to Adolf Hitler. This instruction was confirmed by the Law of the Oath of the Wehrmacht of July 20, 1935. The Oath was as follows: 'I swear before God to give my unconditional obedience to Adolf Hitler, Fuehrer of the Reich and of the German People, Supreme Commander of the Wehrmacht, and I pledge my word as a brave soldier to observe this oath always, even at peril of my life.'

The new oath was essentially different from the old, in that it prescribed loyalty to an individual and not to the State. In his book *The Nemesis of Power* Sir John Wheeler-Bennett has aptly summed up the significance of the new oath: 'It was unequivocal and did not permit of ambiguity. At the moment when the Army believed that all opportunities lay open to them, they had made a capitulation infinitely more complete than their surrender to the Allies in the railway compartment in the Forest of Compiègne. Henceforth such opposition as the Army wished to offer to the Nazi regime was no longer in the nature of a struggle with an unscrupulous partner, but of a conspiracy against legitimate and constituted authority, a fact which was to sow the seeds of a harvest of doubt and moral conflict at all levels of the military hierarchy.'

By August 1934, indeed, a number of leading members of the Wehrmacht had come to the conclusion that Hitler was a menace and that the Nazi regime would have to be removed. This did not by any means imply that such people wanted to restore orthodox democratic government. Thoughts seem to have turned, at least in Army circles at this period, to some form of emergency administration, to President Hindenburg exercising special powers, or even to a restoration of the monarchy. In military as in conservative circles there were very few opponents or critics of the Nazis who wanted to bring back the Weimar Republic, with its known weaknesses and confusions.

With the exception of General Kurt von Hammerstein (the so-called 'Red General') there was practically no high-ranking Army officer who would have been ready to make common cause with the Social Democrats, the Trade Unions or anyone 'left of centre' in the political sense. But the vital importance of the Army was that it remained the only conceivable instrument for removing Hitler and the Nazis from power. Dictatorships can only be crushed by force, and it was a failure on the part of all of Hitler's opponents that they took so long to realize this.

Perhaps the Army should not be too much blamed for its political myopia. The post-1919 founder of the Reichswehr, General Hans von Seeckt, had instilled a sense of rigid 'apartness' into its members. They were to be the servants of the State and community, but were to keep themselves completely clear of all connection with politics. They were not even allowed to vote, let alone offer themselves for election to Parliament. The Army was the only effective instrument which could be used against Hitler, but who was to use it? In the event, it could be manipulated only by its own leaders; and the likeliest way in which the men of action could be induced to act was by persuasion by the men of thought. The only men of thought who wielded real influence in the Army and might bring its leaders to the point of action were Hitler's conservative opponents. Class and caste prejudices ensured this.

Hitler's conservative opponents did not form anything like a homogeneous body. Since 1918 they had been scattered from centre to extreme right wing politically. They had no obvious leader. Hindenburg was immensely old, and verging on senility. The Kaiser was in exile in Holland. Seeckt had grown disillusioned and unsure of himself. The 'official' conservative politicians were a poor lot, and Papen—elegant, vain and erratic—was fairly typical of their divorce from any spirit of political progress and of their vague reliance on an old, outworn and stagnant order of society. The conservative landowners mostly lived out their lives on their estates, even if many of them were model landlords.

This is not written in order to decry Hitler's conservative opponents but only to explain their position at this stage of history, and the problems which confronted them. They included some remarkable men, and something of their story will be told in the next chapter.

three

The Seeds of Conservative Resistance

'A few honest men are better than numbers.'

OLIVER CROMWELL *in a letter to Sir W. Spring*

IN THE summer of 1934 I listened to an ex-colonel of the German Army expounding his views on Hitler, the Nazis and their connection with the destiny of the German nation. This ex-colonel had joined the German Army at the turn of the century and had fought through the whole of World War I. He was a South German, a Catholic and a conservative—no died-in-the-wool reactionary but a man of reasonably enlightened views. He was extremely, but not offensively, patriotic. He believed in Germany having her 'proper place' in the European community, but he did not preach and almost certainly did not believe in German domination in Europe. He loved the Army, but it would have been unfair to dub him a 'militarist'. His views, briefly, were as follows:

Hitler and the Nazis were doing a necessary job, in clearing up the internal chaos left by the Weimar Republic. They would in time presumably become more 'liberal' and less authoritarian, as the influence of the German community as a whole permeated their ranks and watered down their revolutionary ardour. If this did not happen then the German community as a whole would in due course 'reject' them—obviously yet understandably a rather vague concept.

But at the same time, the ex-colonel thought, Hitler and the Nazis were doing another necessary job in working for a rearrangement of the map of Europe which would give back predominantly German-speaking and German-living areas to Germany. They would need more time for this part of their task, in that its fulfilment did not

41

depend on the German people's whole-hearted aptitude for co-operation but on the attitudes and actions of Germany's ex-enemies. The inference was that the German people had here an added reason for being patient with the Nazi regime.

Hitler and the Nazis, according to the ex-colonel, were in some respects admittedly a necessary evil. They were inclined to violence and depended too much on the rabble. They were interlopers and lacking in respect for custom and tradition. But they could be sufficiently checked and controlled—by President Hindenburg, by the Army, by the old officialdom which continued to carry out the lion's share of the administration after 1933.

This ex-colonel did not regard the Germany of 1934 as a notice-ably less pleasant place in which to live than the Germany of 1914. The Nazis made little impression on his daily existence. Some of his friends were in the Party, which was useful. The brown-shirts could be mildly tiresome, with their endless slogans and money collections, but they seemed to have just enough respect for his class and calling. The Nazis' year and a half in power had brought more material comfort to his life, had given him on the whole a more optimistic view of the future. He saw no reason against being averagely and decently contented.

His attitude was probably typical of a great many Germans of conservative views at that time. It was therefore natural that among such conservative-minded Germans opposition to Hitler was initially restricted to a small minority of people who either had a special in-sight into Nazi policies or a special instinct for recognizing the evils which lurked beneath the surface of Nazi drive, efficiency, vitality, patriotism, bluster and back-slapping bonhomie. It was natural, too, that this small minority should initially have lacked all co-ordination.

Two Germans who possessed both insight and instinct and who were therefore destined to become natural leaders of the Conserva-tive Opposition to Hitler were General Ludwig Beck, who took over control in October 1933 of the *Truppenamt* (the 'shadow' General Staff, for the Treaty of Versailles banned an official General Staff), and Dr. Carl Goerdeler, the Lord Mayor of Leipzig at the time that the Nazis came to power. These two men became the twin pillars of constructive, active opposition among the conservatives. For Beck was to gather round him the generals and other high-ranking officers who early on decided that Hitler's aggressive policies should be checked, and who later made up their minds to bring the Nazi regime to an end by the use of physical force. While Goerdeler did much the same job as Beck in the civilian world, although in his case there was a greater emphasis on planning for the period after the Nazis had been overthrown.

Beck was born in 1880, the son of a middle-class, Protestant Rhinelander of liberal views and a keenly scientific turn of mind. On both sides of his family Beck had uncles who had served as generals in the Franco-Prussian war of 1870. He studied at Wiesbaden University, but decided in 1898 to become a soldier. Perhaps the most formative period of service for him before World War I was the three-year course in the War Academy in Berlin. During this course he deeply impressed his superiors with his grasp of military strategy and organization. Beck was cast in the mould of Clausewitz, with a mind wide open to all the implications of the art of warfare. As a fighting soldier he was less impressive; during World War I he reached only the rank of major. After 1919 he soldiered on in the 100,000-strong Reichswehr, and by 1930 had reached the rank of major-general—once again profiting from a prolonged period of peace in which his proficiency as an instructor was given full play.

In his book *The Shirt of Nessus* Constantine Fitzgibbon has pointed out that by a curious coincidence Beck first achieved celebrity outside the ranks of the Reichswehr by defending Nazis. This came about when Scheringer and Ludin, two of his officers of the 5th Artillery Regiment stationed in Württemberg, were arrested for carrying out propaganda activities on behalf of the Nazi Party. This sort of thing was in direct contravention of the spirit and habits of the Reichswehr. Beck reprimanded both officers and reported the matter as a formality. He assumed that this was the end of the affair.

Their arrest angered him. He defended them at their court-martial—not because he approved of what they had done but because he resented outside interference with men under his command. Fitzgibbon regards Beck's action as being no more than what any 'good officer' would have done under the same circumstances. There may be a nuance involved here. The Reichswehr, in accordance with von Seeckt's instructions, kept its nose out of politics; its senior officers were liable to be all the more infuriated if the civil power

43

intervened in the affairs of the Reichswehr. Fitzgibbon is, of course, right in knocking down the legend that Beck was something of a Nazi because he defended Nazi juniors. Probably Beck was strictly 'non-political' at the time and he can hardly be blamed for showing a little of the singular arrogance of Reichswehr officers who considered that their freedom of action had been unjustifiably limited.

In 1932 Beck was given command of the 1st Cavalry Division, and in 1933 he became head of the shadow General Staff, the *Truppenamt*, and, in effect, the planning chief of the German Army. Almost at once he expressed the fear that Hitler might plunge Germany into a premature and disastrous war. In May 1934 his Cassandra-like voice was again lifted up, warning that too quick an expansion of the German Army might provoke France into launching a 'preventive' war. In the same year he swore the oath of allegiance to the Fuehrer, an action which he was subsequently to regret bitterly.

In 1935 Beck offered to resign his plum job when instructed to change his own purely defensive 'Operation Green'—for the containment of Czechoslovakia in the event of war with France—into an offensive plan, involving surprise attack which would almost certainly be carried out without a declaration of war. Two years later Beck refused to work out plans for the invasion of Austria, under 'Special Case Otto'. He had become irrevocably opposed to all kinds of military risks, which he believed could only lead to a war in which European civilization would be smashed and Bolshevism would emerge as the sole victor. In addition, his conscience, that of an essentially honest and upright man, had become sorely tried. His duty—which was to plan for his country's survival—was being turned into a tool for Hitler's aggressive designs. He was being increasingly confronted with the insoluble problem of equating his personal duty to his country with service to a regime in which he disbelieved.

In his comprehensive forecast of a European war in which Bolshevism would emerge as the sole victor—which he expressed in July 1937 in a private talk with the French general Gamelin—Beck was largely right. But he was inaccurate in his other, more detailed predictions. In May 1938 he was forecasting military defeat for Germany in the event of war with Czechoslovakia, based on the assumption that France, Britain and the Soviet Union would come to the aid of the Czechs. In June 1938 he produced a second pessimistic memorandum, criticizing the revised 'Operation Green' plan as being militarily unsound.

Finally, in July 1938 a third Beck memorandum urged the resignation *en masse* of the German generals in order to prevent 'Operation Green' from being launched. In August Beck resigned alone, after Hitler had twice shouted down his generals at meetings in Berchtesgaden and Jueterbog, and had sworn that nothing would stop him from settling the Czech question by force.

One of Beck's fellow-conservatives, Ulrich von Hassell, has written that Beck was 'pure Clausewitz, without a spark of Bluecher or Yorck'. By this Hassell implied that Beck was a mere 'desk general', and neither a leader of men nor sufficiently a man of action to move decisively in his country's true political interest. Sir Lewis Namier, one of the best British historians of the Nazi era, confirms the implied criticism that Beck was a muddler, mistaken in his views and predictions, and unwilling to take positive action. Others of Beck's foreign critics, like Sir John Wheeler-Bennett, suggest that Beck opposed Hitler for the wrong reason—in fact, solely because of the risk of the Fuehrer leading Germany into military disaster.

This sort of criticism is not altogether fair to Beck. He was out to convince other generals that they should help him to block Hitler's war plans. Was he to do this by enunciating moral and political arguments to men whom Seeckt had taught to concentrate on their profession of arms and to serve their Commander-in-Chief and their State? In the event, Beck took the line which offered most prospect of success, by concentrating his fire on his own Commander-in-Chief, Field Marshal Walter von Brauchitsch. How near he came to convincing von Brauchitsch that action had to be taken against Hitler will never be known. But had the latter given the word, Beck would have automatically become the driving-force of a revolt which would have forced Hitler to give up his plans for destroying Czechoslovakia and so moving one step nearer to starting World War II.

Beck, again, should not be too much criticized for over-insistence on the dangers of accelerated rearmament and of the revised 'Operation Green'. He may well have overstated his case deliberately in his attempt to convince his fellow-generals that Hitler had to be resisted. His motives, at least, were good. Finally, Beck was something more than a 'desk general' with a flair for making gloomy prophecies. Long before his resignation he was already in touch with the conservative civilians who opposed Hitler, and after his resignation he was to become one of the leading lights of the *Mittwochgesellschaft* (the 'Wednesday Club'), where the thoughts of a small body of intelligent and resolute conservatives focused themselves on the possibility of driving the Nazis out of power. Beck appears to have had a thoughtful, flexible mind, a sincere belief in justice and an obstinate determination to go on opposing what to him was an alien, un-Prussian dictatorship. Even Namier, who had scarcely a single good word for any German, agreed that Beck had a 'noble' character.

Beck's unusual ability, for a soldier, to meet civilians on a common intellectual plane brought him into touch with Carl Goerdeler, perhaps the outstanding civilian conservative who opposed Hitler. Goerdeler was a near-contemporary of Beck, but was brought up in a far more political atmosphere. When he was fifteen years old his father, who had been a district judge in the West Prussian town of Marienwerder, was elected in 1899 as a conservative deputy of the Prussian Diet. The Goerdeler home was essentially Bismarckian in its politics, in its piety and probity—a very Prussian home, it should be added. Goerdeler's upbringing, as a result, was sound, simple and safe. His father was respected and well-to-do. He had plenty of relatives in good positions who were likewise sound and steady citizens. There was no sense of struggle in his early life, save that implied by the observance of the 'Prussian virtues'.

For several years Goerdeler studied law, mainly at Tuebingen University, and by 1911 was fully embarked on a career in administration, with a special interest in economic subjects. In 1911 he was serving in the municipal administration of the Ruhr steel-town of Solingen, and his civil service career was only temporarily broken in 1918 when he was sent for a short time to White Russia in order to reorganize its financial administration under German armed occupation.

Goerdeler came to dislike the Nazis after he had had time—about three years, as it happened—to analyse them with his somewhat slow-moving, inflexible mind. He came to dislike their revolutionary claptrap and their lack of respect for the established order. He found it impossible to equate their reliance on emotion and mob-action with his own strict and puritanically Prussian way of life. He found the Nazis undignified and faintly ridiculous, and like many of his conservative contemporaries he underrated their capacity for evil. His biographer, Gerhard Ritter, wrote that 'Carl Goerdeler as little as most other Germans fathomed from the beginning the full daemonic nature of the National-Socialist movement. Its rowdyism ran counter to his conservative, essentially bourgeois character, its violence to his strong attachment to law and justice.'

But Goerdeler disliked—at least in 1933—the Treaty of Versailles more than he did the Nazis. Late in 1918 he was for a time in the Polish Corridor, preaching the secession of an independent Prussia from the German State in order to prevent Polish annexation of the Corridor. Goerdeler at that time appeared to be a typical right-wing nationalist, and his sympathies must have been stirred by those men of the irregular 'Free Corps', who formed their independent companies in order to fight pitched battles with the regular forces of the Polish Army. Apart from loathing the Treaty of Versailles, Goerdeler had small regard for the Weimar Republic, which was grinding itself to bits on the rock-like prejudices of the German people.

Goerdeler, again, did not believe fundamentally in parliamentary democracy. He had no conception of a people 'growing up from below', learning to form their own views and contributing to the life of the community in every walk of life. Ritter wrote that 'Goerdeler would have been willing in some circumstance s to dispense with the parliamentary basis of government altogether and to rule for years without the Reichstag'. Goerdeler would have seen nothing retrograde in the idea—he believed in just and efficient administration carried out by an oligarchy, animated by high principles rather than being based on wealth and position, and composed of men of moral fibre, common sense and outstanding ability.

Perhaps it was not surprising that Goerdeler consented to serve the Nazis during their first three years in power. He remained Lord Mayor of Leipzig in spite of an initial set-to with the local Nazi Gauleiter (Goerdeler refused to hoist the swastika flag on the roof of his Town

Hall but, typically, agreed to do so when it had been declared to be the official 'State flag'). In 1934–5 he took on the additional job of 'Price Commissioner' and issued a stirring call to the nation to go forward into battle—against the state of economic crisis which he evidently considered to be Germany's arch-enemy. In 1936 he produced a powerful paper on the economic situation, which Hermann Goering had requested from him. It would appear that he was working hand-in-glove with the Nazis at this time.

Indeed, he was talking freely—and he was an inveterate and untiring talker—about the political merits of Nazism. It aimed, as he saw it at first, at a synthesis of nationalism and socialism. It stressed the element of struggle in life, which Goerdeler, in his old-fashioned way, thought would help to keep normally unambitious, unadventurous citizens up to the mark. It laid down set-piece rules and instructions for a code of social responsibility and personal dedication to the State—and Goerdeler was a devotee of meticulous codification. He wanted, under the Nazis, to go on 'doing his duty', and this meant collaboration during the phase in which Nazism, as he wrongly supposed, would begin to mellow and mature; in fact, grow up.

In 1935 Goerdeler was talking optimistically of 'strengthening the decent elements' in the Nazi Party, while he was working at the time like a demon to improve his beloved city of Leipzig. There is in existence a photograph of him at that time, soberly and approvingly watching the signing of the Golden Book of the City of Leipzig by the Nazi Party official, Dr. Otto Thierack. Ten years later the same Dr. Thierack signed Goerdeler's death-warrant when presiding over an illegal 'Special Court' organized by the Nazi bloodhound Walter Huppenkothen.

In 1935 Goerdeler was still defending the Nazis for carrying out the Roehm Blood-Bath, which he depicted as an 'unfortunate necessity'. But in the same year he suffered a minor setback when he proposed informing all members of the nation-wide Nazi Labour Front of the state of the national economy. The head of that organization, Dr. Robert Ley, bluntly and cynically told him that this would not do: 'We shall leave that alone; otherwise the workers will become too clever.' Was this the voice of the enlightenment in which Goerdeler implicitly believed? It says much for his incurably optimistic outlook that he managed to remain friends with the Nazis for some time afterwards.

In the autumn of 1936 the Nazis blatantly flouted his mayoral authority. The local Nazi authorities, the *Kreisleitung*, proposed removing the memorial in Leipzig to Dr. Felix Mendelssohn-Bartholdy, the famous composer, because he had been a Jew. Goerdeler indignantly turned down the proposal—possibly less in defence of Mendelssohn's Jewishness than because he had been an obvious credit to Leipzig, his native city. Goerdeler thought he had only an officious *Kreisleiter* with whom to deal; in reality, the order for the removal of the memorial came from Berlin, and was an intrinsic if small item of the Nazis' anti-Semitic campaign. While Goerdeler was away on a lecture tour in Finland, the *Kreisleiter* removed the memorial. On his return to Leipzig Goerdeler resigned his post of Lord Mayor; he was officially retired from it in April 1937.

Major developments may sometimes arise from comparatively small and obscure beginnings. After the autumn of 1936 Goerdeler became a bitter and implacable opponent of the Nazis, and his immense energies and capacity for organization were placed at the disposal of Hitler's German enemies. Curiously, the Nazis had offended another leading Lord Mayor, who knew Goerdeler well, in very much the same way, and with similar initial consequences. Konrad Adenauer, the Lord Mayor of Cologne, resigned his office some years earlier than Goerdeler because the Nazis insisted on flying their flags from the Cologne bridges. But Adenauer had none of the stuff of the conspirator in him. He decided to 'sit out' the remainder of the Nazi era, and the corollary of this decision was his refusal to join Hitler's opponents.

It was significant that Adenauer, astute and supremely careful, distrusted Goerdeler, the natural man to secure his collaboration. In Adenauer's view he was too talkative and too indiscreet. But it may well be that Adenauer never thought that the German Opposition to Hitler had much hope of achieving practical success against a powerful and ruthless dictatorship. And Adenauer is a man who has always believed in the virtue of success.

Goerdeler learnt to know Beck at the end of 1936, or very early in 1937. By the summer of 1938 he was in close contact with him. From the point of view of building up the core of a solid Opposition to

Hitler the Beck-Goerdeler combination fell short of the ideal. Beck was too much a 'man of honour', too little of an intriguer and planner. Goerdeler, on the other hand, was tireless in establishing contact with political opponents of the Nazis, and in putting out feelers to men of widely differing political persuasions. But he seems to have combined, along with his other characteristics, a fussiness of mind and manner and a strange inflexibility in his ideas—almost a woodenness—which betrayed his long service as a member of Prussian officialdom.

Beck attracted admiration and recognition but was not well versed in the art of exploiting it. Goerdeler was apt to get on the nerves of many who were instantly ready to recognize his many excellent characteristics. Yet the Beck-Goerdeler combination, if not ideal, was to become the central feature of the conservative opposition to Hitler.

Through the 'Wednesday Club' Beck came into contact with civilians who already knew Goerdeler—men like Ulrich von Hassell, the son-in-law of Admiral von Tirpitz and a member of the German diplomatic service, Erwin Planck, the son of a famous scientist and a civil servant, and Johannes Popitz, another Prussian civil servant who had been a close friend of the murdered General von Schleicher. These men quickly found themselves in general agreement with Beck's aims. But of even greater importance was Beck's influence on men of a younger generation, whose opposition to the Nazis was instinctive and whole-hearted but who needed a mentor and guide. Among the latter were Klaus and Dietrich Bonhoeffer, members of the Evangelical Churches who opposed Hitler primarily on moral grounds; Hans von Dohnanyi and Rudiger Schleicher, both lawyers who had married sisters of the Bonhoeffers; and Otto and Hans John, the former a young conservative with monarchical leanings and close connections with members of the Royal House of Hohenzollern.

A more significant figure in this growing circle of opponents of the Nazis—chiefly because his relations with Beck became so much closer—was Colonel Hans Oster, at that time a leading member of the Abwehr (military counter-intelligence service), and a regular officer in the Reichswehr. Oster was born the son of a Protestant clergyman in 1888, served with great distinction in World War I and was a man of remarkable attainments, studious but sociable, wise and witty, sincere, courteous and inspired by deep and positive beliefs. He had unrivalled dash, tempered by clarity of judgement in the political as well as the military field.

Oster was a man of ideals who could inspire tremendous enthusiasm and devotion among his subordinates. At the same time he was essentially a man of action, with little—perhaps too little—regard for his personal safety. Yet this selflessness, too, was an inspiration to those who knew him. Gisevius, in his book *To The Bitter End*, quotes Oster as once saying to him: 'To our last breath we must remain upstanding men, as we were taught to be from childhood and by our soldierly discipline. . . . We fear the wrath of God will fall upon us only if we are not straight and decent and fail to do our duty.'

Oster's first chief in the Abwehr was Major-General Kurt von Bredow, who was murdered with General von Schleicher on June 30, 1934, at the time of the Roehm Blood-Bath. Oster could never have cared for the Nazis before this, but from June 1934 onwards he worked actively against them. The Abwehr provided him with an excellent operational base. Its ramifications were endless and it was in addition a very large organization (after World War II broke out it reached a total strength of 43,000, of whom 8,000 were officers). Of its three main departments, Abwehr I collected information, Abwehr II organized sabotage abroad and Abwehr III dealt with counter-intelligence.

The Abwehr was largely anti-Nazi and a citadel of orthodox conservatism. In 1934 the heads of Abwehr I and II were anti-Nazis; only the head of Abwehr III had Nazi sympathies. Their underlings, the intellectual élite of the Reichswehr, tended to be anti-Nazi by virtue of upbringing, tradition and instinct.

The successor of Bredow was Conrad Patzig, a naval captain who quickly became involved in quarrels with the Gestapo and the black-shirted S.S., and with their titular heads, Reinhardt Heydrich and Heinrich Himmler. Patzig was replaced by Admiral Wilhelm Canaris, who was destined to play a considerable if controversial part in the Opposition to Hitler. The Nazi Government picked Canaris for this appointment because he was known to be a die-hard conservative and something of a nationalist, who deplored the Treaty of Versailles and despised the Weimar Republic. In addition, Canaris was a convinced, even obsessed, anti-Communist. Possibly this was what did most to convince the Nazis that he would work well under their hand.

Canaris, for his part, distrusted the Nazis but never regarded it as his duty to break with them openly. Instead, he kept a close watch on them, carried out with his individual blend of efficiency and finesse. Canaris came very much under the influence of Oster, so much the bolder, more impulsive and more imaginative character. The two men formed a 'team', each of whose members derived equivalent benefit from the qualities and activities of the other. From Oster, Canaris drew resource, energy and inspiration. In turn, he contributed his near-Borgian flair for intrigue and subterfuge, and a well worked-out 'cover' for Oster's activities. Oster benefited considerably from the Abwehr's 'back-stage' duties; he could move where he would, see whom he would and never lack an easy explanation.

Almost certainly Oster influenced Canaris more than the latter influenced him. The same was true of Oster's relations with Beck. While Canaris was content to sit back, spinning a web of intrigue with infinite delicacy and diligence, Oster began to look for contacts which would enable Hitler's opponents to strike him down. He found two useful allies in the persons of the heads of the Berlin Police and of the Central Criminal Office, Count Wolf von Helldorf and Artur Nebe, both of them Nazi Party members who had quickly become disgusted with Hitler's excesses. Within the Abwehr, and in other sections of the Reichswehr, Oster built up a cadre of loyal followers, men of his own type, sworn to action and contemptuous of a 'parlour Opposition' to the Nazis which took the form of dismal grumbling and seemingly inconclusive discussion.

One of the outstanding members of this cadre of young officers was Fabian von Schlabrendorff, who survived the Nazi era to tell his story in the book *Officers Against Hitler*—and his story included one of the crucial and most nearly successful attempts to kill Hitler. Schlabrendorff was the living refutation of the myth that no Germans opposed Hitler seriously until the war was being lost and it became a matter of policy to end his bloody and brutal tyranny. Schlabrendorff read Hitler's *Mein Kampf* (he calls it the 'two-pfennig book') and Alfred Rosenberg's *The Myth of the Twentieth Century* in the 1920s, while he was studying at Halle University. He took an instant and positive dislike to the Nazis, to their muddled creed, their lack of taste and manners, their physical brutality and racial arrogance.

The Nazis' chief interest in winning over the university students, Schlabrendorff told me after the war, was 'to capture the street'. In his own words, 'the Nazis tried to turn the students into beasts of prey'. Schlabrendorff was thoroughly disgusted when most of the professors of Halle University were terrorized by the students into assuming pro-Nazi postures. His aversion to Nazism was confirmed when he listened to a speech by Hitler's future Minister of Propaganda, Josef Goebbels, which was a unique mixture of magnificent, rolling oratory and filthy, spewed-up invective.

'I was lucky in one sense,' Schlabrendorff told me, 'in that I could see only one point of view where the Nazis were concerned. I was brought up to believe in the value of principles and ideas, and in the individuality of the human being. The Nazis constituted the sort of mass-movement which I was bound to distrust automatically. I loathed their cant and their hysteria. That was why I set out to study them—so few of my friends thought it worth the trouble, and practically none of them read *Mein Kampf*.

'When the Nazis came to power, therefore, I had no qualms of conscience. I believed that Nazism was the worst kind of dictatorship and would lead to war. Dictatorship meant an organized assault on society and on religion, and the surrender of the citizen to the State. War would mean the destruction of Germany. I believed that there could be no compromise with Nazism, and that it would never liberalize, civilize, itself. I take no credit for being right about this; but how many Germans were wrong! Even Jews often refused to face the facts. There is the story of the Jewish prostitute who kept a picture of Hitler on her bedside table. . . .'

One of Schlabrendorff's earliest mentors, Ewald von Kleist-Schmenzin, was equally explicit in his opposition to the Nazis. Early on during the Nazi era he was arrested for refusing to allow swastika flags to be hoisted from the church steeple on his Kuestrin estate in West Prussia. He refused to give money to Nazi organizations, and

his attitude to the Hitler salute may have helped to inspire the
jingle:

> *'Heil Hitler ist ein schoener Gruss.*
> *Die Reichswehr steht Gewehr bei Fuss.*
> *Bald gibt es einen neuen Krach,*
> *Dann sagt man wieder, Guten Tag.'*

('Heil Hitler is a nice greeting.
The Reichswehr stands at "order arms".
Soon there will be another row, and then
one will say, once more, "Good day." ')

Von Kleist was the best kind of German conservative, a sincere
and devout Christian and a believer in the 'old order' in Europe in
the shape of a 'concert' of civilized nations living in friendship with
one another and sharing international responsibilities. With Oster's
backing von Kleist visited London in August 1938, and told Sir
Robert Vansittart, the Chief Diplomatic Adviser to the British
Government, of the danger of war being waged by Hitler over
Czechoslovakia and the Nazi demand for the annexation of the
Sudetenland.

Kleist told Vansittart that all the German generals were opposed
to war, although they could not refuse to march against Czechoslovakia, at Hitler's orders, unless they received every evident encouragement from Britain and France. But given this encouragement—in the form of a Franco-British reaffirmation to stand by
Czechoslovakia, plus a further statement on the horrors of war—
the generals would be in a position to take action against Hitler.
Kleist also saw Winston Churchill, and after he returned to Germany
on August 23 a second emissary was sent by Oster to London. This
was Colonel Hans Bohm-Tettelbach. He, too, saw Sir Robert
Vansittart and other British politicians. His message was much the
same as Kleist's.

The missions of Kleist and Bohm-Tettelbach appear to have been
largely fruitless. Whatever conclusions Vansittart and Churchill drew
from the information given to them, the British Government seems
only to have been confirmed in its readiness to compromise with

Hitler. This was the reaction of the Prime Minister, Neville Chamberlain, to the suggestion that Hitler was ready to go to war over the Sudetenland issue. All that Oster and his friends achieved was the help to prevent a war from 'breaking out by mistake' in 1938. But the Western Powers failed to follow their advice to act with extreme firmness and without delay. Here is one of the origins of the feeling held by many of Hitler's former opponents after the war that the Western Powers could have done much at this stage to help them, as well as helping themselves in the process.

There were many other conservatives who felt as Kleist did in 1938, even if they did not play so clear-cut a part then or subsequently in opposing Hitler. Some of them were banded together in small groups; others acted mainly as individuals, although coming periodically into contact with one or other group. Among the latter was Dr. Hjalmar Schacht, the President of the Reichsbank and Minister of Economics, who quarrelled with Hitler over his financial policies. Ambitious, astute and infinitely careful, Schacht lurked on the fringe of the opposition, sometimes inclined to put his considerable talents at its disposal, sometimes relapsing into a mood of haughty contempt for men whom he regarded as of inferior intellectual calibre.

Another conservative who tended towards isolation, but whose dislike of the Nazis was far more deep-rooted than that of Schacht, was Ulrich von Hassell, the German Ambassador in Rome when Hitler came to power. Hassell opposed the formation of the 'Rome-Berlin Axis' on the grounds that it would act as an incentive to Hitler to pursue an aggressive foreign policy. He quickly came into conflict with Hitler's 'Champagne Salesman Foreign Minister', Joachim von Ribbentrop, who succeeded the Freiherr von Neurath in February 1938. Hassell was recalled from Rome and became a member of the Beck-Goerdeler group. He, too, was desperately keen for France and Britain to pursue a more forceful foreign policy and at all costs not to advertise their moral and physical weakness. It was a pity that his long stay in Italy had left this intelligent, humorous man somewhat out of touch with the French and British diplomatic services.

By 1938 the tireless Goerdeler had established contact with a number of German diplomats besides Hassell. One was Count

Werner von der Schulenburg, a Russophile who remained Ambassador in Moscow until 1941 and who later believed that it might be possible to secure a Russo-German armistice which could lead to a general peace. Another was Ernst Freiherr von Weizsaecker, Secretary of State in the German Foreign Ministry and later Ambassador to the Vatican. Von Weizsaecker was intellectually opposed to Hitler's aggressive policies, but his 'opposition' began and ended there. He favoured the destruction of Czechoslovakia, admittedly not by force but by what he called a 'chemical process', and he talked garrulously of the need to knock Britain out of the war in 1940.

Albrecht von Kessel, a Silesian conservative and a much more convinced enemy of the Nazis, considered that Weizsaecker did what he could, while holding on to a position of authority in which he could be of use to active resisters. Kessel considers that Weizsaecker used his good name abroad, his tact and tenacity, in trying to modify Hitler's and Ribbentrop's foreign policy. There were others in the Foreign Ministry who worked along the same line, often with greater vigour and less regard for their personal safety—like the brothers Theodor and Erich Kordt, and Hasso von Etzdorf, who became the West German Ambassador to London after the war.

Men like these had to lead a curiously 'double' life, serving the Nazi Government with superficial zeal, giving information to its German opponents and sometimes working actively against it. It has subsequently been held against such people that they tried to get the best of both worlds, by saving their skins and holding on to their posts under Hitler, while posing as his enemies after his death. This is more than a little unfair. As sources of information they were useful to Hitler's active opponents, especially in that some of them were able to probe opinion abroad. This last attribute may have been Goerdeler's main reason for enlisting their interest, for he was himself engaged in a round of visits to foreign countries between 1937 and 1939, which do not appear to have been very productive.

The Kordt brothers, at least, conveyed a separate warning to the British Government of Hitler's intentions towards Czechoslovakia, on September 5, 1938. In doing this they had the cautious blessing of Weizsaecker. Even if the latter was still officially propagating the disintegration by 'chemical process' of Czechoslovakia, he was distinctly unlucky to be tried after the war as a war-criminal and sentenced to imprisonment. The Western Allies were often unable to distinguish between men who served Hitler and men who tried to serve their country.

By the very nature of their lives the German diplomats were never inclined to become active conspirators—even though a dozen of them were eventually to be executed by the Nazis. Nor could men like Goerdeler, Hassell and Popitz have engineered Hitler's downfall by a *coup* on their own. Only the generals were capable of doing that, for only they were capable of employing force and organizing the military support which was indispensable if the brown-shirted S.A. and black-shirted S.S. were to be prevented from carrying out an immediate 'counter-*Putsch*'. But at least up to the beginning of 1938 the generals were themselves insufficiently organized to take effective action, and insufficiently convinced of its need. This was amply illustrated by the composite Blomberg-Fritsch crisis, which resulted in the resignations of a Minister of Defence and two Commanders-in-Chief of the German Army, and in Hitler's personal assumption of command of the armed forces. Some historians believe that this crisis gave the Army the most favourable opportunity which was ever to come its way of acting decisively against Hitler.

The Blomberg-Fritsch crisis was divided into two parts. The first act concerned only Field Marshal Werner von Blomberg, Minister of Defence since 1933, a fervent follower of Hitler and nicknamed 'Hitler Boy Quex' after the chief character in a fatuous Nazi propaganda film. Blomberg's loyalty and subservience to Hitler had wavered only once, at the time of the German reoccupation of the Rhineland in March 1936. For a brief moment Blomberg was affected by Beck's doleful forecast that this successful gamble of Hitler's would give the French the chance to reoccupy the Ruhr by taking immediate action with their immensely superior armed forces.

Blomberg's first wife died in 1932 and on January 12, 1938, he remarried—with the official blessing of his Fuehrer. Shortly afterwards it transpired that his second wife had been a prostitute, with a police record. This information was conveyed to Hitler by a roundabout route. The Abwehr first informed Count Helldorf, in his capacity of Chief of the Berlin Police. He, in turn, passed on his information to General Wilhelm Keitel, head of the Wehrmacht-tamt and Blomberg's own son-in-law (he had married the Field Marshal's daughter). Keitel went to Goering, and Goering to Hitler. The Nazi leaders were scandalized and Blomberg was forced to resign. The Officers Corps was furious.

The second act of the drama followed hard upon the heels of the first. General Werner von Fritsch, who had succeeded Blomberg as Commander-in-Chief, was accused of being a homosexual, with a record reaching back at least three years. The charge was trumped up by Himmler and was utterly unfounded (an officer by the name of Frisch had been guilty of homosexual practices, and Himmler confused the names deliberately). Fritsch defended himself successfully against the charge and in due course his honour was 're-affirmed' and he was officially rehabilitated.

But in the meantime Fritsch allowed himself to be badgered into resigning his post of Commander-in-Chief on February 4, 1938. Those of his generals who hoped that he would actively resist and would choose this moment to lead a revolt against the Nazi regime were sharply disappointed. Fritsch was bewildered and, in the words of Wheeler-Bennett in *The Nemesis of Power*, 'resembled a cross between a puzzled virgin and a petrified rabbit'. The picture is an amusing one, but it may have been too much to expect a man like Fritsch—whose life had been dedicated to unquestioning service of the State—suddenly to take violent action against constituted authority. Indeed, the thought does not seem ever to have been seriously entertained by him.

Hitler followed up Fritsch's resignation by proclaiming, on February 4, his own headship of the armed forces. Sixteen generals were relieved of their commands and other senior officers were moved to new jobs. Shortly afterwards three leading conservatives —Neurath, Schacht and Papen—were transferred or retired. Neurath ceased to be Foreign Minister and Schacht Minister of Economics. Papen was removed from the Embassy in Vienna. Two other German Ambassadors were retired at about the same time, Hassell from Rome and von Dirksen from Tokyo. As at the time of the Roehm Blood-Bath, Hitler took this favourable opportunity of removing people inimical to him, who had nothing to do with the particular developments which had occurred.

Did the dissident generals miss a real chance of acting decisively against Hitler in January or February 1938? One German historian, himself an active opponent of Hitler, believed emphatically that they did. After the war Rudolf Pechel wrote that January 1938 was a turning-point for the Army. Pechel considered that Fritsch should have alerted the Berlin garrison and arrested Hitler, Himmler and Goering. 'Then', Pechel wrote, 'the overwhelming majority of German people would have welcomed him as the Saviour of the Fatherland.' The Nazis would have been ejected from power; the Army would have moved quietly in.

Pechel's is a pipe-dream. Fritsch had no following whatever in the nation. His cloistered life as a Prussian officer meant that he had no understanding, on his side, of the nation's mood and views. The German Army could not have established its own government, as Oliver Cromwell's army did at the end of the English Civil War. No military *coup*, moreover, was planned, for the Blomberg-Fritsch crisis caught everyone unprepared, even the Nazis.

Beck, indeed, urged Fritsch to stay at his post and win through in a trial of strength. He even wanted Fritsch to fight a duel with Himmler—although what purpose this would have served has never been made clear. And perhaps only half a dozen generals were at this time committed to opposition to Hitler and would have backed Fritsch. The others would have supported him only in so far as he was maintaining his rightful position and defending his honour. It would never have crossed their minds that Fritsch's 'correct' course was to alert the Berlin garrison and seize the persons of the Fuehrer and his adjutants.

The Blomberg-Fritsch crisis surely did not offer the Army a clear-cut chance of deposing Hitler. But its significance may lie in the fact that it suggested, with sudden, startling clarity, that it was high time that concrete planning for a *coup d'état* should begin. And this is what happened. During the spring and summer of 1938 Beck, Goerdeler and their friends were busier than ever before, consulting and informing one another and gradually arriving at the first fully worked-out plan for overthrowing the Nazi regime. In these preliminary discussions Beck knew that he could count on the support of at least three senior generals: Erwin von Witzleben, Kurt von Hammerstein and Franz Halder, the new Chief of Staff.

In the Abwehr he had the firm support of Canaris and Oster. The conservatives in the Foreign Ministry, the diplomatic service and the civil service would support a *coup d'état*, once it had been successful. As before, the attitude of the Commander-in-Chief of the Wehrmacht was immensely important, and Fritsch's successor, Walter von Brauchitsch, was a man of flabby and indeterminate character, whose lack of decision and purpose more than offset his ingrained but vague distaste for the Nazis.

The outlook for Hitler's opponents, indeed, was not really propitious, but their plans took definite shape at last during the summer of 1938. They were at last utterly convinced of the dangers to Germany which Hitler was ready to risk. The November 5, 1937, conference with his generals, when he said that France and Britain were Germany's arch-enemies, and that a solution in Central Europe could be achieved only by force, had made a deep and lasting impression on them. (It is all the more surprising to find a historian like A. J. P. Taylor, in his *Origins of the Second World War*, claiming that Hitler was only 'day-dreaming' on that occasion. He was, in reality, laying down the axiom of exploiting opportunity by force which he subsequently set out to implement.)

The August 10, 1938, conference in the Berghof at Berchtesgaden furnished final confirmation of Hitler's aggressive designs. At this meeting the Fuehrer bluntly explained his strategy if the Czechs should fight—the German armoured columns were to plough their way straight through to Prague and Pilsen, while a light defensive screen held the embryonic West Wall (the so-called 'Siegfried Line') against the French. It was at this conference that Hitler was reported to have literally howled with rage when some of his generals told him that the West Wall could not be held for more than three weeks. According to the diary of one of the generals present, Alfred Jodl, Hitler told them that the line could be held for three years if necessary, and that any man who failed to do this was a scoundrel.

When the Rhineland had been peacefully reoccupied in 1936 some of the generals had lost their nerve. Austria was peacefully occupied in 1938, but any opposition which the generals might have offered to this project was submerged in the welter of the Blomberg-Fritsch crisis. Now, in August 1938, the situation was radically different. Hitler was proposing to attack a neighbouring state which might be expected to fight and which had a powerful army—estimated at forty-two divisions. Czechoslovakia had natural frontiers on all sides, save perhaps the southern 'underbelly' of rolling hillside which had been exposed to German invasion by Hitler's annexation of Austria. In addition, Hitler was proposing to risk war with France and Britain, possibly with the Soviet Union as well, in order to get his way over the Sudetenland question.

This was the background to the visits to London and to Churchill's Chartwell home of Kleist and Bohm-Tettelbach, to the ant-like activity of von Weizsaecker and the Kordt brothers. It was the background, too, to the discreet soundings of the Italians by Admiral Canaris, who tried to secure through the Royalist Italian general, Roatta, an understanding that Italy would stay out of a war in which France, Britain and Czechoslovakia must surely overwhelm Germany. In these circumstances the German generals drew up a plan which might well have succeeded had all the conditions laid down for success been fulfilled. Its cardinal points were as follows:

Hitler was to be arrested the moment that he gave the orders for the revised 'Operation Green' to be carried out and Czechoslovakia to be invaded. He was to be put on trial before the Nazi 'People's Court' which he himself had created, but that court would, of course, be given a new set of non-Nazi members and the prosecution would be prepared by anti-Nazis like Hans von Dohnanyi and Dr. Carl Sack, the deputy Judge Advocate General.

A plea of insanity would be offered on Hitler's behalf, and it was considered feasible that he could be certified and placed in a lunatic asylum. A panel of psychiatrists, headed by Dr. Karl Bonhoeffer, the father of the anti-Nazis Klaus and Dietrich, had already produced a comprehensive report on Hitler's medical condition, based on information secured by Oster and dealing with his hospital record (Hitler was for a time in Pasewalk hospital after being gassed during World War I, and he was given medical treatment after the unsuccessful Munich *Putsch*).

The moment that Hitler was arrested, the Army was to take over effective control of government. In due course a provisional administration would be formed under some 'blameless' conservative like Neurath (Schacht fancied himself for the post and might well have been the best choice). Some of the conspirators even favoured

Goering. Men like Himmler and Heydrich were, of course, to be dismissed and if necessary placed under arrest. The *Luftwaffe* (Air Force) was to play no part in the *coup*; its officers were mainly Nazis. Nor was the Navy to be consulted, less because of Nazi sympathies than because its leaders felt themselves rigidly bound by their oath to Hitler.

The generals believed that they had all the armed force required to carry out their plans. Their key man in the Berlin area was General Erwin von Witzleben, who commanded the 3rd Military District of Berlin and Brandenburg. His orders were to be executed by Count Erich von Brockdorff-Ahlefeld, the commander of the Potsdam garrison, which included the motorized 23rd Infantry Division. Working in close co-operation would be Count Helldorf, the head of the Berlin Police, and his deputy, Count Fritz von der Schulenburg. The police included many Nazis but could be counted on to carry out orders from their chief.

If additional military force were required it was available in the shape of the 1st Light Division under General Erich Hoepner. This division was normally stationed in the Ruhr town of Wuppertal, but was to be moved up to the Czech frontier to its action-station for the invasion of that country. At the appropriate moment this division would be on the march through Thuringia; it could be diverted from there, either to Berlin or southwards, to intercept the S.S. units in Nuremberg and Munich—which Hitler and Himmler might try to use for a counter-*coup*.

There was no lack of other military commanders who would have backed this plan. Hammerstein was in retirement, but would have come out of it like a shot from a gun—when consulted by the conspirators he told them that his first preoccupation would be to prevent the *coup* from being misused by the crafty Papen, whom he would 'string up' without hesitation. Heart and soul with the conspirators was General Karl von Stuelpnagel, the Army's Quartermaster-General. General Franz Halder, as Chief of Staff occupying the second most important post of all in the Army, had been won over in conversations with Beck and Goerdeler. Halder's most important part in the plan was to give at least forty-eight hours' notice of the implementation of 'Operation Green'.

There remained the Commander-in-Chief. Brauchitsch was to be informed only at the very last moment of what was afoot. This could be done either just before Hitler was arrested or immediately after-wards, when the necessary proclamation that the Army had taken over control had been published. His endorsement of the plan was regarded as a vital necessity by the conspirators.

Why was the September 1938 *coup* never carried out? German historians have given two main reasons. The first is that the Western Powers—in particular the British—failed to give the generals clear enough indications of their determination to fight if Hitler marched into Czechoslovakia. The second reason given is that the signing of the Munich Agreement on September 29, 1938, by the Western Powers cut the ground from under the generals' feet. How could they overthrow Hitler when he had achieved a bloodless victory by uniting the Germans of the Sudetenland with the Reich?

The cession of the Sudetenland by Czechoslovakia did not give only Hitler what he wanted. The great mass of the German people believed that it was wrong that nearly 3,000,000 Germans should live under Czech rule in areas immediately contiguous to their 'native' Germany. Most Germans believed that the Benes regime in Prague was 'oppressing' this German minority. The generals had to offset this feeling by playing on the popular fear of war. Thus their opposition to Hitler and their readiness to overthrow him was based on the main argument that only in this way could war be prevented. They had to assume that Britain and France would go to the aid of the Czechs; otherwise this argument was worth nothing.

Did the Western Powers let down the generals by giving them in-sufficient indications of firmness in face of Hitler's threats? It is not easy to give a straight answer. The Kleist, Bohm-Tettelbach, Kordt and other feelers put out to the Western Powers by Hitler's oppo-nents produced only one positive reaction. This came, typically, from Winston Churchill, who gave Kleist a letter in which he wrote:

'I am as certain as I was at the end of July 1914 that England will march with France, and certainly the United States is now strongly anti-Nazi. It is difficult for democracies to make precise declara-tions, but the spectacle of an armed attack by Germany upon a small neighbour and the bloody fighting that will follow will rouse the whole British Empire and compel the gravest decisions. Do not, I pray you, be misled on this point. Such a war, once started, would be fought out like the last to the bitter end. . . .'

Churchill's letter was delivered to Oster and Canaris. A copy was given to Beck and its contents must most certainly have been communicated to the other leaders of the conspiracy. But Churchill was not a member of the British Government at the time. The missions of the Opposition to London produced nothing more from the British Prime Minister, Neville Chamberlain, than the vague remark: 'I don't feel sure that we ought not to do something.' Other British politicians, including Lord Halifax, Sir John Simon and Anthony Eden, were opposed to giving any undertaking to the German Opposition. Meanwhile the Runciman mission to Czechoslovakia had reported back to London—on the whole in favour of giving the German minority in the Sudetenland the right of self-determination. And Sir Walter Runciman, unlike Churchill, was a member of the Government.

In mid-September Chamberlain travelled twice to Germany to see Hitler, on September 15 at Berchtesgaden and on September 22 and 23 to Bad Godesberg. At Berchtesgaden Chamberlain accepted the principle that the Sudeten areas might have to be detached from Czechoslovakia. Chamberlain had already been advised by the French Prime Minister, Edouard Daladier, to 'seek as good a bargain' as possible with Hitler. By this Daladier indicated very plainly that the French did not want to fight—under any circumstances.

To Chamberlain, Kleist's visit to London was merely an embarrassment. His comment was: 'I take it that von Kleist is violently anti-Hitler, and is extremely anxious to stir up his friends in Germany to make an attempt at his overthrow. He reminds me of the Jacobites at the Court of France in King William's time, and I think we must discount a good deal of what he says.' To Sir John Simon, Chamberlain said, referring to the Czech crisis: 'Here was an intense strain in the centre of Europe which, if it was not to lead from bad to worse, could only be relieved by a concession.'

Meanwhile the London *Times* was loud in its support of a policy of appeasing Hitler. In its leader of September 7, 1938, the paper openly advocated the cession of the Sudetenland to Germany. Sir Robert Vansittart, as his private papers will doubtless show (they are shortly to be edited), was in favour of extreme firmness in dealing with Hitler. But this was due less to any sympathy with Hitler's German opponents than to a deep-rooted distrust of all Germans.

The Kleist and Bohm-Tettelbach feelers produced no clear word of encouragement from him. On the whole it is true to say that not only were the British reactions to the plans of the Opposition cool and reserved to a degree but that Beck, Halder and their fellows were given too little reassurance of Western readiness to answer a Nazi attack on Czechoslovakia by armed action.

The second reason given by German historians for the failure of the Opposition to act against Hitler in September 1938 was the signing of the Munich Agreement. Walter Goerlitz, in his history of *The German General Staff*, expressed the view that the news that Hitler was meeting Chamberlain and Daladier in Munich on September 29 ended the chances of a successful *coup*. The news became known on the morning of September 28, and Goerlitz's comment is: 'Brauchitsch immediately knew that a *coup d'état* was out of the question. One could not arrest a man and have him tried as a war criminal when he was on the point of winning a completely bloodless victory.'

This passage of Goerlitz's book is revealing. For one thing, it indicates that Brauchitsch—who was, in theory, to be informed about the *coup* only after it had begun to be executed—was aware of much of what the Opposition was planning. This has since been confirmed by Halder, who has stated that he saw Hitler's famous letter of September 27 to Chamberlain, appealing to him to join in preventing the 'recalcitrant' Czechs and the 'war-mongers' in Britain from sabotaging a settlement of the Sudeten question, and that he—Halder—went at once to Brauchitsch with a copy of the letter. Halder has further claimed that he urged Brauchitsch to take action against Hitler, even at this eleventh hour.

In *The Nemesis of Power* Wheeler-Bennett wrote:

'Among the many legends which constitute the mythology of the German Resistance Movement—legends as dangerous to the future peace of the world as that of the "stab in the back" after the First World War—there has grown up this story that the only attempt to remove Hitler, which might have been remotely successful, was frustrated and sabotaged by Mr. Chamberlain's announcement of his intention to go to Munich. But, it is submitted, this apology for failure, circulated by interested parties, does not hold water for a moment.'

Wheeler-Bennett goes on to explain why, in his opinion, it does not hold water. The Hitler letter of September 27 opened the way to a peaceful solution of the Sudeten question. The German generals, however, were—on their own admission—only ready to act in the event of war. Could they have misunderstood the terms of Hitler's letter altogether? It is possible, but in that case what did they expect of Chamberlain? Presumably, a blank refusal to negotiate any further with Hitler. This, indeed, could have led to the German invasion of Czechoslovakia. But under these circumstances Brauchitsch—who was clearly being consulted by the conspirators already (see Halder)—would certainly not have directed the German Army to act against Hitler. And the conspirators would have already missed the chance of taking action in defiance of Brauchitsch, and without his prior knowledge of what was going to happen.

Halder, moreover, laid down three conditions which he considered essential for the carrying out of a successful *coup* at this stage—resolute leadership, popular support and the choice of the right moment for action. Popular support might have been forthcoming at any time during the second half of August and the first three weeks of September—assuming that the *coups* were carried out successfully. Popular support certainly did not hinge on a brief moment in time, when Chamberlain decided to go to Munich.

The choice of the right moment for action was a wider one than the apologists of the Opposition to Hitler have indicated. Any moment during a five-week period could have been chosen. Possibly the most advantageous would have been September 23 when the Bad Godesberg talks between Hitler and Chamberlain reached deadlock. The conspirators not only hesitated then and so waited too long; by calling in Brauchitsch on September 28 (and probably even earlier) they showed that this is what they would have done in any case. And Brauchitsch would certainly have discouraged, and almost certainly have frustrated, their plans.

There is, indeed, much to be said for Wheeler-Bennett's view that the conspirators had virtually jettisoned their plans at least a fortnight before September 28. They had become bewildered by the diplomatic manœuvring of the Great Powers, and all impetus had vanished from their planning. They had become even more confused over the question of where Germany's true interests lay. Although

66

Hitler was to be removed, it was arguable that it would be better to postpone his removal until after the Sudeten question, and the Czech question as a whole, had been settled in Germany's favour. In his *In the Nazi Era* Sir Lewis Namier wrote: 'There was little difference between Hitler and his generals in their ultimate aims: the issue between them was technical rather than moral. Both sides were out to rebuild Germany's armed forces, to re-establish her military pre-ponderance, and then, by intimidation or by war, to realize her territorial ambitions.'

Namier's 'by war' is an overstatement. But the humbling of the Czechs must have seemed eminently desirable to most Germans. Weizsaecker, on his own showing, wanted it. Erich Kordt, yet an-other of Hitler's opponents, called the Czech President, Benes, 'the cheated cheat', and referred, after September 1938, in opprobrious terms to 'rump-Czechia'. Albrecht von Kessel considered that Benes was blameworthy in failing to propose a compromise on the Sudeten issue, with plenty of time at his disposal, and in failing to improve German-Czech relations by suggesting a trade treaty.

Von Kessel, again, was to weep tears of emotion when, less than a year later, the Nazis occupied Prague, and Prussian troops, with their usual splendid discipline, beat a military tattoo outside the portals of the Hradschin Palace. Even among anti-Nazis there was a commonly held view that the entire Czech part of the Czecho-slovak State was nothing more than '*Deutsch-Boehmen*' (German-Bohemia) which was ripe for its 'return' to the Reich. Prussia, as von Kessel saw it in 1939, had 'come to Prague'. It was a moving and satisfying experience.

A month after Munich Carl Goerdeler wrote to a friend in America:

'If the warning had been heeded and acted upon, Germany would now be free of her dictator and turning against Mussolini. Within a few weeks we could have begun to build lasting world peace on the basis of justice, reason and decency. A purified Germany with a government of decent people would have been ready to solve the Spanish problem without delay in company with Britain and France, to remove Mussolini, and with the United States to create peace in the Far East.'

Wishful thinking? Very probably—for the 'decent people' in

Germany would have been conservatives with further demands to levy against Germany's neighbours, while Goerdeler was mainly anti-Mussolini because of Italian 'oppression' of the German-speaking South Tyrol. Yet Goerdeler's was a noble dream.

The 1938 conspiracy of the generals was a failure. At least in part it was a failure of leadership. Von Kessel believes that Witzleben would still have acted on his own if the Czechs had fought. But Witzleben, as subsequent events showed, had a limited knowledge of politics, and it would have required a crystal-clear situation to induce him to act. Beck was not, first and foremost, a man of action, and one of his fellow-generals, Heinz Guderian, has since maintained that it was folly to entrust the leadership of a conspiracy to 'this man of known indecisiveness of character'.

Halder was not a good 'substitute leader'. One opponent of Hitler's, Axel von dem Bussche, has called him 'the Bavarian Professor-type'. Another, Hans Bernd Gisevius, thought that 'Halder's imagination was so bold that he was inhibited from doing anything at all'. Halder, again I quote Gisevius, 'was wanting neither understanding nor patriotism . . . he simply lacked the will'.

Yet the efforts in 1938 of Beck, Goerdeler and the others were not wholly in vain. They had thought out their fundamental reasons for opposing Nazism. They had at last envisaged direct action against Hitler. They had established contact abroad—which could have had positive results. They had brought the military and civilian elements of the conservative Opposition into close touch with each other. All this had taken several years to achieve; it would be years more before the next coherent attempts to oust the Nazis would take definite shape.

four

The Opposition of the Church of Rome

'Our patience will achieve more than our force.'
EDMUND BURKE, *Reflections on the Revolution in France*

FROM the beginnings of active opposition to Hitler it is necessary to turn to the more passive resistance offered by various sections of the German community—sections which were neither in the position nor disposed to advocate the use of force to overthrow the Nazi regime. One such section was constituted by members of the Roman Catholic Church, whose struggle was guided essentially by conscience. Their struggle against Hitler was an integral part of the story of the German Opposition.

The leaders of the Roman Catholic Church both in Germany and Rome ought never to have been in much doubt about Hitler's intentions towards their Church and towards organized Christianity. *Mein Kampf,* that little-studied document, brims with pagan, heathen undertones. It attacked 'political Catholicism' and censured the Church of Rome for failure to understand social problems. The activities of the brown-shirted S.A. before the Nazis came to power were, moreover, well known to all students of German affairs. The Vatican had unique opportunities and means of informing itself, partly through the priesthood and partly through predominantly Catholic political parties, about the state of European countries.

Furthermore, the Papal Nuncio in Germany at the time of the first, unsuccessful Nazi *Putsch* had been Cardinal Pacelli, later to become Pope Pius XII. His knowledge of German affairs was very great. Unlike the Germans themselves, the Vatican's advisers could appraise the German situation logically and objectively. Rightly credited with wisdom and far-sightedness, the Vatican should either have found out more than it did about Nazism, and more quickly, or should have drawn more appropriate conclusions from its investigations and its fund of knowledge.

In 1933 the Roman Catholic Church was possibly the only Christian body in Germany which was in a position to defend itself against Hitler with a fair prospect of success. It was not simply that it was united, that it had 30,000,000 members in Germany, that it was supported by its own youth and Trade Union organizations and by its own Catholic Centre Party (*Zentrum*). Behind it stood the Papacy, with its tremendous power and authority in a largely Catholic Europe. Hitler indeed regarded the Roman Catholic Church in Germany as a largely secular force. That was one reason why he disliked it so much. But he disliked it, too, because it was associated closely with the established social and moral order, and because it was essentially conservative, traditional and a part of the older Germany which Hitler despised.

Finally, Hitler disliked the Catholic Church because he was himself a relapsed Catholic. To be a relapsed Protestant is usually no more than synonymous with an easy-going agnosticism. A relapsed Catholic is more often someone with a strong sense of grievance against the established order. For it has required strong feeling for him to break away from the close embrace and discipline of Mother Church. The Vatican, clearly, was aware of the details of Hitler's dingy past and of his readiness to revile the Church of his undistinguished forefathers.

Kurt Ludecke, one of Hitler's earliest biographers, has quoted him as saying: 'National Socialism is a form of conversion, a new faith. . . . Once we hold power, Christianity will be overcome . . . and a Germany—without the Pope and without the Bible—established. Luther, if he could be with us, would give his blessing.' Yet Hitler was always keenly aware of the strength of the Catholic Church. Only for that reason did he not attempt to destroy it at once when he came to power; his policy was to whittle away its prestige and authority.

Obviously the direct political influence of the Church had to be eliminated first of all. Early in 1933 Catholic leaders agreed that there was nothing against German Catholics becoming members of the Nazi Party. In June 1933 Hitler dissolved the predominantly

Catholic Bavarian People's Party. On July 5 the Catholic *Zentrum*, with its main strength in the Rhineland and Baden and more than seventy members in the Reichstag (making it the fourth largest party there), was invited to dissolve itself.

Its voluntary suicide had been predictable for some time. In March 1933 its members had voted for the Enabling Act which gave Hitler the powers of a dictator. The liberal tendencies in the *Zentrum* which had manifested themselves in the 1920s had virtually disappeared, and the Party's outlook had once again become strongly conservative, almost obscurantist. The *Zentrum* made no effort to help the Social Democrats in their single-handed struggle against Hitler, and the story of its placid collaboration in its own demise makes shameful reading. Among those who acquiesced in the extinction of their party was Konrad Adenauer, and among those who arranged the details of its genteel suicide was Heinrich Krone, Adenauer's right-hand man in the West German Cabinet and the Christian Democratic Party from 1955 to 1963. Adenauer's own passivity at this time was one of the main reasons for the post-war fulminations against him of the Social Democratic leader, Kurt Schumacher.

The Vatican would not have been able to maintain political parties in South Germany and the Rhineland in face of Hitler's determination to institute a one-party State, but it could at least have registered a protest against their liquidation and appealed for the earliest possible return to political freedom. The Vatican, however, had no intention of protesting; it was indeed already urgently engaged in negotiating a treaty of its own with the Nazis. This treaty was embodied in the Reich Concordat, signed on July 20, 1933, by Cardinal Pacelli and Franz von Papen, the former Chancellor and devout Catholic whose authoritarian rule a year earlier had paved the way for Hitler's seizure of power.

The details of the Concordat are less important than its effects. For Hitler could never have intended to fulfil its terms, which included a guarantee of the free practice of the Catholic religion and of the right of the Church to manage its own affairs. In return, priests were to be excluded from political activity and no foreigners were to hold important posts in Catholic organizations in Germany. With both Catholic political parties out of the way, Hitler waited

71

only five days after the Concordat was signed before ordering the dissolution of the Catholic Youth League. Very soon the closing-down and 'conversion' of Catholic schools began, arousing widespread resentment which turned into resignation.

So far from preventing persecution of Catholics, as the Vatican must honestly have hoped, the Concordat made it easier for Hitler to cloak his actions with the ostensible blessing of the Pope. Much more important, the Nazi regime acquired a new prestige and 'legality' in the eyes of millions of its unwilling subjects, for the Vatican was the first foreign Power to recognize it. This is all too often forgotten by those who have declaimed against the Western Powers' policy of appeasing the Nazis, and in particular against the British and French 'men of Munich'. The pattern had already been set for them by the Pope, Pius XI, obsessed by his fear of the 'Bolshevik menace', largely advised by Fascist cardinals, and intent on doing honour to Mussolini's potential ally.

A few days after the Concordat was signed Hermann Goering was declaiming with equal violence against the 'red rats' (the Communists) and the 'black moles' (the Catholic clergy). Some Catholics, at least, were not surprised by this, for they had raised warning voices before the Nazis came to power. Thus in the autumn of 1930 the parish priest of Kirchausen, in Hesse, said that no decent Catholic could belong to the Nazi Party, that he himself would refuse the sacraments to any party member, and that the Nazis should not be allowed to attend mass in a uniformed body. Early in 1931 the Bavarian bishops warned their flocks against Nazism and explained that it contained ideas which were contrary to Christian teaching. They, too, forbade attendance of church in a uniformed body and advised priests to consider the case of each Nazi individually when deciding whether to administer the sacraments to him or to give him Christian burial.

In July 1933 the Cardinal Archbishop of Breslau was warning of the impending threat to Church organization, while in Bavaria the first Catholic anti-Nazi society, 'Rhaetia', was formed. It stood for Church and monarchy, published its own newspaper, *Der Gerade Weg*, condemned Rosenberg's crackpot racial theories and proclaimed that National Socialism was a 'plague'.

It was in Bavaria, again, that the first high-ranking Catholic prelate took an unequivocally firm stand against the Nazis. The Cardinal Archbishop of Bavaria, Michael Faulhaber, was sixty-four years old when Hitler came to power and had been Archbishop in Munich since 1917. In World War I he served as Chaplain-General in the Bavarian Army and was the first Roman Catholic bishop to receive the Iron Cross for courage on the field of battle. He was a man of enlightened and surprisingly liberal views. Unlike most of his colleagues he became a pacifist. He refused to attack the Treaty of Versailles. In 1932 he was taking an active interest in the German Peace League (*Friedensbund*) and was very ready to point out the purposelessness and wickedness of war. He took a friendly view of the Jews, and was fond of quoting Cardinal Manning's saying: 'I should not understand my own religion had I no reverence for yours.'

Faulhaber never ceased to stress the value of the Old Testament, referred to by Hitler Youth leaders as 'the Jew history-book full of lies'. In December 1933 he carried out his first act of defiance of the regime by preaching three sermons on the teachings of the Old Testament, with special reference to the fact that the Jews were God's Chosen People. For his sermon of December 31, 1933, Faulhaber chose as his text, 'Love thy neighbour as thyself'. No race, he told his congregation, should learn to hate any other race. Christianity depended on Christ, and Christ did not happen to have been a German.

From 1933 onwards Faulhaber had his sermons printed and copies made available in many churches for anyone who wanted to take one away with him, while other copies were nailed on church doors. From 1933 onwards he was forbidden to have his sermons printed and Munich printers were threatened with heavy punishments if they collaborated in disobeying this order. Yet his sermons continued to be printed and circulated. Extracts from them were added to routine church news posted up in the churches, and I can remember the little crowds that gathered to read them in the late 1930s, their members standing silent and absorbed but casting the occasional surreptitious glance around them.

While the leader of the Hitler Youth, Baldur von Schirach, was declaring that 'Who serves Hitler, who serves Germany, serves God', Faulhaber preached that the conversion of the Germans to Christianity was the true beginning of their nationhood, and that Christ

73

was the only true 'leader' of Germans and of all mankind. In one of his later sermons he called Rosenberg's *Myth of the Twentieth Century* a stone, instead of bread, and in another he cried ont: 'Woe to the country in which youth and the family have been robbed of God!'

Naturally, Faulhaber was primarily concerned with the defence of his Church and his religion, rather than of the whole community. He opposed the closing down of church educational institutions and protested against the dismissal of 600 Bavarian teaching nuns in 1936. Two years later he wrote a vigorous letter to the Bavarian Minister of Education, protesting against the closing down of a further forty-one church schools and claiming that the Nazis were waging war against organized religion. Yet another pastoral letter criticized the Nazis for closing the Catholic Young Men's and Young Women's associations in 1938. At the same time Faulhaber advised young Catholics to 'set aside any thought of underground activity' and to behave like Christian citizens. Even so, some fervent Nazis complained to the Gestapo about the Archbishop.

After their first five years in power, indeed, the Nazis were ready to attack the Catholic Church in a manner which would have seemed incredible in 1933. The Reich Concordat was a buried memory—even though Pope Pius XII, surprisingly, was still claiming its justification and efficacy in 1940–5. Paganism was now publicly commended by the Nazis, and publicly practised. Nazi-sponsored pagan 'cults' revived the pre-Christian shrine to Wotan at the Heiliger Berg near Heidelberg and the pre-Christian temple of the Sachsenhain near Verden. The old stone gods of the Germanic race had been taken out of storage, dusted down and revitalized.

Already in 1935 a paper read to the students of Kiel Academy laid down that 'We Germans are heathens and want no more Jewish religion in our Germany. We no longer believe in the Holy Ghost; we believe in the Holy Blood.' Preaching from the pulpit against Rosenberg's racial theories was forbidden, and Law 130 of the Nazi *Staatsgesetzbuch* (code of law) threatened penalties for any priest who preached 'against the interests of the State'. Goering decreed in Prussia that the *Hitler Gruss*—the right hand flung up with a stiff right arm—should be regarded as 'the only salute to Jesus Christ'. Holy pictures were removed from schools and an order promulgated that school buildings should no longer be blessed by the Church. In some places schoolchildren were forbidden to make the sign of the Cross.

The apostles of the anti-Christian movement were Alfred Rosenberg and Julius Streicher, the foul-mouthed Gauleiter of Nuremberg. In retrospect, Rosenberg seems to have been an almost comical figure, and he went to his execution as a major war-criminal in 1945 still unaware of the pernicious nature of the racial doctrines which he purveyed. Some of them—like his invocation of a Germanic 'Master Spirit of Fire'—in place of Christ's Cross—were purely ridiculous. Born in 1893, a Balt from the Esthonian city of Reval but a German by race and speech, Rosenberg was regarded as the thinker and philosopher of the Nazi Party. His creed was the superiority of the German race, in which he sincerely believed. He gave considerable encouragement to scatter-brained Nazi intellectuals, and his writings were their bible. He was executed primarily for his activities as Reich Commissioner for German-occupied Eastern Euorpe. But his writings had a debilitating effect on German youth.

Streicher, bandy-legged, gross and sensual, led a more direct attack on organized religion. He was a militant atheist. One of his best-known sayings was, 'Christ mixed a good deal with women. I believe he stayed with one who was an adulteress—so I have heard.' Streicher's publication, the *Stuermer*, largely blasphemous and entirely pornographic, adorned the street-corners of German towns, with its lewd and revolting caricatures enshrined in the so-called '*Stuermer-Kasten*'—small wooden frames with glass fronts set at eye-level. Many of the caricatures were directed at the churches. Monasteries were depicted as sinks of bisexual iniquity; nuns were continually being raped by their Father-confessors; the Pope was a High Priest of Sin.

A favourite theme in the *Stuermer* was the lecherous Catholic priest who made indecent advances to young girls (and boys) and who played the Peeping Tom in order to watch women undressing. A secondary theme (for it attracted less attention) was the peculating priest, levying contributions from the poor for his own extortionate use, smuggling goods and currency, living off the fat of the land. The *Stuermer* was instrumental in initiating the trials of Catholic priests which began in 1935-6 and which carried on throughout the whole Nazi era—for alleged immorality, for smuggling and for treason. The purpose of the trials was to smear the whole Catholic Church and blur its image in the popular mind.

What were churchmen like Faulhaber to do in order to stem this tide of atheism? Plenty of them tried to protest. Thus in 1934 Bishop Kaller of the Emsland and Bishop Bornewasser of Trier were declaiming against paganism, and in the same year Cardinal Schulte of Cologne ordered a statement to be read from all pulpits in his diocese, protesting against the intimidation of young Catholics simply because they went to church. In 1935 equally strong protests were made by Bishop Preysing of Berlin and Archbishop Groeber of Freiburg against the 'protective arrests' of priests without trial and without legal charges being brought against them.

In August 1935 the bishops' conference at Fulda produced a pastoral letter which agreed that the Churches should not interfere in the affairs of the State, but which spoke of the Nazi 'war of annihilation' against Christianity. A year later Bishop Bornewasser said in public: 'This week I have seen living martyrs in the diocese of Trier . . . men and women who are suffering a shocking personal martyrdom for the sake of their faith and their loyalty to the Church.'

Faulhaber himself preached openly against the *Stuermer* and the almost equally blasphemous and filthy *Schwarze Korps*. The result was that in 1938 the Nazis organized mobs which attacked his home, smashed all the windows with stones and tried to set fire to the building. The same thing happened to the homes of Cardinal Innitzer in Vienna and Bishop Sproll in Rothenburg. The mob in Munich howled: 'Take him to Dachau!' and 'Away with Faulhaber, the friend of the Jews, who gives his hand in friendship to Moscow!' During fresh demonstrations the Munich mob sang the S.S. ditty— 'Black rats and moles. . . . We shall smite them, we shall drive them out of Germany.'

Faulhaber refused to be intimidated. Two years later he began to preach against the Nazis' euthanasia programme, which entailed the mass murder of hundreds of helpless mental deficients. In November 1940 he risked his neck by writing to the Reich Minister of Justice on this subject. In his letter he said that the general public was now fully aware that mental deficients were being sent to 'homes' at

Grafeneck, Hartheim and Sonneneck, where they were done to death (their families were always served with a notice of a death). Faulhaber urged that euthanasia was a violation of the Concordat and of divine law, and that it was incompatible with Christian teaching: 'The unchangable principle of moral order and the principle of justice cannot be set aside in time of war.'

There was, of course, no answer to this letter but there was also no act of reprisal against the Cardinal. Although Faulhaber's voice was heard less frequently as the war went on, we find him on Passion Sunday in 1942 still telling his congregation in the Munich *Liebfrauenstift*: 'For years now in our country there has been waged a battle against Christianity and the Church.'

While Faulhaber and others were putting up a gallant struggle the Vatican failed in the main to intervene with any authority on behalf of the 30,000,000 Roman Catholics in Germany. One real effort, however, was made. On March 14, 1937, Pope Pius XI ordered that an encyclical, *Mit Brennender Sorge* ('With Burning Sorrow'), should be read from all Catholic pulpits in Germany. The encyclical charged the Nazis with failure to observe the terms of the Concordat and condemned Hitler's racial theories. The Nazis were accused of 'sowing the tares of suspicion, discord, hatred, calumny, of secret and open fundamental hostility to Christ and his Church'. The encyclical went on to forecast 'threatening storm-clouds of destructive religious wars, which have no other aim than . . . extermination'.

The Nazis were gravely alarmed by the Pope's action, at once forbade the circulation of the encyclical and confiscated printing presses from firms which went on printing copies. A special internal inquiry was ordered by the Gestapo for failure to prevent the encyclical from being read in the churches in the first place.

It was a tragedy that the Vatican underrated the effects of its action and the enthusiasm which it aroused in the Catholic Church. Young priests walked and ran miles, bicycled and motor-bicycled all over the country, in order to distribute *Mit Brennender Sorge*. Quite by chance, the encyclical was well timed. The Pope acted only after allowing the Concordat to be systematically violated for a period of around three years, but Hitler—unknown to the Pope—was just entering a new period of increasingly dangerous diplomatic activity. Had the encyclical been followed up by diplomatic pressure from the Vatican, or had the Pope produced a further, more sweeping condemnation of Nazism, the course of history might have been changed. Would Mussolini have been able to keep Italy on the side of a Nazi Germany involved in conflict with the Vatican? Would the German Catholics, in their vast majority, have continued to obey Hitler's orders? Would the Western Powers have been so ready to appease him?

Unfortunately, *Mit Brennender Sorge* remains an isolated incident in the history of the Vatican's relations with the Nazi regime. Because of this, more than for any other single reason, the Roman Catholic Church failed to become the principal focus of conservative opposition to Hitler. This should have been its natural role.

This did not, of course, prevent Catholics of the calibre of Faulhaber from opposing the Nazis. By far the most outstanding among those who stood up for their Church and for Christian principles was the Bishop and later Cardinal Archbishop of Muenster, Clemens Count von Galen. Here was a figure, with his square jaw, bullet head and bold stare beneath bushy eyebrows, who has gained an almost legendary reputation since his death just after the war. A member of an old Westphalian noble family, an aristocrat who gave himself no fine airs but possessed an unbounded confidence in himself, a fighter—even though he carried no arms—of the stamp of Bishop Odo of Bayeux, Galen was a potential Christian leader whose endurance and periodic audacity impressed even Hitler. This was the real reason why Galen survived the war and the Nazi era.

Clemens Count von Galen was born in 1878, the eldest son of a family rooted in the hard soil and among the *stur* (obstinate) people of Westphalia. He was brought up and remained a conservative. He believe in the justice of Germany's cause in World War I and was acidly sarcastic about the democracy of the Weimar Republic. A man of no great political acumen, he succumbed to the 'stab in the back' legend of 1919, which laid down that the Imperial German Army was never beaten in battle but was treacherously betrayed by the striking workers and the mutinying sailors. He was appointed Bishop in September 1933 and on October 23 took the oath of loyalty to the regime—as provided for under the terms of the Concordat—before Marshal Goering in Berlin.

Von Galen did not, in 1933, look like a potential enemy of the

Nazis. For one thing he was opposed to Church interference in the affairs of the State. His conservatism was tinged with a rabid anti-Bolshevism and an only partially subdued nationalism. In 1939 he delivered an exultant pastoral greeting at the end of the Spanish Civil War—godless Communism had been routed and the forces of evil defeated 'with God's help'. On another occasion Galen concluded a letter to Goering with the ultra-Nazi salutation, '*Mit deutschem Gruss—heil Hitler!*'

The outbreak of war against Poland, Britain and France produced the sort of message to his clergy which must have delighted the hearts of Hitler and his minions: 'War, which outwardly was ended by an imposed peace in 1919, has now broken out anew and has drawn our *Volk* and *Vaterland* into its clutches.' With much of the warrior-priest in his make-up, Galen was slow to recognize that war in the twentieth century must be both evil and nonsensical; he accepted the ideal of the German soldier who was a model citizen and a practising Christian and he talked in typically Germanic terms about chivalry on the field of battle.

Even from the pulpit he called on his flock to resist the alien foe. What is more—for he was a studiously honest man—he certainly believed in what he said. Nor was this as grotesque as it must sound, years afterwards, to anyone who remembers Hitler's War as a thing of concentrated horror, of oppression and torture, of the massacres of Lidice and Oradour. Most German soldiers who went to the wars in 1939–40 genuinely believed in chivalry in battle. They looked after enemy wounded like their own, and they were often highly embarrassing in their determination to give their chocolate and cigarettes to the first prisoners-of-war whom they captured.

Galen, like most of his colleagues in the Catholic Church, tended to subscribe to talk about the Christian's duty to his Leader, about the chance of his winning glory in combat and sanctification by dying a soldier's death. A dozen Catholic newspapers—the *Klerusblatt*, the *Muenchener Kirchenzeitung*, the *Bayrische Katholische Zeitung*—did likewise. To them, as to Galen, what was supremely important was that the Catholic Church was identifying itself with the German national cause, with the reversal of the Treaty of Versailles, and with the mighty struggle of a people which had first acquired nationhood, under Bismarck, through war.

Yet well before the beginning of the war Galen was beginning to come into conflict with the Nazis. As early as 1934 he began to cast doubt on Nazi racial doctrines by preaching the brotherhood of all mankind. In September 1936 he preached in the fourteenth-century collegiate church of St. Victor in the Rhineland town of Xanten. His words contained more than one clear indictment of dictatorship: 'Obedience which places souls in servitude is the most base form of slavery. . . . It is worse than murder, for it is the subjection of all human personality. . . . It is an assault on God Himself.'

No less clear were Galen's thoughts on the attitude of the Nazi dictatorship to the Roman Catholic Church: 'See how Holy Church . . . and its loyal children in Germany are today insulted and reviled! How many Catholics, priests and laymen, have been attacked and insulted in the papers and at public meetings, driven out of their professions, imprisoned and illtreated without judicial sentence being passed! There are fresh graves in German soil in which lie the ashes of those whom Catholic people regard as martyrs for the Faith.'

On November 4, 1936, the Nazi authorities ordered the removal of crucifixes as 'symbols of superstition' from schools in the Oldenburg area. This was a predominantly Catholic part of Germany and belonged to Galen's diocese of Muenster. Galen ordered nine days of prayer for the retention of crucifixes in the churches. On the next Sunday the churches in Oldenburg and Muenster were filled to overflowing with the faithful, and the Nazis retorted by sending the Gauleiter of Oldenburg, Roever, to speak at a mass-meeting in the Cathedral Square in Muenster, the heart of the resistance. The Muensterlanders are noted for their dourness, their distrust of outsiders and their lack of spontaneous self-expression. More than 4,000 of these stolid but sturdily loyal people assembled to meet Herr Roever, but they had not come to listen. They howled him down. Police used truncheons and firehoses on the crowd.

On November 25 the ordinance of November 4 was cancelled. But only a few weeks later the Muensterlanders were once again up in arms—because in spite of the cancellation of the ordinance crucifixes were being removed from the school classrooms by local authorities. In some villages large crowds demonstrated for hours, shouting in chorus whenever Nazi-appointed local officials tried to

Ludwig Beck, Hitler's leading opponent in the German Army during the
early years of the war and immediately before its outbreak

Cardinal von Galen, the 'Lion of Muenster' and the outstanding
Roman Catholic opponent of Hitler

address them. Parishioners replaced the crucifixes, and some of them were arrested for doing this (this happened in one or two villages on the Rhine and Moselle too).

Could this spontaneous opposition to the regime have burgeoned into something bigger—even into the kernel of a national resistance? Possibly it did not do so because the Nazis were so adept at stifling and emasculating opposition of every kind. They set out to rob the Roman Catholic Opposition of two of its most vital assets by undermining the Catholic youth movement and by destroying the Catholic Press.

The Nazis were always intensely aware of the need to get German youth on their side. Non-Nazi youth groups, after a time, could no longer be tolerated. In 1935 members of Catholic youth groups were forbidden to appear in organized bodies in public, or to take part, in a team-sense, in sports meetings. In 1936 they were instructed to join the Hitler Youth, in addition to whatever other youth organization they belonged to. In 1938 the Nazis closed the Catholic Action organization, which gave advice to young people of school-leaving age. The same thing happened a few months later to the Catholic sports association, the *Deutsche Jugendkraft*.

By the end of 1936 Catholic youth groups had been managing to assemble only on strictly church occasions. Wisely, the Nazis left them unmolested as a rule when these occurred. Most young people were dragooned into the Hitler Youth without too much difficulty. Only in 1938 was the order passed around by the Hitler Youth that members of Catholic youth groups were in future to be 'made to look ridiculous'. Their names were taken, they were black-listed and barred, whenever possible, from responsible jobs. Pressure was brought to bear on their parents by the Party. All effective organization of Catholic youth gradually withered away in face of this campaign, although some small groups were still surviving in 1940–1 in Bavaria and the Tyrol.

The destruction of the Catholic Press, which had begun in 1933, was to be carried out with greater speed. The 416 Catholic newspapers and periodicals, with a total circulation of over 12,000,000, were systematically obliterated. Among them were papers like *Michael* and the *Ketteler Wacht*, both with circulations of over 150,000. The craft of the Nazis lay in their ability to back-pedal whenever they chose. With the Catholic Press and youth groups out of the way, the Nazis relaxed pressure in face of the demonstrations of the doughty Muensterlanders. This was followed in turn by a relaxation of vigilance on the part of the Catholic communities.

Galen himself certainly did not relax his vigilance. In 1937 he was openly attacking Nazi propaganda organs like the *Stuermer* and denouncing the Nazi vilification of Christian saints and martyrs. He protested strongly against the ban on collections for the poor and needy by the Catholic aid-association, Caritas (its collections had previously averaged about 33,000,000 marks a year). His pastoral letters continued to be distributed, and in March 1937 young Catholics used physical force to defend girls who were distributing them and who were molested by the brown-shirted S.A.

Galen's attitude to World War II—that of a patriot who believed that the Fatherland was in danger, and who attributed the war largely to the Treaty of Versailles—contributed to the modification for a time of his opposition to the Nazis. For two years he was surprisingly quiet, for this was a period of increasingly open Nazi oppression of the Churches. In a score of different ways they sought to make the Catholic Church look impotent and absurd. They banned religious processions, beginning with a ban of the 1939 Corpus Christi processions (in spite of it, 16,000 people took part in Munich, including 600 university students). They prevented church collections and pastoral work in the hospitals. They enforced the law that any child over the age of fourteen could withdraw of his free will from the Church, without reference to his parents.

The Nazis indulged in frequent acts of sacrilege. S.A. and Hitler Youth columns marched past churches chanting anti-religious ditties; cemeteries were desecrated, and crosses were sometimes taken from the churches and used by the Hitler Youth for target practice. Every effort was made to encourage apostasy—although apostates often returned to the Church. Thus, in 1938, sixty-seven did so in the single diocese of Salzburg. Priests were bullied, threatened and even imprisoned for refusing to betray the secrets of the confessional.

It must have cost Galen a tremendous effort of will and imposed a severe strain on his conscience to have remained, for him, comparatively silent at this time. By 1941 he had decided that his duty did not lie in keeping silence any longer, and in July and August of that year he preached a series of sermons which contained the bravest and most trenchant criticism of the Nazi regime that any Catholic churchman had so far dared to make.

The first of these sermons was delivered in the Lamberti church in Muenster on July 13, 1941. Galen openly attacked the power and brutality of the Gestapo, pointing out that the average citizen remained utterly impotent and helpless in face of it. 'No single one of us is safe,' Galen told the congregation, 'and however guiltless he may know himself to be, he may still be taken one day from his home, deprived of his liberty, and locked up in the cellars or concentration camps of the Gestapo.' He concluded the sermon with this appeal: 'I publicly declare: we demand justice! If this call remains unheard, if the rule of Justice is not restored, then our German *Volk* and *Vaterland* will perish of inner decay and rottenness, in spite of the heroism of our soldiers and their glorious victories.'

The second sermon was preached in Muenster's *Liebfrauenkirche* on July 20. It contained Galen's most stirring appeal of all, for devotion to Christian duty. 'Be strong! Stand firm! Just now we are not the hammer, but the anvil. . . . Take a lesson from the forge! Ask the smith and learn the truth from him; what is hammered out on the anvil takes its form not only from the hammer but from the anvil too. Be strong! Stand firm and steadfast, even as the anvil beneath the hammer's blows! It may happen that obedience to God, and loyalty to conscience, can cost you or me life, freedom or home. But it is better to die than to sin. May God's mercy, without which we are nothing, give and preserve for you and for me this unshaken steadfastness."

Not for nothing was Galen nicknamed 'The Lion of Muenster'. In his third sermon, on August 3, he attacked the Nazi euthanasia programme, and asked that 'through prayer and sincere penance we call forth God's forgiveness and mercy upon us, our city, our country and our whole beloved German *Volk*'. In the course of the sermon he gave an account of the killing of poor imbeciles in the euthanasia 'institutions' of Warstein and Marienthal. Members of his congregation wept.

The three sermons infuriated the Nazis. Some of their leaders wanted Galen executed for treason and proposed this to Josef Goebbels. But Hitler decided against this step on the grounds that Galen's execution would result in the population of Muenster and district being 'written off' for the duration of the war. A Gestapo report was drawn up on Galen's activities and early in 1942 Hermann Goering was agitating for action to be taken against him. Hearing of this, Galen wrote a firm and dignified letter, claiming that he had done no more than exercise his citizen's right to criticize when criticism was in the interest of the community.

There is a legend that the Gestapo did, early in 1942, call on Galen, in order to take him from his Bishop's Palace for interrogation. According to the legend, Galen asked them to wait downstairs for a moment. He went to his room and dressed himself in full bishop's regalia, returned downstairs and told the waiting Gestapo that he was ready to accompany them. They decided to leave him in peace. Relatives of Galen have not confirmed this story, which may be apochryphal. What is sure is that Galen, although greatly daring, remained a free man.

One historian of the German Opposition to Hitler, Frau Annedore Leber, believes that Galen's courageous and outspoken sermons had two results—Hitler ordered the confiscations of Church property, at least in Galen's diocese, to cease, and the organized murder of mental deficients was temporarily stopped. In his diary Ulrich von Hassell wrote: 'Why does Rome let Galen fight all alone? And what are our lordly princes of the Church doing?' The Vatican, indeed, outwardly did nothing to help its gallant servant in Muenster. Galen's success is in some degree an answer to those apologists of Popes Pius XI and XII, who claim that they were unable to act, because nothing constructive would be gained and because the Nazis would have taken reprisals against the Vatican.

His 1941 sermons marked the climax of Galen's active opposition to the regime. On no subsequent occasion did he show such an entire disregard of the consequences. Although he continued to administer his flock and do his Christian duty, it may well be that the war against Russia restrained his readiness to criticize the Nazis. Galen regarded atheistical Communism as a terrible menace to Europe. Certainly he never became one of those few Germans who felt that Germany could atone for the Nazis' crimes only through total defeat. When the advancing British troops crossed the Rhine in 1945 Galen did not look on them in any sense as 'deliverers'. His comment on their entry into his badly bombed city of Muenster was 'This is a shattering experience.'

Galen's survival of the war—he died in 1946 and there have since been demands for his canonization—was no slur on his courage. He would doubtless have been prepared for martyrdom, but honestly believed that his flock needed his continuing presence among them. In this sense his opposition remained 'orthodox', an amalgam of audacity and common sense, exercised in the interests of his Church and community.

But Catholic martyrs did exist in the Nazi era; some of their stories comprise another part of this account of Catholic resistance. One of the outstanding stories of this kind was that of Father Bernhard Lichtenberg, the dean of the Cathedral of St. Hedwig in Berlin. Lichtenberg was born in 1875 and took up his post at St. Hedwig's in 1938. He was an ardent pacifist and was warned by the Nazis that propagation of pacifist ideas in time of war could be regarded as treason. Lichtenberg was also scandalized by the Nazi heresy which put the Fuehrer, Adolf Hitler, above religion; his comment on this heresy was 'I have only one Fuehrer, Jesus Christ.' This remark was reported to the Nazis.

If he had concentrated on discreet propagation of pacifism and on his normal religious duties Lichtenberg might have been largely ignored by the Nazis. By the time that war broke out he was nearly sixty-five, a plump, shy man who was not likely to impress German youth. But Lichtenberg decided to do something which was not attempted by the Papacy or by paladins of the Church like Galen and Faulhaber—he defended the Jews publicly. By so doing he was signing his own death-warrant.

In October 1941 Lichtenberg offered up prayers in church for the Jews. As an answer to viciously anti-Semitic Nazi leaflets which were being circulated at the time, Lichtenberg had this announcement read from the pulpits in his diocese: 'An inflammatory pamphlet anonymously attacking the Jews is being disseminated among the houses of Berlin. It declares that any German who, because of allegedly false sentimentality, aids the Jews in any way, is guilty of betraying the people. Do not allow yourself to be misled by this un-Christian attitude, but act according to the strict commandment of Jesus Christ—Thou shalt love thy neighbour as thyself.'

Lichtenberg was arrested on October 23, 1941, and was charged with having prayed for Jews and the inmates of concentration camps, who were the 'enemies of the State'. During his trial it was established that Lichtenberg had been offering up prayers for the Jews ever since the 'Reich Crystal Night' of November 8, 1938. He had also asked to be sent to the Jewish ghetto in Lodz, in order to share the sufferings of its wretched inmates. He had accused the Nazis of vandalism from the pulpit.

His fate was certain. He was sentenced to two years' imprisonment only, for the Nazis were aware of his personal popularity. But they intended to ensure that he would never be a free man again. He was removed from his prison in Berlin-Tegel on October 22, 1943, and taken on his way to Dachau concentration camp, in so-called 'protective custody'. He died on the journey, in the north Bavarian town of Hof.

In the same selfless spirit Father Rupert Mayer, born a year later than Lichtenberg and a member of the Jesuit Order from 1900 onwards, opposed the Nazis openly and stated his opinions with suicidal bluntness. Mayer served through World War I and was awarded the Iron Cross for his courage in the front line. He was wounded, and lost a leg. In 1923 he declared in Munich that a good Catholic could never simultaneously be a good member of the Nazi Party. In one sermon he produced a phrase which must have maddened the Nazis: 'That which makes more noise does not usually possess more soul and strength.' In 1937 he preached an anti-Nazi sermon in the convent church of Varsberg: 'In all political, economic and social questions we are prepared to go along with our fellow-citizens; but in religious matters we must say to all others—Hands off!'

On May 28, 1937, the Nazis banned Father Mayer from preaching. He ignored the ban and was arrested on June 5. Strong protests were sent to the regime, notably by Cardinal Faulhaber. But he was sent to Lansdberg prison for five months and the judges found that —although he could not be categorized as a common criminal—he was 'a menace to the State'. On release he was forbidden to preach publicly, but members of his congregation continued to come to St. Michael's Church in Munich to ask his advice.

Mayer was rearrested in January 1939 and once more released after warnings of dire penalties. In the autumn of 1939 he was sent to Sachsenhausen concentration camp. Here his health gave way as a result of near-starvation and he was released simply because he was too weak to give any more trouble. Father Mayer died in 1945, as a result of his privations, in the monastery of Ettal in the Bavarian Alps.

Heinrich Feuerstein was another Catholic who died as a result of persecution by the Nazis. Born in Freiburg, he served in a number of Catholic churches in the South German province of Baden. An outspoken man, he referred to Hitler as a 'catastrophe' and asserted that he would 'prefer to be called a fool than a coward'. Feuerstein regarded it as his personal duty to explain that Christ's martyrdom was intended as an example and was not a mere incident in the Christian story. This led him to examine the bases of martyrdom and to reach the conclusion that the Nazis' victims in Dachau were martyrs. He did not hesitate to say so publicly, and to condemn the murder of mental deficients. He was imprisoned in Dachau in June 1942 and died there two months later.

There were innumerable other brave and active Catholic opponents of the Nazis, among the foremost of them the unnamed heroes of the St. Raphael's Association who helped numbers of Jews to get out of Germany before the outbreak of war. There was Father Joseph Lechner, a professor at Eichstaett diocesan seminary who produced his *Goebbelsbrief* (Goebbels-Letter) broadsheet roundly attacking Hitler's Propaganda Minister. Lechner accused Goebbels of spreading immorality and falsehood. He signed his broadsheet 'Michael Germanicus' and distributed thousands of copies of it.

There was 'Brother Paul', Father Max Joseph Metzger, who founded his own 'White Cross' peace movement, was arrested four times and executed in 1944 in Brandenburg gaol. There was Sister Josefa, a Bavarian nun who between May 1944 and April 1945 succeeded in smuggling food and clothing to the inmates of Dachau, and who made a particular point of bringing in, concealed on her person, the sacramental bread and wine for the clandestine communion services of the Catholic prisoners. There was the priest, August von Rathenow, who was murdered in Dachau for striving with courageous chivalry to prevent Polish girls from being beaten-up and humiliated.

There was Father Otto Mueller, who helped individual Jews, his members of the active resistance when they were on the run, and passed on truthful news about the war by listening to foreign broadcasts. Mueller was arrested in August 1944 and was taken to the Berlin-Tegel prison. There he was tortured so badly that he went blind from shock and died.

A very special place in the history of the Catholic Opposition is occupied by Father Alfred Delp, a Jesuit priest who believed that it was not enough to set a Christian example and preach the Word of God without fear or compromise. Delp was unique among the priesthood (a handful of evangelical pastors thought as he did) in believing that it was a part of his duty to help to plan for the political future of his country. Born in 1907 and accepted into the Jesuit Order in 1926, his opposition to the Nazis was primarily intellectual. He thought that the Churches had mistakenly encouraged a 'collectivist' view of democracy, that the spreading of political responsibility had brought a decline in the individual's sense of citizenship, and that government should repose in the hands of a 'creative élite'.

As a South German Catholic, Delp had small regard for the expansionist Germanism, based on the hard core of Prussia, which the Bismarckian era had initiated. He looked on Hitler as a 'National Bolshevik', a nihilist and an anti-Christian. But he had a horror, too, of the 'Slavic hordes' which lacked leadership and creative talent, and he distrusted Britain and the United States, regarding them as devoid of spiritual content and obsessed by material well-being. Delp, indeed, seems to have passed on some of his views to West German Catholics who, like Konrad Adenauer, have fashioned the post-war policies of the Federal Republic. He wanted a reconstructed, integrated Western Europe, based on Franco-German friendship, and a 'balanced' German State, compounded of German custom, classical tradition and the Christian ethic.

Delp, the deep thinker, came into contact with the members of the primarily conservative 'Kreisau Circle', and through them made the acquaintance of Stauffenberg. His part in the conversations of the Kreisauers was the reason for his being arrested after the failure of the July 1944 conspiracy, and he was executed in February 1945. In his last letter from gaol Delp wrote: 'It is the time of sowing, not the time of harvest. God sows; and in due course He will reap. I will strive at least . . . to fall as a fertile and good seed on the soil.' Certainly his wish has been granted; the seed of his thought has not been forgotten and is a part of the origin of progressive European thinking and flourishing European institutions.

What was the real extent of Roman Catholic resistance to Hitler, and how can one best measure, appraise and analyse it? According to most estimates around 5,000 members of the clergy were sent to German concentration camps and more than 2,000 of them died there. There were certainly more Roman Catholic priests than Evangelical pastors in German concentration camps, chiefly because a proportion of them were Poles (no Protestant country occupied by the Nazis was treated with the same ruthlessness as Catholic Poland). The numbers of German Roman Catholic clergy imprisoned in the camp,s ran at least, into many hundreds; and scores of them died there.

Here is one yardstick to Catholic resistance. In addition, many other German Catholics, who were not priests, suffered primarily because of their faith. This was particularly so in Bavaria, where the monarchists of the *Heimat und Koenigsbund* were almost all Catholics and were led by aristocrats like Baron Harnier and the Baroness von Stengel, and the head gardener of Schleissheim Palace outside Munich, Heinrich Weiss. This was so, too, among the Catholic youth groups in the Rhineland and Austria, and among the South German peasantry who opposed Hitler's scorched-earth policy at the end of the war—sometimes losing their lives in the process.

Certain factors militated against the organization of a bigger and more effective Catholic opposition to Nazism. The first was the fact that—in spite of the unity of the Catholic Church—opposition remained localized and was never co-ordinated throughout the country. As soon as the war broke out, again, opposition was sapped by emotional attachment to the Reich, by personal attachment to friends at the front, by the feeling that Germany was engaged in a national struggle for survival, by hatred of the Treaty of Versailles, by the effects of Goebbels' brilliant propaganda and by an ingrown fear of the 'Red Menace' of Communist Russia. Active resistance was discouraged by conformism, and by the vague hope that Nazism was only a temporary phenomenon which could be endured for the time being.

It may well be that some of the Catholic bishops were afraid that opposition to the Nazis and to the war would only weaken the position of the churches. Some of the bishops, certainly, were far too ready to identify themselves with a 'national' war. This was what Conrad Groeber, Archbishop of Freiburg, had to say in 1940: 'Should one of you lose his life, it becomes far more than the ordinary tribute demanded by Death the Conqueror in repayment for man's mortal guilt. It is the ultimate offering to *Vaterland* and *Volk*. A soldier's death is . . . a sacrificial death. A sacrificial death is a hero's death.'

And this came from Father Franz Rankowski, who made a habit of talking unmitigated nonsense about the German mission to 'civilize' and 'Christianize' (with gas-chambers!) Europe: 'Because our Fuehrer . . . became acquainted with the inferno of war when he was a simple soldier at the front, he has tried as no other statesman to spare Europe from armed conflict.'

Finally, there is the vexed question, which will not be resolved for many years to come and may never be resolved at all, whether or not the Vatican did enough to stimulate and support the Church leaders. Presumably the Vatican inspired the 1941 and 1943 declarations of the bishops that to kill was a sin (the 1941 declaration added a careful rider to the effect that it was not a sin to kill in war). Faulhaber, Galen, Preysing in Berlin and others must have consulted the Vatican at vital moments and it may be assumed that they followed its advice. Pius XI did, in addition, produce the encyclical *Mit Brennender Sorge*, and the Vatican City extended its protection and the right of asylum to all who sought refuge there—including escaped prisoners-of-war—and even while the Germans were occupying Rome.

For one brief interlude, too, the Vatican entered into negotiations with members of the active Opposition to Hitler in Germany. This was in October 1939 when Josef Mueller, a friend of Faulhaber and a former member of the Bavarian People's Party, travelled to Rome with the express purpose of establishing contact with the Pope. He achieved this with the help of two Germans living in Rome—

Monsignor Kaas, a former leader of the *Zentrum* Party, and Father Robert Leiber, the Pope's personal secretary. Mueller wanted the Pope to act as a go-between with the Western Powers, and so secure from them some sort of guarantee of fair treatment for a future non-Nazi Germany.

The indications are that Pius XI was ready to act, up to a point, as intermediary. The British Minister to the Vatican, Mr. D'Arcy Osborne, forwarded information to Whitehall and received some pointers from the British Government in return. Some interest was aroused in London by the suggestion that peace might be secured if the Nazi regime were removed, a democratic government installed in its place and a promise made that there would be no German attack in the West. In return, Germany's eastern frontier was to be revised to her advantage and a part of the work of Versailles undone.

A report outlining these 'terms' was, in fact, presented to Field Marshal von Brauchitsch, and to his Chief of Staff, General Halder. Brauchitsch refused to consider action against the Nazi regime, in view of its popularity with the German working-man. Halder claimed that his conscience would not allow him to act and that the military situation could not justify his breaking his oath of loyalty to the Fuehrer. Halder's final rejection of this chance of a negotiated peace seems to have come about April 1940. Mueller was to be arrested three years later and imprisoned, but survived the war. Through no fault of its own the Vatican's most serious effort to assist towards a negotiated peace came to nothing.

But that—if not all the story—is most of it. The Vatican certainly failed to take sufficiently positive and open action to help even the persecuted Catholics of Germany and of countries occupied by the Nazis. The evidence supplied by Professor Gerald Reitlinger, in his book *The Final Solution*, and by other students of Nazi history, suggests that the Vatican procrastinated when its help was sought for the far more brutally persecuted Jews of Central Europe. Pius XII, admittedly, helped a few dozen Jewish families. But did the Vatican lift a finger to help the German Jews—for this must be an operative question in this study? The answer seems to be, No.

In 1963 a young West German dramatist, Rolf Hochhuth, wrote a play *Der Stellvertreter* (produced in England as *The Representative*) which caused a sensation in Germany. The play was a frontal assault on Pope Pius XII who, as Cardinal Pacelli, had played a major role in the negotiation of the 1933 Concordat. Hochhuth depicted Pius XII as a careerist, a 'political priest' who totally failed to register a single effective protest against Nazi barbarism. In particular Hochhuth castigated the Pope for failing to make some effort to help the Jews of Italy in 1943, when Rome was no longer occupied by the Germans and the Italian monarchy had come out on the side of the Western Powers.

One West German who at once sprang to the defence of the Pope was Albrecht von Kessel, himself closely connected with Hitler's German enemies and a member of the German Legation in the Vatican City in 1943. Kessel believed that Papal intervention would not have saved a single Jewish life and might have only spurred Hitler to worse excesses—a natural reflex of the Fuehrer's when he felt frustrated and thwarted. But Kessel used some misleading arguments (he discussed the case in an article in the newspaper *Die Welt*). He suggested that Pius's only chance of intervention was, in fact, in 1943. But there were, of course, many earlier opportunities, which were not taken. Kessel suggested, too, that the Pope would have run the risk of being arrested. This is quite true. But Kessel added that nobody has the right to ask 'even his nearest relation' to risk martyrdom.

The Pope, in the sense of his high office and his manifest responsibilities, has no earthly 'nearest relation'. But if his martyrdom could have served to discourage the persecution of Jews and Catholics alike, then his duty was plain—to denounce evil. The thought is unavoidable that the Pope failed to speak a word for the persecuted Jews after the Germans retreated from Rome, only because he did not want to draw attention to his significant silence at a previus period when the Nazis could have revenged themselves on him.

Kessel, finally, made the surprising suggestion that the Pope's martyrdom would have been as 'purposeless' as that of Hans and Sophie Scholl, the infinitely gallant Munich students who laid down their lives with an almost nonchalant courage. This suggestion is in itself a condemnation of the educated German of the Nazi era. For the force of example of the men and women who did oppose Nazi barbarism can become one of the most formative influences in German history in the years ahead.

Even in 1945 Pius XII was writing that the Concordat with Hitler had saved German Catholics from worse persecution. It is possible that he believed that his silence, where the Jews were concerned, was equally of benefit to the Catholic Church. This may be the true explanation of his abysmal silence. It may explain why the Vatican had nothing to say about the unprovoked and ruffianly Nazi attacks on small and friendly neighbouring countries like Holland, Belgium, Luxemburg, Norway and Denmark. In his penetrating study *The German Catholics and Hitler's Wars* Gordon Zahn, an American writer, concluded: 'The idea that the Church, as a temporal social institution, can accommodate itself to any regime which affirms its willingness to respect Church property and prerogatives seems almost to have become an unchallengeable truism in Catholic political philosophy.'

Leaving aside the failures of the Vatican—and I am afraid these failures are incontestable—it is still hard to sum up the achievement of Hitler's Catholic opponents in Germany. On the whole, they failed to oppose aggressive war. Save for some links with the conservative Opposition, they did not make common cause with other groups of resisters. They were for the most part preoccupied, understandably, with the defence of Catholic Christian teaching and the preservation of Catholic institutions. They took too long to recognize that Nazism was intrinsically evil.

But their contribution should not be underrated. One Catholic, Hermann Lange, wrote: 'If it be God's will that I die—then let God's will be done.' The stuff of the early Christian martyrs was still there—even in Hitler's regimented Germany. The spirit of self-sacrifice burned bravely in the hearts of many bishops, priests and Catholic laity. It is undeniable that the Christian faith and the Roman Catholic Church had their martyrs, in the twentieth century, in Hitler's Germany.

five

The Protestant Conscience

'Constantly speak the truth, boldly rebuke vice, and suffer patiently for the truth's sake.'

Bible. Book of Common Prayer

COULD the German Evangelical Churches have achieved more than the Roman Catholics in opposing Hitler? This is a question which many German Evangelicals have asked themselves, sometimes shamefacedly, since the end of the Nazi era. For the Evangelical Churches comprised nearly 60 per cent of the German people. Eighty per cent of the people of Prussia—the 'hard core' of the German nation—were Evangelicals. Devout Protestants were well entrenched in the civil service, the Government, the General Staff and even in the Nazi Party. Up to 1945 the unified German Reich was a predominantly Protestant State.

The Evangelical religion was closely identified with the life of the bulk of the German people. It expressed itself in the piety and puritanism of which the Prussians were so proud, and in the traditional Old Testament attitude to women—who were restricted to the 'Three K's' of *Kirche, Kinder, Keuche* (church, children, kitchen). One of its visible symbols was the belt which the soldier buckled on, engraved with the words '*Gott mit uns*' (God with us). There was something Cromwellian about the Germans who marched into battle in the 1914–18 war singing hymns, and about their womenfolk, offering up prayers to a strictly German God who, they were convinced, would give their country victory.

It was Evangelical, nationalist philosophers who pronounced that the State was God-invested and the apex of human goodness, and that the German *Volk*, or race, was a divine revelation. Here, again, the Evangelical Church may have been closer to the heart of the German people than the Roman Catholic. Its influence should have been correspondingly greater. Prussian Protestantism, tough, upright and enduring, might have played a major role in the Opposition to Hitler.

But certain factors told against the Evangelical Churches. In the first place their leaders seem to have misunderstood the lessons of World War I. Hardly one of them suggested that the arrogance and shortsightedness of the German nation had played a major part in causing war and bringing Germany defeat. No less than the politicians and the rest of the laity, the churchmen were affronted by the Treaty of Versailles and aggrieved by a military disaster which they refused to recognize. Even clergymen who subsequently opposed Hitler (Pastor Martin Niemoeller is an obvious example) tended to conform to the general nationalistic pattern (the nonconformers were mainly anti-Church socialists). There is no evidence even of the Churches offering worthwhile support to the Weimar Republic.

In the second place the Evangelical Churches—like the rest of the politically neutral members of the community—underrated the Nazis and failed to understand their intentions. Hitler's *Mein Kampf*, it seems, was read by many Germans but only understood by a few foreigners. As early as 1923 Hitler said publicly: 'We will have no other God but Germany.' He made no secret of his belief that religion should be subordinate to the national 'ethos' and to the mixed-up ideal of 'loyalty to the race'. *Mein Kampf* was basically an anti-Christian book, and forecast—even if in guarded terms—the suppression of Christianity by force and terror.

Hitler's tame racial crank, Alfred Rosenberg, was even more openly intent on undermining orthodox Christianity. In his *Myth of the Twentieth Century* he propagated his own personal myth of the physically courageous, rabidly militant Christ. (It is interesting and may be significant that a curious cult has grown up in post-war Germany, which bases its Christian concepts on the belief that Christ never died on the Cross, but suffered his agony and survived, in order to demonstrate the earthly triumph of the fighting spirit over adversity.)

Rosenberg disbelieved in a Christ who died to save humanity, and regarded crucifixion as the mark of failure. This turned Rosenberg

and his Nazi disciples violently against the teachings of St. Paul. An
Aryan Jesus was just bearable, but a Jewish Jesus was intolerable.
One particular Nazi, who believed rather more in Rosenberg than
in the Bible and who became Hitler's Minister for Church Affairs,
was Hans Kerrl. His statement on the subject of the Jewishness of
Christian beginnings was: 'The priests say Jesus was a Jew, and
speak of St. Paul the Jew, and of salvation coming from the Jews.
This *won't* do!'

Thirdly, the Evangelical Churches were divided and their view of
the State was based on a misreading of Martin Luther's teachings.
There were so many independent branches of the Evangelical
Churches that historians cannot settle on their exact number. There
were at least twenty-eight independent provincial synods and there
may have been as many as thirty. The biggest branch, the Church of
the Old Prussian Union, had around 18,000,000 members; some of
the smallest branches had only a few hundred thousand. Like other
Protestant Churches the world over, the German Evangelicals established pitifully little contact with the Churches of foreign countries.
Unlike the Roman Catholics, they had no international organization
or support.

The German Evangelicals, moreover, followed the teachings of
Luther—or what they visalized them to be—very closely. St. Paul
had proclaimed the doctrine 'Render unto Caesar', and this doctrine
is open to almost limitless misinterpretation. The particular misinterpretation accepted by many Germans was that they had no
right of resistance against rulers who could, in the broadest sense,
be regarded as 'legitimate'.

Luther sided with the German princes against the peasants,
preached a brand of nationalism which had its own medieval anti-
Semitic twist (just one of his many anti-Semitic statements: 'I would
rather be a pig than a Jewish Messiah, for a pig is not afraid of the
devil and his hell-fire'), and venerated the State. Luther did, indeed,
declaim against tyrants, but this part of his message was too easily
forgotten after he had sided with the tyrants himself. Most German
churchmen adopted a woodenness of approach to the problems
posed by secular authority. The result was a virtually universal
obedience—irrespective of what sort of secular power it happened
to be.

NACHFOTO
Ry. 1948

Buchdruckerei J. Fefckert

Pastor Schneider, who suffered martyrdom because he believed in,
and carried out, the First Commandment

Verlag Annedore Leber

Julius Leber, a Social Democrat who never ceased resisting Nazism

German Evangelicals were heartened by the fact that Hitler's first cabinet contained only three Nazis—himself, Goering and Wilhelm Frick. The 'wild men' of the Party were evidently going to be excluded from administrative office. The old, conservative and superficially respectable Germany was going to reassert itself by virtue of its administrative talents. An apparent additional guarantor of the established order was the massive figure of the Reich President, Field Marshal von Hindenburg. He, at least, would—so a great many decent Germans thought—keep Rosenberg, Martin Bormann and their kind in place. For he was a devout and honourable man who was bound to be disgusted by the Nazi heresy that the Christian and Nazi ethics were incompatible, and that a Nazi ethic had to be superimposed on the German character and the German community.

Those Germans who considered the Nazi threat to the Christian Churches at all, and who remained optimists, were quickly proved wrong. Even before Hitler came to power the Nazis, with the co-operation of the Nationalist para-military *Stahlhelm* organization, had founded the 'German Christian' movement (its earliest beginnings were in 1930 and it first became a force in 1932). Among the co-founders of the movement were two of the Kaiser's sons, the obese Prince Eitel Friedrich and the spruce and already keenly Nazi Prince August Wilhelm. Hitler's propaganda chief, Josef Goebbels, was another of the powers behind the movement, whose titular head was an obscure schoolteacher, Herr Wilm. In 1932 the movement came under the control of Pastor Joachim Hossenfelder, aged only thirty-three, born in Silesia, and a former member of the illegal 'Free Corps' which fought in Eastern Germany after the end of the First World War.

The German Christians linked the Cross of Christ with the swastika of the secular arm. They equated Germanism with Christianity, and godlessness with Marxist Communism. The Church, according to Hossenfelder, was 'a community of believers, which is under the State'. Hitler had been sent to the German people by God, as Hossenfelder told a gathering of prominent German Christians in February 1933. At their April 1933 congress in Berlin the German Christians proclaimed that 'God has created me a German; Germanism is a gift of God. . . . For the German, the Church is a community of believers, which is under an obligation to fight for a Christian Germany. . . . Adolf Hitler's Reich calls to the Germans.'

Warning voices had already been raised. Otto Dibelius, General Superintendent in Brandenburg, circulated a letter to the pastors of Berlin and Brandenburg in March 1933, telling them that they must be ready to defend their faith against all intolerant ideologies, including the Nazi. The Bishop of Mecklenburg, Rendtorff, told the churchmen of his diocese in April that the Nazis were bound to interfere in the internal affairs of the Churches. (How right they were was very quickly shown. Dibelius was dismissed from his post by the State-appointed Evangelical Church Commissioner for Prussia, Dr. Jaeger.) In the September 1933 elections Friedrich von Bodelschwingh was elected and confirmed as head of the Evangelical Churches. But his candidature was refused by the Prussian Government, and a German Christian, the fifty-year-old ex-naval chaplain and violent nationalist Ludwig Mueller, was appointed in his place. Mueller's appointment was confirmed by a 'National synod' at Wittenberg, Luther's birthplace, on September 27, 1933.

On July 2, 1933, the reorganization by the Nazis of the Evangelical Churches was celebrated by a huge congregation in Berlin's Kaiser-Gedaechtniskirche. It assembled for a 'Day of Praise'. The interior of the church, which stood at the end of the brash Kurfurstendam, was hung with the Nazi swastika flags. Outside, martial music sounded. This was the official act of the so-called rebirth of the soul of the German people.

In November 1933 the German Christians held a mass meeting at the Sport-Palast in Berlin. One of their most irrational spokesmen, Dr. Krause, demanded the ejection from the Evangelical community of everybody with Jewish blood in his veins, the rejection of a large part of the Old Testament as being a 'book for Jewish cattle', and the removal of certain passages from the New Testament—in particular the writings of St. Paul, the 'Jew rabbi'. Krause's proposals, tabled in the form of a resolution, were approved with only one dissenting vote.

The writing was on the wall, with a vengeance. Hitler's evangelical agents intended to propagate their new, Germanic myth of Jesus the Hero, Jesus the Storm Trooper, Jesus the prototype of Horst-

Wessel, the debauched young Nazi who died in a drunken brawl and gave the Party its plagiarized anthem.

It was this German Christian meeting, more than anything else, which probably prompted Hitler's remark: 'You can do anything you like with them [the German Evangelicals]. They will submit . . . for they are insignificant little people, submissive as dogs.' The Fuehrer, a relapsed Catholic, may have found a special, sadistic pleasure in dragging German Protestantism through the dirt.

Inevitably, Hitler was determined to capture the souls as well as the bodies of Evangelical youth. German youth was already inured to the 'hard life' of the *Pfadfinders*—elderly and mature versions of Boy Scouts, with a much more detailed programme of physical and mental exercise. The *Pfadfinders* and *Wandervoegel* between them produced a healthy tradition of combined thought and effort, and a magnificent race of young people, full of ideas and resource, moulded in the image of Sparta and the warriors who stood shoulder to shoulder with Leonidas at Thermopylae.

The young Germans who, before World War I and in increasing numbers after it, set out with healthy bodies and full hearts to learn something of the world outside Germany should have become model citizens. Most of them were killed on the battlefield. Their post-1919 successors, still full of vigour and a desire to learn, were lapped up by the surge of Nazism. Even before the Nazis came to power these young Germans were thinking in terms of devoting their physical fitness and brute force to a nation which intended to destroy the Treaty of Versailles. Youth, they believed, had to have an elemental radicalism, or it would degenerate into an effigy of the older generation. This was one reason why Hitler conquered German youth.

In 1933 the Evangelical youth groups had 700,000 members. Baldur von Schirach, already the budding Nazi youth-leader, sniped at them as separatists and sectionalists who did not have the true interests of the community at heart. He implied that they no longer kept step with the tempestuous national revival. In December 1933 the Evangelical youth groups were forcibly incorporated in the Hitler Youth. Little effort was made to protest, and who should blame these young people? The political bankruptcy of the Weimar Republic was an established fact. The Treaty of Versailles, which these decent enough young people had been brought up to regard as an infamous document, was going to be torn up. The 'new Germany' needed them; and even if it were not a perfect new Germany it was their duty to serve it.

Hitler may have supposed that control of the machinery of Church administration, as well as of Church youth, would give him control over the future of the German Evangelicals, and that he need fear no further opposition from these 'insignificant submissive dogs'. But plenty of German Protestants were very quickly aware of the dangers which Nazism posed to their Churches and their faith. Early in September one-third of the Prussian synod refused to confirm the election of Reich Bishop Mueller. Hitler acted instantly: all Church synods were abolished by State decree.

Resistance at this point became centred on the Evangelicals of Westphalia and the Rhineland, and they had no intention of bowing to the authority of the secular State in religious matters. Their first gestures of defiance were seized on by Pastor Martin Niemoeller in order to challenge Nazi interference in Church affairs. Niemoeller formed his *Pfarrer-Notbund* (emergency league of pastors) in late September 1933. More than 1,300 pastors from all over Germany joined at once. By Christmas the league had more than 6,000 members, or roughly one-third of all the Protestant pastors in the country. The German Christians were left with, at the most, 3,000 out of 17,000 pastors. Roughly half of the pastors remained neutral, in a struggle whose outcome was uncertain and whose implications were largely beyond their comprehension.

Resistance was under way. In December 1933 it began to take more definite shape. It was two-forked. In the south of Germany the religious leaders fought a gallant if unspectacular campaign to preserve their churches from secular influence and their flocks from losing all sense of the purpose of Christianity. In the north of Germany something more basic emerged—a concerted effort of Christians, who would not compromise with their consciences, to resist a declared enemy, Nazism.

At first these two different types of resistance were closely associated with one another. In December 1933, for instance, 6,000 pastors from all over Germany signed a resolution that the existence of the German Evangelical Churches as a whole was endangered. In the same month the Lutheran bishops protested as a body against the forced take-over of the Evangelical youth groups by the Nazis. In January 1934 a representative body of Church leaders called on Hitler with a list of complaints, but were bluntly told that the duty of the Churches was to get into step with the Nazi movement and stay there.

In March 1934 the bishops once again tried to secure some under-standing with Hitler by meeting him in person. The South Germans were leading them—Bishops Theophil Wurm of Württemberg and Hans Meiser of Bavaria. They claimed that they had undertaken a final attempt to work with Reich Bishop Mueller (according to Dibelius they had in fact agreed to dissociate themselves from the *Pfarrer-Notbund*), but that nothing had come of it. Two bishops who were present said that any further pressure by the Nazis would force them to go into 'loyal opposition'.

The upshot was a typically violent explosion of wrath from Hitler. He said that the Evangelical Churches had collapsed completely in 1918, and had become a mere 'appendage' of the Roman Catholic Church on the one side and the Marxist Social Democrats on the other. He howled at the bishops, calling them traitors and enemies of the State.

Something went out of the orthodox, South German Evangelical Opposition to Hitler after this meeting. Is this at all surprising? Men like Wurm and Meiser were not simply interested in maintaining their administrative systems; they honestly believed that their essen-tial duty was to enable the Christian faith to continue to be preached and practised. Was it their duty, like early Christian martyrs, to retire into the catacombs? As they saw it, this simply did not enter into the controversy, which was waged between a secular and a religious authority in a modern age, with the latter wanting only its due and not questioning the evils of the secular administration. The mistake of men like Wurm and Meiser was that they totally under-rated Hitler's ingrained nihilism, his utter disregard of the interests and wishes of the community and his determination to impose his will on the German nation. Plenty of well-versed politicians made the same mistake as Wurm and Meiser, and with less excuse.

Still the 'orthodox' South German Evangelicals continued to oppose the encroachments of the State in a resistance which became increasingly local but which never deviated from its original objectives. Wurm and Meiser were twice arrested in 1933 and 1934, chiefly because they refused to merge their provincial churches with the new Reich Church which was based on middle Germany, on that characterless area of forest, rolling hillside and manufacturing townships in Thuringia, Anhalt and West Saxony. The Reich Church had no roots and Wurm and Meiser remained for a time confident in the sturdily independent instincts of their Swabians and Bavarians. Those instincts resulted in mass-demonstrations when the two bishops were imprisoned in September 1933, after they had discreetly protested against discrimination against non-Aryans. They were immediately released.

Wurm was in trouble again in 1934. In August of that year the Evangelical Churches of Württemberg and Bavaria formed a 'Fighting Front' in Augsburg, which rejected regimentation under a national synod organized by the Nazis and asserted its own right of independence. In September Wurm was asked to retire by Mueller. He was simultaneously arrested for alleged diversion of Church funds to the political opponents of the Nazis. From September 15 to 18 he was under arrest, and the German Christians announced that 'He who sets himself up against the Reich Church, sets himself up against the Fuehrer'.

Wurm was released, but still refused to retire voluntarily. On October 9, 1934, Mueller had him forcibly retired, and the Nazis felt able to act against him without compunction. Bishop Wurm was declared a traitor to the State ('*Volks und Staatsfeindliche Elemente*'). Once more he was arrested.

On October 21, 1934, around 7,000 German Protestants assembled in front of Bishop Wurm's house in Stuttgart—he was being held incommunicado in his own home—and shouted: 'Give our pastor to us! Set him free!' He was released. Curiously, almost the same thing was happening to Bishop Meiser of Bavaria at almost exactly the same time. The reorganization of the Evangelical Churches in Bavaria was proclaimed by the Nazis in October 1934. On October 12 the steadfast Meiser was arrested, but violent protests in Nuremberg, Bamberg and other cities led to the local Nazi Gauleiter and notorious Jew-baiter, Julius Streicher, issuing a statement that no Evangelical Christian need abuse his conscience. Meiser was reinstated. For a moment it seemed that orthodox Church resistance had won the day.

Yet orthodox Church resistance could never have achieved much against dynamic Nazism. It is not surprising to find it tailing away during the next ten years of the Nazi era. Men like Wurm and Meiser never stopped trying. Late in 1934 they met Hitler (they seem to have held their own at the meeting, but nothing concrete came out of it). In February 1935 they played their part in organizing demonstrations against the encroachments of paganism, and in April Meiser spoke out boldly against the *Neuheidentum*, the new heathen ideology which was sweeping the Hitler Youth. In 1937 Meiser was put under a sort of house arrest, had to report himself to the police and was expressly forbidden to visit 'pagan' Thuringia and Saxony. Wurm was engaged in a new, local battle in Württemberg in 1938, when pastors in his diocese were beaten up, insulted in public and even shot at (the Pastor of Oberlenningen was badly injured and the Pastor of Boeckingen had the windows of his house smashed by bullets).

In July 1940 Bishop Wurm was complaining to the Ministry of the Interior about the organized murder of mental deficients and epileptics. His protest was based on a report—doubtless accurate—that an average of forty-three organized murders a day took place in the Grafeneck hospital, which had a total complement of 100 beds. In 1941 Wurm was fighting hard to prevent the banning of Church newspapers and magazines. Later on in that year and in 1942 he wrote personal letters to Hitler protesting against Nazi interference with Church organization.

From 1942 onwards both Wurm and Meiser were trying to save the Christianized Jews (around 340,000 in all), explaining that their conversion was an act of faith which involved the whole Christian community and that, once converted, they belonged to that community and could not be discriminated against. In 1943 Wurm and Meiser began to argue openly against the hideous persecution of the Jews, and in 1944 Wurm said that the bombing of German cities by the Allies was God's judgement for the things which had been done to Jews. The Gestapo called on him. Surprisingly nothing more happened for the moment. On March 3, 1944, the Reichsminister of the Reich Chancellery, Dr. Hans Lammers, gave Wurm a 'final' warning, chiefly because his criticisms of Nazi Church policies had been reprinted first in Swedish and then in English, French and other languages.

Wurm and Meiser survived the Nazi era. One may be forgiven for setting down some of the bare facts of their efforts to oppose Hitler, because these two men and their loyal helpers in Southern Germany are simply unknown outside Germany itself. Of course, 'orthodox' resistance by the Evangelical Churches was not very effective. But what had to be the objective of men like Wurm and Meiser? They believed that their position and responsibilities did not entitle them to seek martyrdom. As they saw it, their main task was to ensure that the word of God continued to be preached. There had to be, so to speak, an above-ground retreat to the catacombs of spiritual existence.

It can very well be said that Wurm and Meiser failed but it cannot be said that they did not try, and go on trying, down to the very end of the Nazi era. And one concrete result of their sturdy refusal to give up was the post-1945 reblossoming of common sense and dependability in the South German Evangelical communities. Swabia has become once again one of the citadels of progressive German political thinking; and the Bavarian Protestants have played their full part in the development of the West German State. Perhaps Wurm and Meiser did not fail completely.

Orthodox Evangelical opposition could not, naturally, halt the course of the Nazi juggernaut. Other German Evangelicals very quickly realized this, and set out to oppose Nazism in their own, far more active, way. The essence of that way was to stop the Nazis from reaching their first objective, an administrative reorganization of the Churches which would gradually stultify all sort of opposition and prepare the Evangelicals for their conversion to the 'new heathenism' of the 1,000-year Reich. Active opposition became centred in the 'Confessional Churches' (*Bekennende Kirchen*) and rather particularly in the person of their greatest leader, Martin Niemoeller.

First, a word on the Confessional Churches. Their counter-organization to the German Christians emanated from the *Pfarrer-Notbund* which Niemoeller formed in September 1933. This emergency organization, it will be recalled, collected 6,000 out of the

17,000 pastors in the whole of Germany by Christmas of that year. It was inspired by Niemoeller's proclamation: 'We appeal to all pastors . . . to anchor themselves on Holy Scripture and the beliefs of the Reformation, and to protest against every attack on their beliefs.' Niemoeller's own church in the Dahlem borough of Berlin became the centre of the *Pfarrer-Notbund* movement. Two of his ablest lieutenants, Pastors Jakobi and von Rabenau, also worked in Berlin. Pastor Luecking was in Dortmund; and the Westphalian industrial cities, Dortmund, Wuppertal and Essen, became strongpoints of the active resistance to the Reich Bishop and his State Church.

In January 1934 the Reich Bishop announced that disciplinary meaures would be taken against any pastor who failed to carry out his orders. On January 26 Niemoeller was deprived of the Dahlem living and forced to retire. A few days later, after energetic protests had been made to Mueller by the *Pfarrer-Notbund*, a bomb was thrown at Niemoeller's rectory, in which he was continuing to live. In February Mueller proclaimed his doctrine of 'One people, one State, one Church', echoing Hitler's '*Ein Volk, ein Reich, ein Fuehrer*'. For the next two months he counselled a policy of compromise and a settling of differences which he maintained were 'purely internal'. Mueller relied on the traditional discipline of the Lutherans, and believed that resistance to the Reich Church would blow itself out.

Meanwhile, Meiser and Wurm had made their dignified but fruitless protest to Hitler, and the active resisters realized that they must lose no more time before organizing an integrated opposition to the German Christians. In April the Confessional Church leaders in Berlin, Westphalia, the Rhineland, Bavaria, Württemberg and a number of communities in other parts of Germany bound themselves into a united front and proclaimed that the Church was in danger. In May the Confessionals protested to the Reich Minister of the Interior, Wilhelm Frick, against the intervention of the State in religious matters and organization. They insisted that no compromise with the German Christians was possible, and bitterly criticized the secular Church administration for using force and giving the German Christians unconditional backing. In the same month of May the Confessionals held a synod in Barmen (today one

of the twin towns which comprise Wuppertal). There they pro-
claimed themselves to constitute the 'true Church of Christ', which
would remain united in face of schism contrived by the State. Karl
Barth, the philosopher, declared a state of emergency for German
Protestantism. He had sounded the same warning note already in
July 1938.

The Confessionals were now committed to all-out opposition, not
to the secular administration of the State but to the German
Christians and to State interferences in the affairs of the Church.
Evangelical opposition to Hitler was, indeed, bound to be kept at
first within exact limits. Political and racial persecution was only in
its early stages, and the Confessionals can scarcely be blamed for
being mainly preoccupied with their own affairs, and with the free
practice of their faith—although they expressed solidarity with their
Jewish brethren. Thus at their second and third synods, in October
1934 and March 1935, in Dahlem, they organized their own leadership, confirmed their aims and denounced the paganism preached
by Alfred Rosenberg: 'We see our people threatened by a deadly
danger. This danger consists in a new religion.' A declaration to this
effect was due to be read from all pulpits occupied by Confessionals
at the end of March. The Ministry of the Interior proscribed its
reading in public, but a large number of Confessionals deliberately
disobeyed the government order.

Here, for the first time, was an act of open rebellion, and the
Ministry of the Interior acted with speed and rigour. At least 500
pastors (according to some authorities, 700) were arrested and imprisoned. Protests from citizens of all kinds poured in, and most of
the pastors were released within a few days. But at the end of April
thirty-six pastors were still under arrest, and twenty-seven more had
been sent to Dachau concentration camp. Another sixty-one were
forbidden to preach in public. The Nazis counter-attacked by
sending the notorious Jew-baiter, Julius Streicher, to Bavaria and
Hesse, where he carried out a virulent anti-Church campaign and
compared the Eucharist with Jewish 'ritual murder'. Battle was
joined.

Martin Niemoeller may well have been glad. This man was one
of Hitler's most courageous opponents but a weirdly contradictory
character. He had been a U-Boat commander in the First World

War and an acknowledged expert in the art of sinking defenceless merchant ships. At the end of the war he scuttled his boat rather than let it be taken over by his British conquerors. He entered the Church in the 1920s, in spite of his flaming anger over the Treaty of Versailles and his strongly nationalist leanings.

At first sight he was an incongruous figure in the pulpit. Small, upright and alert, he looked—and indeed had been—a typical Prussian officer. His temper was fiery, his voice harsh and staccato, and he spoke in the clipped accents which recalled his previous rank and vocation. Philip Friedman, in his book *Das andere Deutschland. Die Kirchen*, called him 'dynamic, friendly, natural and eloquent'. The words do not quite create the right picture—that of a fire-eater in clergyman's cassock, an apostle of truth but an unwitting symbol of certain human frailties.

Niemoeller was spoiling for a fight. He would himself have preferred it to have been even more open (one has the mental picture of a submarine commander who would not have hesitated to surface his tiny craft, and engage a superior enemy with his own miniature guns). The view held in some quarters at that time was that the Church should take its stand on the faith and loyalty of the people, declare itself a *Freikirche* and be ready to go into the wilderness in defence of the pure Christian ethic and Christ's teachings. In spirit, Niemoeller would have subscribed to this view, although he did not propagate it publicly.

Yet Niemoeller's judgement, not just at this time, but both before and after the Nazi era, was suspect. He was a keen Nazi as far back as 1924. When the Nazis came to power he had just published his book *From U-Boat to Pulpit*, in which he wrote of the fourteen years of the Weimar Republic as 'years of darkness' and expressed his regard for the Nazis' arrival in power as a 'national revival'. In 1933, according to some authorities, he preached more than once in favour of Nazism. Years after the Second World War Niemoeller took a contrary pleasure in opposing Western Germany's integration in the Western alliance and in travelling freely in Communist Eastern Germany. In between, he volunteered—while Hitler's 'special prisoner'—for military service on the outbreak of the Second World War.

Niemoeller gloried in his own contrariness. It was all very well to talk in 1934 of getting rid of the 'baggage-train' of Evangelical organizational impedimenta, and of relying on God's word and the strength of the Holy Spirit. But the Lutheran Church was organization-minded and its members had the normal German's veneration of authority. They would not have gone gladly into the wilderness (the same has been proved true of the Evangelical Churches in post-war Eastern Germany, when Niemoeller has been at pains to support their policy of compromise, while enduring). On one point, however, Niemoeller was right. His instinct told him (for his judgement was faulty) that Hitler intended to root out Christianity from Germany, and that there could be no compromise with Apollyon. Early in 1935 he said openly that 'The Jews were not the only people who nailed Christ to the Cross'. How true! At about this time the deputy leader of the Nazi Party, Rudolf Hess, was announcing that atheists had infiltrated the churches and 'modified' their teachings; Hermann Goering was jabbering about 'finding our way back to the primeval voices of our race'; and the Hitler Youth leader, Baldur von Schirach, was telling American visitors that German youth intended to 'overcome' orthodox Christianity. In the Berlin Sport-Palast 15,000 Evangelicals listened to Count Reventlow saying that it was unnecessary to revive Wotan, because the spirits of the 'ancient deities' lived on in the breast of every German true to his 'blood and soil'.

In 1935 and 1936 a ding-dong battle went on between the Nazi State and the Confessionals, with both sides notching up minor successes. In July 1935 the Reich Bishop Mueller resigned, wearied by the struggle and quite possibly shaken in his belief in Nazi enlightenment and benevolence. To save the crumbling German Christian movement Hitler appointed a special Minister for Church Affairs, Dr. Hans Kerrl. He in turn appeared to make a concession by including Confessionals in a 'Reich Church Committee', ostensibly an advisory body but in reality a nullity and a piece of camouflage to convince Christians that the State respected their religious scruples and beliefs.

In May 1936 the Confessionals compiled a memorandum for Hitler, pointing out that blood, race and nationality did not confer a special grace on the German people. Their Whitsun memorandum, which was intended for Hitler, ran as follows:

'When blood, race, nationality and honour receive the status of eternal values, the Evangelical Christian is obliged by the first Commandment to reject this scale of values. When the Aryan man is exalted, God's word testifies to the sinfulness of all men. When, in the framework of National-Socialist ideology, anti-Semitism is imposed on the Christian, obliging him to hate the Jews, for him the Christian Commandment of brotherly love remains binding.' For the first, and indeed only, time the Confessionals denounced anti-Semitism in an official declaration.

This led to the second rash of Nazi reprisals. Kerrl announced: 'The Church stands on the basis of positive Christianity, and positive Christianity is National Socialism. God's will reveals itself in German blood. True Christianity is represented by the Party, and ... the Fuehrer is the herald of a new revelation.' The memorandum of the Confessionals led to the arrest of several hundred of them, to the confiscation of church funds and to the control of church collections. Arrests continued during the autumn and winter. A leading lay supporter of the Confessionals, the judge Friedrich Weissler, was seized by the Gestapo, taken to Sachsenhausen concentration camp, and beaten and trampled to death there early in 1937.

In June 1937 at least forty pastors were arrested for disobeying 'regulations'. Some refused to have swastikas flown on church premises, others had published brochures for their congregations or had carried out church collections for unspecified purposes. On July 1 Niemoeller was arrested and brought to trial, as undaunted and unrepentant as Thomas à Beckett. He was flung into the Moabit prison in Berlin, subjected to various indignities but not tortured. His demeanour, a compound of uprightness and the ex-officer's 'hohe Kragen' (literally, 'high collar') bearing, may have helped him.

Niemoeller was tried by a special court on March 2, 1938. Surprisingly he was acquitted of the trumped-up charge of conspiring against the State, but he was fined 2,000 marks and sentenced to seven months' imprisonment. Since he had been just that time in gaol already, he was released, but was seized by the Gestapo as he left the Berlin courtroom. He was taken first to Sachsenhausen, then to Dachau, as Hitler's 'special prisoner', living in solitary confinement and not being subjected to the gross cruelties practised on most of the other prisoners. Although Otto Dibelius read a statement from the Dahlem pulpit, pointing out that Niemoeller had never used provocative language as a preacher and had sought only pure Christianity, this was in the nature of an epitaph. For Niemoeller, even though he survived the war, was lost to the Evangelical resistance from then on.

Niemoeller's personal part in that resistance may be capped by a curious story. At the outbreak of war he applied to his gaolers to be set free and to be allowed to put on naval uniform again. He was only forty-seven years old and would no doubt have been a welcome addition to the *Kriegsmarine*. Niemoeller has been asked often enough why he made this application to fight for Hitler's Germany. With his usual mischievousness he has refused to tell the truth. In 1960, indeed, he told members of the Foreign Press Association in Bonn that his action was due to his sense of shame on behalf of his sons, of fighting age, having a father locked up in prison. In reality his friends in the active Evangelical resistance to Hitler wanted to get him out of gaol and thought that this method was worth trying. Fifteen years after the war Niemoeller remained something of an *enfant terrible*.

After Niemoeller's trial the resistance of the Confessionals was forced back to an increasing extent into 'orthodox' channels—becoming not unlike that of Bishops Wurm and Meiser. Brave and honest men continued to speak their minds. More important, the word of God continued to be preached and the German Christian movement faded into virtual oblivion. Resistance, of a kind, went on during the whole length of the Second World War. Here is the briefest summary of events.

The situation of the Evangelical pastors was a frustrating one. Germany was resounding to calls to battle and to pledges of loyalty to the Fuehrer. An immense national effort to stave off total defeat was genuinely needed—at least, the very moment that the Russian campaign was under way. The hearts of decent, patriotic churchmen must have been pulled in half a dozen directions. Their duty was to go on preaching the word of God. Their duty, too, was to succour the poor and the needy—and many of the latter had Nazi husbands fighting at the front. Their duty was to discover their country's true interests and the way of serving them best. They had an obvious and unavoidable duty to the men of the armed forces, most of them youngsters filled with mixed-up ideals and cracker mottoes, ready to die for a Fatherland which still seemed wonderful to them. The pastors had to defend and maintain their Church. . . .

This last task was quite beyond them. The Nazis, like medieval monarchs, were keenly aware of the power of the purse. Between 1934 and 1941 they cut State grants to the Evangelical Churches by 4·4 million marks. In 1931 Church revenues were 65 per cent from State grants and only 35 per cent from Church levies and collections. By 1944 only about 30 per cent of Church revenue came from the State. And by 1944 barely 2 per cent of Church revenue came from Church property and investments, which had been subjected to wholesale Nazi confiscations. The Nazis set up finance departments for all regional Church bodies. No secrets could be kept from them. Financial strangulation was one of the most effective weapons used to break down Church resistance.

Bishop Hans Lilje, a churchman who did not resist openly but who strove to do his duty towards his flock, has described the difficulties of his apparently mundane task in a book *In the Dark Valley*. Lilje honestly believed that he should steer clear of open or overt resistance and continue to look after his flock. He preached, in basic Christian terms, to congregations of 2,000 and 3,000, whose members needed reassurance in order to keep their faith alive. He was approached by the political resisters to Nazism, chiefly because of an outspoken sermon on 'The possibility of living a Christian life at this present'. He refused to join the political resisters (he was, as a matter of interest, appalled by the Conservative resister Carl Goerdeler's lack of discretion and his habit of discussing his plans over the telephone). But this caution did not save him. He was continuously harassed by the Gestapo, interrogated and intimidated. For long periods he was forbidden to preach, his passport was taken away from him and his church journal was banned.

Eventually Lilje, who really could not be blamed for much by the Nazis and has been more blamed since the war for failure to resist them more openly, was arrested. He was interrogated for fifteen hours and more at a stretch and imprisoned in Berlin from August 1944 onwards. Lilje escaped murder by the Nazis by a narrow margin. All this could happen to an honourable and decent man, who did not set himself up against the regime. It can be imagined what happened to those who did.

One of them was Prebendary Ernst Wilm, who started preaching against total war around 1942. A year later he was arrested for denouncing the Nazis' euthanasia programme and for comparing the fate of German Protestants with that of the Christians of the primitive Church. Wilm went to Dachau but survived the war. After it was over he said: 'We are not ashamed of our resistance. We are only ashamed that we failed to resist more resolutely and openly.'

Another who set himself up against the regime was Pastor Heinrich Grueber. In 1936, in company with Pastor Martin Albertz, he helped to found the 'Bureau for Christians of Jewish Birth' in Berlin, a sort of aid-office for Christianized Jews who were being persecuted under the Nuremberg racial decrees of 1934. In addition, he formed a more clandestine association which worked solely to protect Jews and half-Jews. There were branches of both organizations outside Berlin, and Grueber helped numbers of Jews to emigrate before the outbreak of war, with the aid of forged passports and visas procured in Holland, Switzerland and Britain. Grueber was arrested in December 1940 and thrust into the inevitable concentration camp. At Sachsenhausen he had most of his teeth knocked out. But his work was carried on by Albertz, Hermann Maas, Werner Sylten and others, and by Pastor Zwanziger of Munich, who is credited with having smuggled sixty-five people out of Germany in February 1940 alone.

By the end of 1941 Maas, Sylten and Albertz had all been rounded up for helping the Jews, along with thirty to forty other Evangelicals. Many of them had done no more than protest against the Nazi practice of forcing Jews to wear the yellow 'Star of David' as a badge of shame for their Semitic birthright. Grueber spent long years in Sachsenhausen and Dachau, and after the war strove once again with great courage and tactical skill for his Evangelical flock in Communist East Germany. There, too, he had to bow to brute force, eventually seeking refuge in the West in 1960.

There were Evangelical clergymen who refused to take the oath of allegiance to Hitler, and others who defied a ban imposed on their preaching. There were many who spoke up bravely and did not hesitate to warn their flocks of the dangers of Nazism. Such a one was Karl Stellbrink, the pastor of the Lutheran Church in Luebeck. Stellbrink was in his early forties when the war broke out and had earlier spent eight years looking after the German Evangelical communities in Brazil. In Luebeck he became firm friends with several Catholic priests, Johannes Prassek, Hermann Lange and Edouard Muller, and collaborated with them in circulating letters and sermons of anti-Nazis like Cardinal Graf Clemens von Galen.

After Allied planes bombed Luebeck on the night of March 28, 1942, Stellbrink and his Catholic friends told their congregations that the bombing was God's judgement on all Germans for their sin in serving a tyrannical regime. Stellbrink and the three priests were arrested in April, tried by the People's Court in June, sentenced to death and executed in November. Stellbrink is reputed to have said of his joint resistance with Roman Catholics: 'What a community we could become if we were united!'

A different kind of opposition was waged against the Nazis by Justus Perels, one of the earliest members of the *Pfarrer-Notbund*. Perels, still in his twenties at the time, set out to help anyone who was persecuted by the Nazis. He gave advice and material help to the wives and families of pastors who had been imprisoned by the Nazis. He hid Jews and helped them to escape from Germany. He did the same for political opponents of the regime, and he was one of the comparatively few members of the Churches who came into contact with the military and lay members of the active Opposition to Hitler. He led a charmed life until he was denounced in October 1944, arrested and sentenced to death. He was held in a Gestapo cell until April 22, 1945. That night he was taken out into the street and shot there in one of the last of the holocausts perpetrated by the guilt-ridden S.S. In gaol he declared: 'So many are falling in battle fighting for this system. I believe it is better to fall fighting against it.'

One could go on indefinitely recounting the efforts of individual churchmen to show their loathing of Nazism. Possibly the story of a single one of them can serve best to trace the path of martyrdom which so many of these unsung heroes trod. That is the story of Paul Schneider, the pastor of the little town of Dickenschied, in the Hunsruck hills which run to the south of the valley of the Moselle.

Schneider was born in 1897 in the village of Pferdsfeld, near

Kreuznach, the son of a country parson. He studied to join the Church, interested himself in a mild way in politics (he thought and talked much of the desirability of creating a 'Christian Socialist' state), and became Pastor of Hochelheim, near Giessen, when his father—who had moved there some time previously—had a stroke. Paul Schneider quickly made a name for himself as a super-active and 'modern' parson. He rode on his motor-bike to visit the members of his flock, had a great way with the sick whem he visited with scrupulous frequency, was loved by young and old alike. The picture of Paul Schneider at this time was of an intensely manly person, physically strong and virile but with an outstanding quality of tenderness and understanding.

Schneider disliked the Nazis from the bottom of his heart. He thought that they distracted the youth of Germany from a Christian way of life by dragooning them into military exercises (as soon as the Nazis were in power, seven- and eight-year-olds began to learn the arts of handling dummy hand-grenades), and into athletics conducted with military rigour and disciplined seriousness. Schneider saw beyond these outward trappings of the Hitler Youth movement, recognized that Nazism was basically anti-religious. In October 1933 he was already in trouble. He told members of the Hochelheim congregation that the Nazis, in particular Ernst Roehm, the head of the brown-shirted S.A., were wrong to try to build a Third Reich without seeking the internal regeneration of the German people. The local consistorial council took exception to this statement—it was just the sort of thing which could get them into trouble—and asked Schneider to leave Hochelheim. He earned an additional reproof from his bishop. What Schneider had to say about regeneration could not well have been nearer the mark—Roehm, a blatant homosexual, was murdered eight months later in peculiarly disgusting circumstances by the orders of his friend Hitler.

In the event Schneider was allowed to stay on at Hochelheim until February 1934, but by then his name was high up on the black list kept by the local Nazi district headquarters. He spoke openly against the German Christian movement, criticized the Nazi Government, and produced some apt and acid comments on the speeches of Josef Goebbels. He was accordingly moved 120 miles west, to Dickenschied, in a mainly Catholic area but with an Evangelical congregation of 500. Within a few months he was in trouble again with the Nazis.

In June a leading member of the Hitler Youth died and Schneider conducted the funeral service. The Nazi *Kreisleiter* interrupted the funeral service in order to make a political speech in which he said that the dead boy had gone to join the 'Horst-Wessel Brigade' in heaven. Schneider protested in front of the *Kreisleiter*, pointing out with his usual blunt humour that there was no evidence that St. Peter gave automatic entry into heaven to members of the Hitler Youth. He followed this up with a formal letter of protest to the *Kreisleiter*.

This time he was arrested and put in prison in the neighbouring town of Simmern. He was there for a week, but was released when even members of the S.A. in Dickenschied protested against his imprisonment, and his congregation drew up a petition. He left Simmern gaol after being instructed not to make any further statements which were 'hostile to the State'. Unabashed, his first action on reaching his home was to sit down and write a letter protesting against the use of this unjustified phrase.

For some weeks Schneider evidently decided to tread with care, and in one letter wrote resignedly that the strains imposed on Christians must 'be borne, with God's help'. But in 1935 he was in almost continual trouble with the authorities. He spoke his mind freely when more than 500 Confessional pastors in Prussia were arrested, and he was denounced for collecting money for the Jews and allegedly calling Hitler an agent of the Devil (fortunately the accusations were not believed). Once again he was reported to the authorities, this time by two young Nazi schoolmasters. Then came the 1936 elections, when 99 per cent of the German people (allegedly, according to the figures published by the Nazis) voted '*Ja*' to Hitler's policies.

It was impossible to vote 'No', so Schneider simply did not vote at all. Nazi louts daubed his house in the night with the inscription: 'He did not vote for his Fatherland! Germans, what do you say to that?' But parishioners washed the inscription out the next day. Schneider, however, went over to the offensive, because the Nazis flew flags from his church steeple and rang his church's bells, in celebration of their 'victory' in the sham-plebiscite. In his protest he said that Nazism was coming into increasing conflict with Christianity and that German youth was being led astray. In reference to Hitler's reoccupation of the Rhineland, Schneider said that 'Germany's fate does not depend on the presence of German troops on the Rhine, but on the German People's attitude to the word of God'.

In March 1937 Schneider had a bad motor-car accident. One leg was broken in three places, and he was laid up for two months while it was operated on and shortened. On May 30 he preached his last sermon in Dickenschied. He chose his text from St. Luke xviii, verses 31 to 43. It was the story of Jesus passing on the road to Jericho and giving the blind man back his sight. Schneider's message to his congregation was to have trust in God. The blind man was Germany, and only faith could make Germany whole. On the next day he was arrested by the Gestapo and removed to Coblenz for questioning. He was held in gaol until July, when he was taken to Wiesbaden and told that he could not return to his parish. His answer was to tear up the expulsion order and take the next train back to Dickenschied, but his friends there persuaded him to leave again at once and take refuge in a Black Forest village until the storm blew over.

For Schneider it was unusual not to follow the dictates of his conscience. He was desperately unhappy in Southern Germany. In due course he wrote to his parish council to find out how things were going in his absence. They painted a black picture. In the four months since he had left there had been no religious instruction for children and no confirmation classes. Pastors of neighbouring parishes were helping out with morning and evening services, but on several Sundays there had been no evensong. Practically nothing was being done by the church for the sick. His parishioners were forlorn and frightened, and they asked him if he could not arrange to come back to them.

Schneider wrote to the Confessional synod in the Rhineland, asking for advice. He was told that he should consult his own conscience, but that his duty lay with his flock. The synod was unwittingly sending Schneider to his doom. On September 30 he sent a dignified request to the Reich Chancellery to be allowed to go back to his parish. He did not wait for the answer. On October 1 he travelled to the town of Kirn, where he spent the night. From there he went to Dickenschied. He was arrested, for the last time, on his way to evening service. As the Gestapo took him away, he cried out to his wife: 'Tell my congregation that I am and always will be their pastor.'

This time he was put in a prison in the town of Kirchberg, where his wife, paying him a visit the next day, found him cheerfully whistling *Ein feste Burg ist unser Gott*' in his cell. But the Nazis were not going to let him out again. This turbulent priest, as they regarded him, was certain to go on giving them trouble. His parish was already in an uproar and the plucky protest of his parishioners —they wrote to the Prussian Ministry of the Interior, complaining that his arrest was illegal—could not help him. His spirit could not be broken, and in November 1937 they sent him to Buchenwald concentration camp.

Schneider's month in Kirchberg gaol may well have been the most difficult of his whole life for him. He was so near his old parish—a mere three miles. One word from him and he would have been released and restored to his parishioners—to teach them the word of God and eschew politics. Freedom was so near and possibly the most touching documents of the German Opposition to Hitler are Schneider's goodbye letters to his three older children, aged ten, eight and four, which say nothing of his worries but recall the joy of having them crawling over his bed early in the morning, when the birds have long since begun to sing. From his cell Schneider smuggled out a letter in which he said that the fate of German Christianity would depend on the individual and that no amount of compromising 'church politics' could help. In his prison Schneider busied himself, as far as he could, with the spiritual welfare of his fellow-gaolbirds. In between he watched the leaves falling from the chestnut tree outside his window. He was disillusioned to some extent, but he remained steadfast. His wife was allowed to come to the outside of the gaol when he was driven away from it. She recalls that he was sitting erect—and smiling.

According to Eugen Kogon, in his book *The S.S. State*, Schneider refused, at one of the first prisoners' parades which he attended in Buchenwald, to take his cap off when the Nazi swastika flag was hoisted. He was at once seized, and summarily punished by being given twenty-five strokes of the whip on the dreaded *Bock*—a rack on which the victim was stretched, with his legs drawn up and his buttocks exposed. Half a dozen lashes were usually enough to make a prisoner howl in agony. There is no record that Schneider uttered a sound. He was taken down from the *Bock* and flung into a solitary cell.

The cell was unlit. Schneider had to sleep on its bare floor which was often an inch deep in water. He was put on a bread-and-water diet. He was beaten up continually by the S.S. overseer, Martin Sommer, who used to make a habit of kicking, cuffing and punching him every time he visited the cell. He was tortured. Sommer had him strung up by his arms, which were tied behind his back, from the bars of his cell window. His hands could be tied higher and higher behind his back, forcing his head down into a bent position. The Agony on the Cross was being re-enacted, but not as a single, awful ordeal. Schneider was strung up for hours at a time, day after day and week after week, as he fined down to a broken, bruised skeleton, clad in rags and with his body crawling with lice.

Fellow-prisoners emptied his slops and brought him his pitiful ration of food. One of them told him that he should spare himself (it was known that he had been promised his release if he would sign an undertaking not to try to go back to Dickenschied) and think of his wife and six children. His answer was: 'I know why I am here. Do you think that God gave me children that I might only provide for their material welfare? Were they not entrusted to me so that I might safeguard them for eternity?'

More than once he was taken out of his cell and told once again that he had the chance of going home. When he said nothing he was asked: 'Do you prefer a concentration camp, then?' He told a fellow-prisoner that he had answered: 'I do not prefer it. But if it is ordained that I must bear it, then I shall bear it also.' What great Christian martyr of history gave plainer evidence of his faith and constancy?

His captors put him in a cell which looked out, at ground-level, on to the camp parade ground. They probably did this so that his sufferings would discourage indiscipline among the other prisoners. They did not reckon with the astonishing courage of the man whom they were torturing to death. He prayed aloud, in a resonant voice which carried across the parade ground, filled with its human scarecrows. His voice would ring out, at moments of silence while the prisoners were being counted: 'Jesus said—I am the beginning and the life.' The S.S. occasionally shot prisoners on parade—it broke the monotony of the proceedings. Sometimes, when this happened, Schneider's great voice would cry: 'I have seen this! And I will accuse you of murder before God's judgement-seat!'

Schneider's awful survival was protracted for two years. According to Julius Leber's widow, he was brought to the camp hospital on July 18, 1939, and given five lethal injections, each of them sufficient to kill him. His body was a single festering mass of cuts, scars and bruises. The bones of his legs and other joints were swollen to elephantine proportions by starvation, and his wrists were coloured blue, green and red, in huge blotches. He was beaten on his death-bed by the flower of Hitler's Aryan youth. His coffin was delivered to his widow, but was sealed, with strict orders that it should not be opened but should be lowered into the soil at its appointed resting-place.

Kogon's version of his end is slightly different. Kogon had a job in the camp hospital for a time, and knew some of the other prisoners who worked there. He maintained that Sommer decided to kill Schneider and put large quantities of poison in his food. Schneider went into a coma but did not die. He was taken to the hospital to have heart stimulants, but died of heart failure when cold compresses were used to bring him out of his coma. The ultimate irony may have been that he was delivered from his agony when the Nazis were trying to preserve his life.

Schneider determined to live his life according to the First Commandment. For him there could be no compromise with the forces of evil, for by compromising he would break that commandment. Of his end a fellow-prisoner, Alfred Leikam, wrote afterwards: 'In camp life the greatest of all trials for me was to stay silent in the face of unimaginable wrongs inflicted on the people there, or even to be forced to participate in such things. . . . As far as I know, there was only one man in Germany who did not share in this guilt. This was Pastor Schneider, who even in the concentration camp protested by word and deed against injustice, and for this died a martyr's death.'

What more could any man have done than Pastor Schneider in order to testify to his faith and to make his personal contribution towards retrieving the good name of the German nation? What other sort of resistance was possible? Christ said that they who take up the sword shall perish by the sword. Could churchmen, then, use physical force against the Nazi tyranny? The great mass of them cannot be blamed in any way for believing that they could not do so. But a very few Evangelical churchmen came to a different conclusion. They decided to identify themselves with the active Opposition to Hitler. This meant, eventually, preparedness to kill him. Here, too, no compromise was possible.

Those who have been wise after the event have been quick, since the war, to point out the failures of Hitler's Evangelical opponents. They should have united in face of the palpable threat of Nazi paganism. They should, for that matter, have been much more united in the first place, and not divided into their twenty-eight to thirty independent provincial organizations. They should have been more diplomatic (if they happened to be Confessionals), or more forthright (if they were followers of Wurm and Meiser). They should not, if filled with a furious courage, have thrown away their lives, like Pastor Schneider. For was his martyrdom not lacking in point or purpose, watched as it was by the helpless inmates of a concentration camp? Of course, thinking in those terms, the whole New Testament would appear to be nothing more than a chronicle of failure. Yet the world at large has evidently come to the conclusion that the essence of real resistance was to strike a blow, in the most obvious physical sense, at Hitler.

Of those who decided, after desperate searching of their consciences, to do just this, I would select three. They were Eugen Gerstenmaier, since 1954 the President of the Bundestag in Bonn, Dietrich Bonhoeffer, a theologian of real depth and originality, and Eberhard Bethge, one of Bonhoeffer's disciples, and long after the war, once again, a pastor in his native Rhineland.

Gerstenmaier's story can be dealt with briefly, chiefly because he is today unwilling to talk about it, and has written nothing so far which casts any new light on the Opposition to Hitler. When Hitler came to power Gerstenmaier was only twenty-seven years old. He had been trained as a business man, and worked for eight years in commerce. Only at the time of the Nazis' seizure of power did he begin to study theology and philosophy at the universities of Zürich and Rostock. He disliked Nazism at the very outset, but it seems that his active part in the Opposition to Hitler began only after the outbreak of war. A Swabian, with a Swabian's stolid common sense, Gerstenmaier became one of the apostles of action after being brought into touch with Count Moltke and the Kreisau circle of intellectual opponents of the Nazis, and with Carl Goerdeler. Gerstenmaier, trained as a man of God, is credited with having been one of those who helped Stauffenberg to decide on Hitler's assassination.

This was remarkable. Assassination is a long step beyond the simple obedience to the First Commandment which Schneider and his sort observed. Gerstenmaier was aware that the majority of the Kreisau circle never, even at the end, believed that assassination was right and justified. One of them, Count Yorck, regarded it, and with great reluctance, as a necessary evil; Moltke would have nothing to do with it before his arrest. Gerstenmaier was heavily implicated and was at the Bendlerstrasse, the headquarters of the conspirators, on July 20, 1944. He was arrested, but defended himself so cleverly before the People's Court that he got away with a sentence of seven years' imprisonment. After the war he pursued an equally notable role in helping to rebuild a democratic West German State.

Gerstenmaier has said little since the war about a theologian's justification in using actual force against a tyrant. It may well be that he has realized that the arguments for and against priestly militancy can be argued out until Doomsday. What he has set down very plainly, if shortly, are his reasons for opposing Nazism. In his view no German owed loyalty to a tyrant. Hitler's opponents had the right to follow the dictates of their own consciences. Their duty to their country was to 'rescue' it from Hitler's clutches, and if possible to protect it from utter collapse, and so save millions of lives. Resistance was self-help, and had nothing to do with Allied war aims and plans. Ultimately, logically, Hitler had to be 'removed' by any possible means. Murder is an ignoble word; assassination, as Gerstenmaier saw it, could equate with duty. Some day he may make a worthwhile contribution on paper to the history of the Opposition to Hitler.

Unlike Gerstenmaier, Bonhoeffer died in trying to save his country. And unlike Gerstenmaier he has handed much of his philosophy and reasoning down to posterity. Dietrich Bonhoeffer, too, was born in 1906, in Breslau, and was one of eight brothers and sisters. From an early age he was destined for the Church, and became a student-pastor in Berlin at the time that the Nazis came to power. In 1935 he was head of an Evangelical teacher-training college in Berlin, and he was already a much-travelled man. He had spent months in Barcelona and two years in London as pastor of the German Lutheran church there, and he was to travel to the United States as well.

He was in process of becoming a theologian in his own right. His later theories were beginning to develop—that God is not 'magic' and 'supernatural', but the essence of all 'being', which is sentient, rational and capable of self-fulfilment; that God is not a source of succour (to be invoked most of all in the hour of need or fear) but the seed of self-help and elemental power latent in us all. Bonhoeffer seems to have believed, in the last resort, that God lives in each of us—a phrase which has been used more often than it has been either understood or meant. Certainly he contrived to show that this phrase could be true.

In 1935 Bonhoeffer returned to Germany from London to take part in the struggle against Hitler. He regarded the Fuehrer, quite simply, as Anti-Christ and he came in due course to believe that he had to be 'removed', almost certainly by force. He was, in his own way, uncompromising—there could be no room for 'expediency'. Two of his sisters had married men whom he converted into enemies of Hitler, the lawyer Hans von Dohnanyi and Ruediger Schleicher; and a brother, Klaus, was implicated too in the Opposition to Hitler. A niece married Pastor Eberhard Bethge. This was very much a 'family' resistance group. As early as 1936 Bonhoeffer tried to get the Confessional Church to pass a resolution that the Nuremberg Racial Laws against the Jews were violating human rights. As a leading Confessional he helped to have young pastors-to-be trained and ordained, and educated in seminars conducted in secret.

Bonhoeffer came into contact with other conservative opponents of Hitler, as well as with the Kreisau circle. In addition he was not content with the slow processes of conspiracy inside Germany; he tried to seek help and encouragement from outside the country. This led to his visit to Sweden at the end of May 1942. Just before, and quite independently of him, Pastor Hans Schoenfeld, of the foreign-relations bureau of the Evangelical Churches, arrived in Stockholm on exactly the same mission—to establish contact with Dr. George Bell, the Bishop of Chichester and the president of the Universal Christian Council for Life and Work. Both Schoenfeld and Bonhoeffer knew Bishop Bell. They saw in him a man who could tell the outside world what they thought true of the majority of the German people—which was that they wanted peace, distrusted or even disliked their own government, and would subscribe to a successful conspiracy against Hitler which was now reaching fruition.

Schoenfeld and Bonhoeffer gave very similar accounts of the situation to the Bishop. They made similar proposals to him. They wanted him to inform Allied governments of the existence and extent of the conspiracy against Hitler, and to describe its make-up. They wanted the Allies to send a private message to the active conspirators (and Bonhoeffer was now one of the most active) that they would negotiate with a post-Hitler regime, or would at least guarantee to offer terms to such a regime as soon as Hitler was overthrown. (Sir John Wheeler-Bennett, in his *Nemesis of Power*, suggests that Schoenfeld and Bonhoeffer wanted a statement of this kind published even before Hitler had been overthrown. Obviously this would have been an unwise thing to do; it would have automatically betrayed the Allied link with the resisters.)

Schoenfeld and Bonhoeffer indicated a basis for Allied terms for a post-Hitler regime. This basis would be provided by undertakings given by the German conspirators. All persecution of the Jews would end. German troops would be withdrawn behind the 1919 frontiers. The new German State would renounce the alliance with Japan. It would co-operate with the Allies in the reconstruction of Europe. According to some authorities, Bonhoeffer gave the Bishop the names of the key members of the resistance—Carl Goerdeler, Generals Ludwig Beck and Kurt von Hammerstein, Wilhelm Leuschner. The Bishop saw Mr. Anthony Eden, then Foreign Secretary, on June 30. Eden decided that nothing could be done and that no good purpose could be served by entering into any sort of agreement with the conspirators. He wrote in this sense to the Bishop on July 17.

Eden may have been afraid that the opponents of Hitler wanted a 'cheap peace' for the Fatherland which they continued to venerate. He may have been afraid that they would try to consolidate some at least of Hitler's territorial gains and that they would, perhaps unintentionally, contrive to split the Grand Alliance against Germany by bargaining with the West and ignoring the East. It has been widely suggested that Bonhoeffer was himself dubious about this 'resisters' peace offensive'; he had already come to believe that Germany had to lose the war and seek regeneration afterwards. Hans Rothfels quotes Bonhoeffer as saying: 'I pray for the defeat of my Fatherland. Only through a defeat can we atone for the terrible crimes which we have committed against Europe and the world.' And to this thought Bonhoeffer added, at a later date: 'Hitler is the Anti-Christ. We must therefore continue with our work and root him out.' Bonhoeffer possessed both the power of thought and the readiness to act, a rare combination.

Bonhoeffer's active part in the conspiracy was terminated by pure chance. In October 1942 an Abwehr agent was arrested on a charge of smuggling currency between Germany and Switzerland. He was forced by the Gestapo to confess what he knew of Hitler's opponents in the Abwehr and elsewhere. It took months to follow up the random clues which he betrayed to his captors. But in April 1943 Bonhoeffer and his brother-in-law, Dohnanyi, were arrested. Bonhoeffer was only tried a year and a half later and was not executed until April 1945. His brother Klaus died too; so did Dohnanyi and Ruediger Schleicher. Bethge was put in prison and his trial should have taken place in May 1945. He was freed by the Red Army, whose approach he and his fellow-prisoners in the Lehrterstrasse prison in Berlin watched from the roof of the gaol.

Bonhoeffer's writings from the dank twilight of his cell wring one's heart. This plump, balding, kindly man had an immense love of humanity, and a veneration of life itself. A fellow-prisoner in Buchenwald described him in these terms: 'Bonhoeffer was all humility and sweetness; he always seemed to be able to diffuse an atmosphere of happiness, of joy in every smallest event in life, and of deep gratitude for the mere fact that he was alive. . . . He was one of the very few men that I have ever met whose God was real and ever close to him.'

In Buchenwald Bonhoeffer was given little to eat, isolated from his fellow-prisoners, given practically no reading matter (he was allowed a Bible, because he was a pastor and because of the curious Nazi foible of being 'correct' in their treatment of their victims). He never complained and even believed that his time in gaol was not wasted. He wrote poems, essays, letters, and some of his letters were smuggled out uncensored. They contained two particular messages. One was embodied in two phrases: 'Lord Jesus Christ: You were poor and wretched and forsaken and so am I', and 'Christ suffered alone and in disgrace and, ever since, so have Christians suffered with Him'. The second message was an oblique warning to the Germans of both 1945 and 1919: 'Talk of a heroic defeat is not heroic, because it means failure to face the future.' But the message may have been meant for the men of the Opposition to Hitler too.

The snuffing out of Bonhoeffer's evocative spirit and the brilliant promise of his youth—he was under thirty-eight when he was murdered—was a tragedy. His brother-in-law, Eberhard Bethge, has described to me what he believed were his salient virtues, which went beyond his obvious goodness, godliness, courage and sense of responsibility. Bonhoeffer, according to Bethge, wanted to save the established order in Germany—in order to build something better on its ready-made base. He was ready to compromise his own conscience by telling lies and participating in conspiracy. He was ready, too, to break the Fifth Commandment: 'Thou shalt not kill'. He deliberately stepped aside from the strait and narrow path of Christian orthodoxy, knowing that his crusading soul would find its way through the labyrinth which he had entered of his own free will. Bonhoeffer's personal salvation was the more certain because he risked it so readily in the interests of his fellow-men.

Did the opposition of the German Evangelicals to Hitler 'fail'? The word failure can scarcely be used, when believing Christians did their duty. But could the Evangelicals have done more? Bethge, looking back at events nearly thirty years later, said:

'Many of us thought that Hitler would concentrate on politics and leave the fabric of German society alone. Many of us thought that the fabric of German society was all-important. I was a clergyman's son, and I did not like leftish political radicalism.

'The Churches were divided—and weak. The Confessionals had to fight to maintain true Christian religion in the community; they had too little time for the rest of humanity, and they may have done too little in this respect because they were watched by the Nazis. They were sometimes rather afraid. They may, in the last resort, have had too great a spirit of obedience, and this hampered their opposition to the Nazis. But they tried—yes, they tried—to help.'

This judgement is modest and fair. During the first years of the Nazi era the Evangelical Churches strove to shore up their organization and authority. They honestly believed that they could best serve the community in this way. During the later years they were gradually driven into different attitudes of resistance. A very few churchmen assisted in the conspiracy to eliminate Hitler, and so save German and European civilization from further terrifying sufferings. They failed. And in a material sense it might be said that all Evangelical Opposition to Hitler failed. But that would be to misunderstand the underlying purpose in endeavour and suffering. The story of the disjointed Evangelical Opposition to Hitler is part of the pattern of the story of the human race, so full of technical successes but so full, at the same time, of the sense of spiritual failure.

six

The Last Remnants of Weimar

'When bad men combine, the good must associate; else will they fall, one by one, an unpitied sacrifice in a contemptible struggle.'

EDMUND BURKE, *Thoughts on the Cause of the Present Discontent*

IT HAS become a convention to blame the Social Democratic Party for Hitler's rise to power, far more than the Catholic and Evangelical Churches, the decaying German Liberals or the disjointed elements of German conservatism. The Social Democrats, it is often pointed out, were the strongest single party during the first twelve years of the Weimar era. As such they bore a major share in the responsibility for making democratic government work. Even in the November 1932 elections they won 121 seats in the Reichstag and remained the second strongest party there (the Nazis won 196 seats). They held their vote in the March 1933 elections (119 seats).

Why, some critics have asked, did the Social Democrats not combine with the Communists, who held 100 seats in November 1932? Why, alternatively, did they not form an 'anti-Nazi Front', with the smaller parties of the centre and the Catholic *Zentrum*? The latter actually increased its representation in the Reichstag in March 1933 from seventy-one to seventy-four seats. Why, when all else failed, did they not call a general strike, paralyse the anti-democratic forces in power and repeat the successful defence of democratic order which they achieved in the first years of the Weimar Republic?

In his comprehensive book *The Rise and Fall of the Third Reich* William Shirer wrote, with some justice: 'Fourteen years of sharing political power in the Republic, of making all the compromises that were necessary to maintain coalition governments, had sapped the strength and zeal of the Social Democrats until their party had become little more than an opportunist pressure organization, determined to bargain for concessions for the trade unions on which their strength largely rested.'

The tragedy of the Social Democrats, Shirer went on, 'could not be explained fully by bad luck. They had had their chance to take over Germany in November 1918 and to found a state based on what they had always preached: social democracy. Now at the dawn of the third decade they were a tired, defeatist party, dominated by old, well-meaning but mostly mediocre men. Loyal to the Republic they were to the last, but in the end too confused, too timid, to take the great risks which alone could have preserved it.'

Shirer blames the Social Democrats for failing to answer von Papen's proclamation of military law in July 1932—which gave Hitler a useful precedent of undemocratic rule—with a general strike. He blames them for not calling out the workers when Hitler laid before the Reichstag his 'Enabling Act', which gave him the powers of a dictator. He blames them for weakly supporting Hitler's foreign policy statements in May 1933, shortly before their dissolution as a party.

Only when the Enabling Act was debated on March 23, 1933, did the Social Democrats show a temporary revival of their fighting spirit. Before this debate began, the eighty-one Communist members of the Reichstag were arrested and the Communist Party was outlawed. A number of Social Democrats—estimates vary between twenty and thirty—were prevented from entering the Reichstag building by the Nazi storm troopers. But eighty-four out of ninety-four Social Democrats present voted against the Act, which was passed by a huge majority (441 votes for it).

The Social Democratic spokesman, Otto Wels, made a historic speech in defence of democratic rights. 'Freedom and our very lives,' he said, 'can be taken from us, but not our honour.' He defended the right to criticize government, 'which is both necessary and healthy'. And he concluded: 'We German Social Democrats pledge ourselves solemnly in this historic hour to the principles of humanity and justice, of freedom and socialism. No Enabling Act can give you the power to destroy ideas which are eternal and indestructible.'

Wels's speech should have done much to redeem the reputation of the Social Democrats in the eyes of future generations. But the justification for Shirer's strictures rests on two factors—the isolation of the Social Democrats, and their inevitable identification with the policy of fulfilling the universally unpopular Treaty of Versailles (*Erfuellungspolitik*). These two factors not only prevented the Social Democrats from maintaining Weimar democracy; they hamstrung effective resistance to the Nazis at a crucial period of history. The first factor might be held to have been, in part, their fault; the second was their affliction.

Their political isolation was partly historical. Up to 1919 the Social Democratic Party's sole achievement in co-operating with other parties was in the prosecution of World War I. Otherwise the party was divorced from potential allies by its Marxist, free-thinking and anti-clerical dogmas, and its post-1919 pacifism. Its anti-clericalism made it suspect to a great many practising Christians, of all creeds and classes. Its post-war pacifism made it an object of distaste to the Army and to the 'army caste' which extended far beyond the limited bounds of the 100,000-strong Reichswehr. There has for long been a tradition in German politics (it has continued since the Federal Republic came into being) of 'non-fraternization' with members of other parties; the Social Democrats, with their dogmatic thinking and 'under-dog complex', were strong protagonists of this tradition. Even the advent of Nazi tyranny did not induce them quickly to drop it.

Critics of German Social Democracy have identified it with woolly-minded humanitarianism, with a sort of soapiness of political outlook which has impeded pragmatic thought and constructive action, with a lack of political common sense. This is an accusation commonly levied against all Socialist parties which have failed to reach a position of political predominance in twentieth-century Europe. But the German Social Democrats suffered under the huge additional disadvantage of having accepted the Treaty of Versailles and then striven to implement it. Versailles meant the loss of eastern territories, the creation of the Polish Corridor, the sheer threat of reparations (which were largely never paid), the acceptance of a 'subject' role for Germany in Europe and in the world. Versailles, or rather the German people's paranoic hatred of it, did most to prevent the Social Democrats from 'stopping' Hitler.

Since the war I have asked Social Democrats why their party failed so signally in 1933—apart from Otto Wels's brave and dignified protest. This is what a leading member of the Party had to say about this in 1963. Fritz Erler's view was:

'You must first consider the Weimar era as a whole. The Weimar Republic collapsed because of the military defeat of 1918, and because the bulk of the German people looked on the Weimar Republic as the offspring of that defeat. Because of this there were very few Germans who were ready to go on to the barricades to defend Weimar democracy. Apart from active minorities on the Right and Left which were anti-democratic, most Germans were simply neutral.

'Then authoritarian rule did not arrive with a single jump. We went through semi-authoritarian phases under Bruening, Papen and Schleicher. And various factors conspired to prevent an active protest—the economic crisis, the bankruptcy of the farmers, the lack of any sort of co-operation between two working-class parties, the Social Democrats and Communists. Possibly there was one moment when resolute action would have saved the day—July 1932, when Papen dissolved the Braun-Severing Social Democratic government in Prussia. Then, indeed, the Social Democratic workers might have acted and might have been supported by the Prussian police and civil service. There could have been strike action, directed against the infringement of the constitution. But—the party leaders decided against direct action of this kind.'

Why, then, I asked Erler, did the Social Democrats not organize massive strike-action when the Nazis came to power and revealed themselves as a far greater menace to German democracy than Papen or Schleicher had ever been? His answer:

'In a totalitarian state you must have the overwhelming majority of the workers behind you in order to be successful. Our party was supported by only 22 per cent of the electorate. The Communists would not have helped—in fact they collaborated with the Nazis in organizing the transport strike of November 1932, which was directed against the Trade Unions and against us. Both the Nazis and Communists called our party "the figleaf of the bourgeoisie" and the "Social-Fascists". The workers would not have been ready to act, because they still hoped that Hitler would do a great deal for their material interests. A general strike in 1933 would, in short, have been a total failure.'

Erler might have added that a pathetic illusion lingered for some time that Nazism could be opposed, even defeated, by legal means.

Concerted working-class action was rendered virtually impossible, moreover, by the bewildering speed with which the Nazis acted as soon as they were firmly entrenched in power. On May 2, 1933, the Nazis closed down Trade Union headquarters throughout the country, dissolved the Unions, arrested their leading members and confiscated their liquid assets and premises. A number of Trade Unionists were hustled off to the first of the concentration camps. On May 10 Nazi officials and police began to occupy Social Democratic party offices, close down party newspapers and seize party funds, files and other property.

Strikes were outlawed by decree and collective bargaining was abolished. The Social Democratic unformed *Reichsbanner*—formed to prevent the brown-shirted S.A. from terrorizing the streets unopposed—was dissolved. Its members had fought endless street-battles against both Nazis and Communists, trying to preserve order in face of organized extremist provocation. In July 1933 the Nazis passed a law forbidding the formation of political parties, so leaving themselves in exclusive control of the political field.

Many Social Democrats were removed to the concentration camps. Among the most distinguished of them was Carl von Ossietzky, one of the first Social Democratic 'martyrs'. Born in 1887, he was a member of an aristocratic Prussian family, a most improbable recruit for German Social Democracy! He became a pacifist after World War I, denounced clandestine German re-armament under Stresemann and the violent nationalism of the early post-war years. His outspoken comments in the *Weltbuehne*, a left-wing weekly which he edited, brought him into conflict with the Bruening government in 1931. He was arrested, tried for treason and sent to prison for eighteen months.

Ossietzky had the chance of leaving the country at Christmas 1932 when he was released under a pre-Hitler amnesty. He refused to do so, for, as he maintained: 'If one intends to combat the diseased spirit of one's country successfully, then one has to share its fate.' He returned to the *Weltbuehne* and to his writing. He was rearrested by the brown-shirts on the night of the Reichstag Fire, in February 1933, and was thrust into a concentration camp. He could still have saved himself. For in 1935 he was awarded a Nobel Peace Prize while still in gaol. Hermann Goering had him brought from his cell for a personal interview.

He had already been told that if he would recant his openly expressed pacifist views and cease opposing the Nazis he might be released. Goering made this clear to him in their interview—subtly reminiscent of the meeting of Faust and Mephistopheles but producing an exactly opposite result. For Ossietzky, a small, prematurely bent but indomitable figure, flatly refused to make any promise whatever.

He went back to gaol and died there after persistent and brutal persecution. One particular picture of him has survived—standing fearlessly, in his pitiful prison-garb, before a gross, uniformed Nazi bully. He was one of the outstanding political martyrs of the Nazi era, but twenty-five years after his death there had still been no biography of this infinitely gallant man, no edited volume of his writings and letters, no real recognition of his essential worth and of his contribution to the German heritage.

The speed, toughness and perfect organization of the Nazi moves in 1933 crippled Social Democratic powers of resistance. Many Social Democrats, including some of the most active younger members, went into exile, thus weakening the democratic remnant left in Germany but surviving until after the war and helping to refound a united and thriving party since then. The 1954–63 Chairman of the West German Social Democratic Party, Erich Ollenhauer, was in exile throughout most of the Nazi era, as were some of his ablest lieutenants, Herbert Wehner, Waldemar von Knoeringen and Erwin Schoettle. Party leaders who remained in Germany were arrested or went underground. Meanwhile, the average worker contented himself with expressing the vague hope that things were 'not as bad as they looked' and that the political situation might improve. The material situation, at all events, quickly became better, and this is what interested him most of all.

Lack of immediate resistance by them did not modify the Nazis' treatment of the Social Democrats. Literally thousands went into the concentration camps, starting as soon as the Nazis were in power. By the end of July 1933, according to one estimate, there were 26,789 Germans in the concentration camps or being held as political prisoners in gaol. A great many of them, possibly even a majority, were Social Democrats. In the single electoral district of Bayreuth nearly 500 Social Democrats were reported to have been arrested in 1933. This immediate wave of arrests was designed to break the powers of resistance of the Social Democrats. But it was not altogether successful.

For one thing the exiles quickly became very active. Often with the support of the Social Democratic parties of other countries they established centres of activity in places like Prague (the principal exile headquarters until the Nazi invasion of Czechoslovakia in 1939), Basel and St. Gallen in Switzerland, Eupen in Belgium, and Mulhouse in Alsace. During the first year of Nazi rule at least 3,000 Social Democrats went into exile, many of them determined to carry on their resistance to the regime from abroad. They founded such newspapers as the *Neue Vorwaerts*, published in Prague from mid-1933 onwards, and the *Sozialistische Aktion*, with a circulation of at least 12,000. The *Sopade* reports on German conditions, published in Prague, were invaluable in informing the outside world about the true meaning of Nazism.

These reports could be compiled only by smuggling information out of Germany. For this purpose a 'courier service' was set up which operated across the German frontiers, finding loopholes in the frontier defences, over the hills of the Bavarian Forest and the Erzgebirge, through the marshes along the German-Dutch frontier, or across the Rhine into France and Switzerland. The couriers also brought into Germany foreign newspapers and those produced by the exiles.

This was intensely dangerous work, involving the risk of being shot by trigger-happy frontier guards and the certainty of brutal manhandling and imprisonment if the courier were caught. Yet there was never a shortage of people, usually young men, to carry out this work. The result was that the exile organizations for years received a regular and invaluable flow of information. Necessarily, this began to dry up when frontier control services were perfected, and during the war it dried up completely.

Two particular sections of the courier service deserve special mention. The first was the Chemnitz-Karlsbad (Karoly-Vary) service across the German-Czech border, through what since the war has become the East German uranium-mining area. Here the hills of the Erzgebirge rise to a shelf around 3,000 feet high with numerous little river-valleys winding down on both the German and Czech sides. The Chemnitz-Karlsbad service functioned splendidly until the Nazis seized the Sudetenland. This led to wholesale arrests of Social Democrats living on the Czech side of the frontier. One of the leaders of the service, Kurt Nadebuhr, committed suicide after capture in order to avoid incriminating his friends, under torture.

Equally active was the so-called *'Vereinigte Kletterabteilung'* (the 'United Scramblers') which brought thousands of copies of the *Brown Book of the Reichstag Fire* into Germany, and distributed them inside bogus bookbindings—generally those of Schiller's *Wallenstein*. According to one source—Guenther Weissenborn, in *Der Lautlose Aufstand*—twenty-four members of this group were murdered by the Nazis and another eighty-nine imprisoned.

One 'resister in exile' also deserves particular mention, chiefly because his story links that of the Social Democrats in exile with that of the post-war Social Democratic Party which has made such a big contribution to the re-establishment of a democratic West German State. Willy Brandt lived through the war years to become Lord Mayor of West Berlin in 1955, and since then has been one of the outstanding figures on the German political stage.

Born illegitimate in 1913, working his way up as a journalist, a socialist progressive who cared little for dogma but a great deal for humanity, Brandt had to go into exile at the very start of the Nazi era. He escaped from Germany on a fishing-boat which brought him to Rodbyhavn on the Danish island of Lolland in a storm.

Brandt was only twenty years old at the time but was bursting with energy and ideas. He opened a Social Democratic party office in Oslo, helped to organize illegal newspapers and leaflets which were smuggled into Germany, paid visits to exile headquarters in Prague, and became one of the Party's principal spokesmen in Scandinavia. One of his jobs was collecting money for Social Democrats who were being tried in Nazi Germany for crimes which they had not committed. Another was in convincing foreigners that

German socialists were not professional trouble-makers. One memorable story of his is of the Social Democratic conference at Laaren, in Holland, in February 1934. The local Lord Mayor was violently pro-Nazi. He had the Germans arrested and four of them taken in handcuffs to the German frontier and handed over to the Nazis. Brandt was himself taken to police headquarters in Amsterdam for interrogation, and then deported from Holland.

In the summer of 1936 Brandt returned, illegally, to Berlin and was put in charge there of a Social Democratic underground (the 'Metro'). He stayed in Berlin until February 1937, building up cells of five trusted members each, creating a small underground army of between 200 and 300 people and, as a convenient 'cover', studying Nazi lore at the Humboldt University! In 1937 Brandt was in Spain, organizing medical supplies for the Spanish loyalists as well as writing for the newspapers. In 1939 he was in Finland, mainly as a Red Cross worker during the Russo-Finnish war. Later he worked with the Norwegian Resistance, was arrested and imprisoned during the Nazi occupation of Norway, and was only released because the Nazis thought he was a Norwegian. Brandt's was a remarkable record of audacity, ingenuity and perseverance.

Back in Germany, after the first shock of Nazism in power had worn off, work began on the organization of a Social Democratic underground. Its beginnings were modest. The first task of the badly shaken Social Democrats—most of whose leaders were either in prison or in exile—was to collect small cadres of the faithful. This was not as easy as someone who did not experience the Nazi dictatorship might suppose. Nazism was a nation-wide movement, which transcended class and income group. The Nazis were quick to infiltrate any group hinting at sedition. The art of denunciation was sedulously taught and expertly practised. Social Democratic resistance had to 'begin small', in discussion groups which moved tentatively into the channels of resistance—the printing of illegal pamphlets and brochures, their distribution, and the scrupulous collection of truthful information.

Total secrecy was needed for all of these operations. Discussion groups had to have a 'cover story' in case they were surprised by a roving Nazi official or agent. Information of importance had to be hidden and, if possible, camouflaged. Leaflets usually carried bogus title-pages, with such headings as 'Miniature Library of Philosophy', 'Eccentric Hair-Styles' or 'Persil remains—Persil'.

The danger to this sort of underground work did not come only from the Nazis: it came from the Communists too. After 1933 large numbers of former Communist Party members came over to the Nazis, exchanging one form of totalitarian dogma for another. This made ex-Communists, or even Communist resisters, highly suspect to the Social Democrats. For they might either be Nazi agents or might be members of Communist 'cells' which were Nazi-infiltrated. The Social Democrats in exile flatly refused to have anything to do with the Communists, not because of any fear of betrayal but because they reckoned, generally with reason, that they were simply agents of Soviet Communism. The Social Democrats in Germany recruited as few ex-Communists as possible. Later events were to prove the wisdom of this 'go-slow' in relations with the other party involved in the 'War of the Marxist Brothers'.

Underground work was rendered yet more difficult by the Nazi practice of installing *Blockleiters*, even in small housing settlements or blocks of flats. These Nazi 'men of confidence' were everlastingly on the prowl. Yet underground work actually increased during the first three years of the Nazi era. Typical of the groups which were active during these early years was that of the 'Eilbek Comrades', led by Walter Schmedemann, who became Minister of Health in Land Hamburg after the war.

Eilbek is a borough of Hamburg and no great distance from the centre of the city, lying just to the east of the Aussen-Alster lake. Schmedemann was the leading Social Democrat in this part of Hamburg. Very soon after the Nazis came to power he was arrested —almost as a matter of form—along with members of the local party executive committee. Schmedemann went to prison with his committee members for several weeks. When they were released, the new Nazi 'Senator' for Police (Hamburg is an old Hanseatic port and still has its own 'Senate'), a Herr Richter, solemnly warned them not to take part in any future political activity.

Schmedemann and his followers ignored this warning. In one sense they possessed an advantage over many of the other Social Democratic 'cells' which were forming at the time—they were old friends who knew and trusted one another. They set to work to produce an illegal newspaper—a modest affair of four pages but something which was prized and cherished at a time when the entire official Press was controlled and censored by the Nazis. The newspaper reached a circulation of 5,000 but its readership may have been eight or ten times as large. Copies were smuggled as far afield as Hanover, Hildesheim and Bremen, distances of from eighty to 100 miles.

Schmedemann and his followers collected money. This was illegal, and a sixpenny contribution to a 'non-approved' organization could bring the contributor a three-month prison sentence. So the Eilbek group collected money by selling picture-postcards. In this nobody was caught. The Eilbekers established their own courier services with Czechoslovakia and Denmark, and even smuggled news in and out of Oranienburg concentration camp. Their wives helped; sometimes they acted as distributors of the leaflets, which were taken to different parts of Hamburg with the washing and under a couple of layers of laundry.

Schmedemann was caught eventually, after three years of invaluable underground work. He was sent to Fuhlsbuettel concentration camp, kicked, beaten-up and bullied. He saw some of his close friends literally thrashed to death. At least sixty-eight of them were arrested at one time or another, most of them after a single mass-trial in 1936.

But in two respects Schmedemann had the last laugh on the Nazis. When arrested for the first time he had his fountain-pen confiscated. The Gestapo official who was carrying out his interrogation decided to use Schmedemann's pen, and cursed when he found that there was no ink in it. He used it all the same, dipping the nib continually into an ink-pot. The reason why there was no ink was that the inside tube had been removed and a piece of paper inserted. It carried the names of Schmedemann's contacts outside the Social Democratic Party. They remained undiscovered.

Finally, when discharged from his concentration camp, Schmedemann carried out a new form of anti-Nazi propaganda. He distributed a leaflet which contained a full list of the brutalities perpetrated in the concentration camps in which he had been imprisoned, including dates and the names of Nazis responsible. These leaflets were dropped in the letter-boxes of all the leading

Nazis in Hamburg. After the war Schmedemann said: 'At least they could not claim that they didn't know what was being done in the name of their Party!'

The Schmedemann group was one of many which were uncovered by the termite-like agents of the Gestapo. In 1936 alone, 11,687 people are known to have been arrested on account of illegal work carried out for the Social Democratic underground. The number in 1937 has been estimated at just over 8,000 (these figures were published in Frau Annedore Leber's *Das Gewissen Entscheidet* and are probably the most accurate which have yet been compiled). One underground group after another was infiltrated and broken up. Their members were arrested for every sort of 'offence'—for making jocular remarks about the Nazis, for simply meeting clandestinely and so being 'organized', as well as for more positive underground activities. It was an 'offence' to make a joke about the Nazis on the stage; equally it was an offence to laugh at the joke. Essentially, former membership of the Social Democratic Party constituted an offence in itself.

In 1934 there were mass-trials in the industrial towns of Waldenburg and Dresden. A year later there was a mass-trial of 'Osterloh and others' in Bremen. In 1936–7 there were nine big trials in the Central German town of Halle, involving upwards of 100 Social Democrats and resulting in the imprisonment of at least 90 of them. In 1938 the infiltration of the 'Spengemann Group' in Hanover led to 1,000 arrests and the trials of 240 people. At the Duisburg mass-trials 233 people were sentenced; 79 more were sentenced in Berlin and 98 at the Saxon mining town of Zwickau.

The limbs and sinews of German Social Democracy were being steadily hacked off and destroyed. Two expertly organized underground groups, *Neu-Beginnen* and *Der Roter Stozstrupp*, were infiltrated. *Neu-Beginnen* included men like Fritz Erler and Waldemar von Knoeringen, and concentrated on the building-up of small cadres, from which it was hoped that a mass-movement would later be created. The group succeeded in creating an astonishingly far-flung network over Central Europe. Its main centres were Berlin and the Ruhr, but it had branches in Budweis and Bratislava (Pressburg) in Czechoslovakia, in Salzburg and Kufstein in Austria, and in Switzerland and Spain.

The long-term aim of this organization was to maintain sub-groups which would play their part in the reconstruction of Germany after the Nazi collapse. *Neu-Beginnen* produced a leaflet, *Das Gruene Otto*, which specialized in up-to-date news gleaned from the radio programmes of foreign countries and from newspapers smuggled in from abroad. The group was particularly active in 1936–7, when its 'activists' opened up arms and ammunition trains at railway sidings and sent details of the Nazi preparations for war to the Social Democrats in exile. Members of *Neu-Beginnen* were smuggled out to Spain to fight for the government side there. The group managed, in spite of the arrests of hundreds of its members at different times, to remain active until 1944.

The *Roter Stosztrupp* introduced *Fuenfer-Gruppen*—teams of five reminiscent of the *Troika* of three men each used by the Communists in Eastern European countries occupied by the Nazis. The *Roter Stosztrupp* produced a leaflet which ran into twenty-eight numbers, with a circulation of at least 3,000 in Berlin and neighbourhood. At one stage a new leaflet was being published every ten days. The groups helped the wives and children of men imprisoned by the Nazis. Even at the time of the November 1933 'elections' staged by the Nazis, the group managed to circulate thousands of leaflets telling people to vote 'No'.

The *Roter Stosztrupp* was one of the very few groups to establish contact with the Communists. This may have led to its infiltration. In November 1933 one of its leaflets fell into the hands of a Berlin civil servant, who passed it on to the police. The leader of the group, Rudolf Kuestermeier (since the war he has been the correspondent in Israel of the West German News Agency D.P.A.), was arrested. By Christmas the group had broken up in disorder.

The Nazis made a point of weeding out Social Democrats from the police, the civil service and the armed forces. They were hunted out of the teaching profession, for in the schools were remorseless, dedicated children who had been trained to denounce their elders, including their own fathers and mothers (the same thing has happened in the Communist East German Republic since the war, where children are publicly commended and sometimes even paid 'head-money' for denunciation). Wherever possible, Social Democrats were closely and continuously watched. All over Germany their cells were broken up, and by 1937 their leaflets were being collected by the Nazis at a rate of 4,000 a month. The marvel is that their resistance went on, and often in the most unexpected places. One of these, surely, was in the heart of Catholic, conservative Bavaria.

In 1934–5 more than 700 Social Democrats were arrested in Catholic Bavaria and the Tyrol. Their main centre had been in Augsburg and was based on the M.A.N. heavy engineering works there. The Bavarians have always had a cosmopolitan turn of mind and have been proud of their connections with Austria, Italy, Hungary and Switzerland. The members of the M.A.N. resistance group established a great many contacts abroad, mainly in those countries. After early trouble from the Gestapo they reorganized around 1940 and even began to collect arms. They might have played a useful part at the end of the war in dealing with Hitler's so-called 'werewolves', the last-ditch fighters, but were unfortunately wrecked in 1942 by a wave of arrests. More than fifty of their leading members went to prison. At least fifteen of them were executed, and another six committed suicide.

Among those executed was the chief organizer of the M.A.N. group. Bebo Wager was a typical Bavarian, stocky, tough, bullet-headed and addicted to the 'national' costume of *Lederhosen* (leather shorts), braces and embroidered monkey-jacket. He was one of the comparatively few Social Democratic resisters who thought primarily in terms of armed action. But he wanted to re-serve this armed action for the appropriate moment, when it would have a chance of success. Wager would certainly have become in-volved in the 1944 conspiracy against Hitler had he survived until then. But he was arrested in 1942 when the Gestapo pounced on his group. Even so, he was able to smuggle out an anti-Nazi manifesto which he composed in gaol. He was murdered in the Stadelheim gaol in Munich in August 1943. His last words in a letter to his wife were: 'Be brave for our children's sake, and I will try to die bravely for my beliefs.'

What of the Social Democratic rank and file, who were not directly involved in one or other clandestine group and who had to go on living normal lives under the tyranny which they loathed and despised? A totally false picture has been built up of Hitler's '*Ja* plebiscites', which appeared to give him the heartfelt support of the overwhelming majority of the German people. Other, more representative, votes correct this picture. Thus in March and April 1933, when Hitler was already in power, works-councils elections in some factories showed that the spirit of the workers was still unbroken. Here is one small selection of results, in which the Nazis polled about 5 per cent of the votes cast:

Factory	Non-party candidates	Christian	Communist	Nazi
Bewag, Berlin	3034	—	156	83
Tramways, Hamburg	4319	—	189	158
City Railway, Hamburg	1152	—	416	160
Explosives Works, Troisdorf	1249	309	189	199

At the Naszdorf works-council election in April 1935 2,900 out of 3,125 workers voted, but 1,700 anti-Nazi votes were declared invalid. The Nazis obtained 1,014 votes and claimed to be easy victors, with 84 per cent of the 'valid' poll. In reality their vote represented 35 per cent of the poll.

Of course, the Nazis soon found ways of dealing with resistance of this kind. The Naszdorf results, indeed, ran counter to those obtained elsewhere by systematic 'arrangement' by the authorities, through intimidation and discrimination against anyone failing to toe the Nazi line. But the workers had other ways of registering their independence of mind. One was by turning out in force at the funerals of people who were known to have opposed Nazism. Thus in 1934 hundreds of working people, silent and soberly dressed, attended the unveiling of a memorial in Breslau to Hans Alexander, a Trade Unionist who had been murdered in a concentration camp. In 1935 there were large crowds at the funerals of Johannes Stelling, the former Social Democratic Prime Minister of Mecklenburg, and Fritz Husemann, a coal-miners' leader who was murdered by the Nazis in the Ruhr. Even as late as 1942 people flocked to the funeral of Franz Kuenstler, a former Social Democratic Party official in Berlin who died shortly after his release from a concentration camp.

The workers had their own resistance groups. One was the *Goldene Sechs*, consisting of six young musicians—one of them a girl—who played in working-class quarters in and around Berlin and who produced leaflets on their own duplicating-machine. Another was the partly Communist *Gruppe Herbert Baum*, which had Jewish members and which in 1942 actually set on fire a Goebbels exhibition called 'The Soviet Paradise'. All of its members were caught and fourteen at least were executed. One man managed later to escape to Hungary. Many members of the families of these resisters were rounded up and sent to the extermination camp of Auschwitz where they were all murdered.

On a larger scale was the 'Robby Group', again partly Communist, which was formed by a Berlin worker, Robert Uhrig. Uhrig was arrested in 1934 for stirring up opposition to the Nazis in the Osram electrical works in Berlin. After his release he organized a network in the city, with 'cells' in Osram and in the Siemens electrical and Borsig engineering works. But the organization became too large and was infiltrated, possibly because some of its Communist members had been under Gestapo observation for a long time past. In 1942 dozens of its members were arrested; at least sixteen were murdered in gaol and another thirty-six sentenced by special courts and executed.

Many of these people were systematically tortured in order to gain information about other groups of resisters. One such group, under Beppo Roemer, a former 'Free Corps' officer who had sworn to kill Hitler, was almost certainly discovered as a result. Roemer was executed at the end of 1944, and around fifty of his followers were killed too.

Primarily left-wing in its sympathies was the 'Uncle Emil' (*Onkel Emil*) group in Berlin, which consisted mainly of actors and actresses and writers. This group collected food for people in hiding from the Gestapo, forged papers for those 'on the run' and procured doctors' certificates for conscientious objectors. They helped the dependants of people who had been murdered by the Nazis.

In particular they helped to hide Jews, who had readier and more numerous friends in Berlin than anywhere else in Germany—according to one estimate, 30,000 Jews were hidden at one time or another in Berlin, but the figure may be on the high side. The internal security of the *Onkel Emil* group seems to have been excellent and some of its members were still active at the end of the war, when they were chalking up 'No!' on Nazi placards calling on the Berliners to resist to the last and carry out 'werewolf' terrorist activities if their city fell into enemy hands.

The Trade Unions made a major contribution to resistance groups during the Nazi era and to the maintainance of a spirit of independence among the workers. The Unions probably played the principal part in the drawing up of the 1936 'People's Front' manifesto, which was widely circulated among enemies of the regime. Among its 'Ten Points' were the destruction of the Nazi regime, the establishment of the rule of law, the re-establishment of all basic democratic freedoms, the nationalization of heavy industry, the ending of competitive rearmament and a *rapprochement* with France.

The Unions might, indeed, have managed to organize themselves better for underground opposition to Hitler. For they had known, well in advance, what their fate was likely to be if Hitler came to power. But like so many other Germans they were a prey to vague hopes—that the Nazi regime would not last and that it would liberalize itself. There were no grounds for such hopes. As far back as 1931 the Nazis made it clear what their attitude to the Unions would be. In November of that year the Land Hesse police seized the so-called 'Boxheimer Documents', a series of draft decrees which the Nazis intended to put into force on seizing power. One decree laid down that a worker who refused to be directed into a job, or who went on strike, could be shot for 'sabotage'.

In April 1933 Josef Goebbels was noting in his diary: 'I discussed the questions at issue thoroughly with the Fuehrer up here [Berchtesgaden]. On the 1st May we shall organize a massive demonstration of the will of the German people. Then on the 2nd May the Trade Union buildings will be occupied. . . . There may be trouble for a day or two, but they [the Unions] will belong to us from then on.' Goebbels was as good as his word. On May 2, after the first, tumultuous, Nazi-organized May Day demonstrations, action against the Unions began. The Labour Unions (*Freie Gewerkschaften*) were dissolved, and the Christian Unions suffered the same fate in June. All labour representation was taken over by Dr. Robert Ley's Labour Front, a 100 per cent Nazi organization.

The Labour Unions had 5,000,000 members in May 1933, and the Christian Unions around 1,000,000. Liberal Unions and trade associations had another 465,000 members. Here was, or should have been, one of the basic props of Weimar democracy. Why did the Unions, then, take no action to save themselves in May 1933? The answer, of course, is much the same as that given to the question of the Social Democrats' inactivity. The brown-shirts dominated the streets, and on the streets—in a literal sense—were a great many of the 6,000,000 unemployed. The morale of the workers could scarcely have been lower; even so, the Unions considered calling a big 'trial' strike in 'red' Saxony, where the Nazis were weakest in the whole of Germany. But they failed to organize anything, partly because of lack of enthusiasm and partly because the Communist *Rote-Gewerk-schafts-Opposition* would not co-operate. Saxony was the chief Communist stronghold.

After their initial measures against the Unions, the Nazis behaved as they liked with the representatives of organized labour. Hundreds were arrested—often being hauled from their beds in the small hours of the morning. Others were beaten-up or threatened. One Nazi procedure was to force potential opponents of Hitler to sign statements renouncing all trade union activity. Another was the systematic falsification of the voting in works-councils elections. Bullied, badgered, frightened and frantic, union members, with one or two exceptions, could at first think up no plan of resistance.

An outstanding exception was Wilhelm Leuschner, a woodworker by trade who had become deputy chairman of the *Freie Gewerk-schaften* in 1932. As Minister of the Interior in Land Hesse he called out the police earlier that year to prevent an S.A. *Putsch*. He had established close relations with the Christian Unions and especially with one of their leaders, Jakob Kaiser (he was Federal Minister for All-German Affairs in Bonn from 1949 to 1956). Leuschner wanted resolute action in May 1933.

Leuschner was an almost exact contemporary of Hitler. He had been a member of the Darmstadt Town Council at an early age, and a member of the Land Hesse Parliament before becoming its Minister of the Interior. Hesse has for a long time past produced much of the life-force of German democracy, deriving in part from the proud role played by the Free City of Frankfurt, Hesse's largest city, in the 1848 Revolution.

Leuschner saw an immediate chance of resisting Nazism, outside Germany's borders. He had been temporarily imprisoned in May. In June he was released, in order to attend an International Trade Union Congress in Geneva. This may seem a surprising thing for the Nazis to have done. But they argued that the Geneva Congress would not recognize some completely bogus delegate from Ley's Labour Front. But it would recognize Leuschner, and the Nazis assumed that he would be very careful indeed in Geneva. He had already had a taste of gaol, and the Nazis could take reprisals against his family if he misbehaved. He was merely required to keep quiet in Geneva, but for an occasional 'constructive' word explaining to the organized labour of the world that the Nazi regime had come to stay.

Leuschner—with an invitation to join the Labour Front in his pocket—instead remained totally and consistently silent. His silence was the most eloquent testimony of all against the Nazi regime. On his return to Germany—he bravely decided against exile—he was rearrested and spent the next two years in prison. He emerged quite undaunted from prison and established contact with all sorts of enemies of Hitler—conservatives, liberals and even soldiers. 'Even', because Leuschner was a left-winger with an ingrained suspicion of the Army. Yet by 1944 he had emerged as one of the men who would have helped to rule Germany, had Hitler been killed and the Nazi tyranny swept away. During the years before that he became, by degrees only, convinced that Germany could best be saved by a 'revolution from above'. This concept was contrary to traditional Union beliefs.

Leuschner's arrest did not only deprive the Unions of their natural leader; it robbed them of much of their spirit of resistance. Trade Union 'cells' were established all over Germany, but their initial purpose seems to have been mere survival. Former union leaders were well known to the Nazis and were often arrested on 'preventive 'grounds, taken to concentration camps and killed there.

Union groups which formed in different parts of the country had only a limited lease of life. The 'Iron Front' cells in Duesseldorf, Essen, Neuss, Cologne and Krefeld lasted for a time, based mainly on former members of the Railwaymen's Union. The last chairman of the Metal Workers Union, Alwin Brandes, created another circle which was broken up in 1936. The smallest cells of all were organized inside sports societies, choirs, fire-brigades and, of course, the factories. The Christian Unionists toyed with the idea of a deal with the progressive 'Strasser' wing of the Nazi Party (Gregor Strasser was murdered in the 1934 Roehm Blood-Bath and his brother Otto escaped abroad).

Possibly the most useful resistance work of the Unions was their establishment of links abroad. They set up a liaison-office in the Czech town of Komotau (Chormutov) which organized daring escapes of marked men from Germany. Links were established with the Scandinavian countries, with Holland and Belgium and with the United States. Ernst Reuter, later to be Lord Mayor of West Berlin, formed his own cells in Turkey, and Willy Brandt in Sweden. Another Brandt, but no relation, Walter, escaped to Switzerland, went from there to Paris, fitted himself out with a forged passport and returned to Berlin in 1937. He worked for a time in the Trade Union underground, posing as a foreign student, was arrested and hanged himself in gaol to ensure that his secrets should die with him.

Consider the ultimate loneliness of such an end! Walter Brandt was very young and had so much to live for. He died regarded as a traitor, after brutal torture, with no hope of escape and with no word of recognition or praise from any quarter. He was indeed one of those '10,000 forgotten heroes' to whom the newspaper the *Manchester Guardian* later referred. Ten thousand, incidentally, was an under-estimate. Just before the outbreak of war, according to a Gestapo report, there were 27,367 political prisoners in German gaols, while in the previous six years 112,432 more had been sentenced by Nazi courts.

The outbreak of war, of course, made working-class resistance to Hitler more difficult than before. Pre-war the Gestapo had been active enough, but now the whole country was turned into a hive of security forces. Everywhere notices went up, '*Vorsicht beim Gespraech—Feind hoert mit!*' ('Take care what you say—the enemy is listening!') Soon the importation of hundreds of thousands of foreign workers brought endless checks of the population, in trains, restaurants, places of work and entertainment.

146

Denunciation became second nature to all loyal Nazis. During the big air-raids orders went out to frontier and railway police, to the Hitler Youth and the girls of the *Bund Deutscher Maedel*; these were the occasions when the resister might be caught up in a spot-check, interrogated and exposed. Nazi officials often caught Hitler's German opponents by chance, when they were searching for escaped prisoners-of-war or foreign workers.

Naturally the tendency of the Social Democratic resisters was to go further 'underground'. As the war went on, and ever stricter security regulations were introduced, resistance—for most of those thousands of Social Democrats who were still resolute—became increasingly a matter of keeping opinions alive, learning and passing on truthful news about the war, and waiting for it to end. This may sound unadventurous, but it was inevitable. Yet, it was precisely during the war years that leading Social Democratic opponents of Hitler set out to overcome one of their biggest obstacles—their lack of contact with other German enemies of the Nazis. Three men played the chief parts in this exodus from traditional isolation— Theodor Haubach, Carlo Mierendorff and Julius Leber.

Haubach was thirty-seven years old when the Nazis came to power. Mierendorff was an exact contemporary and so close a friend of his that their stories are intertwined like the branches of a vine. Both men were convinced Social Democrats from an early age. Both became journalists, after studying at Heidelberg University. In June 1922, when the half-Jewish Walter Rathenau, then Foreign Minister, was murdered by nationalist thugs in broad daylight in the streets of Berlin, Mierendorff forced the anti-Semitic Professor Lenard to fly the national flag at half-mast from the physics institute of Heidelberg University. Haubach put up a spirited defence of Mierendorff's somewhat unconventional action before the Rector of the University and its hastily assembled governing body.

Both men joined the uniformed *Reichsbanner* and fought up to 1933 to keep the brown-shirts off the streets (Mierendorff was as strong as a bull and gave an excellent account of himself in the street-fighting). 'The new Germany is not yet here', Haubach was writing in the *Hamburger Echo*. 'But it will come, and we are fighting for it already. And if we fight for a new Germany, we fight for a new Europe too.'

Both men carried on underground resistance after the Nazis came to power, were arrested and imprisoned, and released again. Haubach was two years in concentration camps, Mierendorff four. The Nazis probably hated the robust Mierendorff more than the ascetic Haubach, because of his vitality, love of life and immense physical and moral courage. The Nazis liked to depict socialists as mean, down-at-heels, cringing creatures who had subscribed to their country's defeat in war and would offer it a shameful subjection for posterity. Mierendorff was the antithesis of this picture— which was a false one with regard to Social Democrats, anyway.

During the war both men went to Berlin, and turned the 'Mehlgarten' public house in the Olivaer Platz into one of the centres of anti-Nazi discussion and planning. It was in Berlin that they entered into contact with non-socialists, largely through the 'Kreisau Circle' built up to plan for Germany's future by Count Moltke and his friends. In the Kreisau Circle they met active resisters, who eventually took part in the principal conspiracy to kill Hitler. Both men might have held high office in an anti-Nazi government, but Mierendorff was killed, by ironic chance, by an Allied bomb in an air-raid at the end of 1943. Haubach worked on until July 1944, when he was arrested and sentenced to death. He was executed in January 1945.

Julius Leber was probably the outstanding member of this trio, and the leading Social Democratic opponent of Hitler. Born in 1891 in Alsace, he fought in World War I and became an officer—for the son of a mason an unusual feat, even in war-time. In 1920 he led his Reichswehr soldiers against the nationalists of the *Kapp Putsch*. From the Army he went to Luebeck, to become editor of the *Luebecker Volksboten*, where Willy Brandt worked under him for a time. In 1924 he became a member of the Reichstag.

Leber was imprisoned by the Nazis in 1933 and brutally maltreated in concentration camps. For a whole year he was in an unlit and unheated cell, sleeping on the stone floor without a coat or blanket. Yet while there he managed to write a thesis on the causes of the failure of the Weimar Republic, and to outline his concept of a socialist state with a 'strong core', in which extremist parties of both the right and left would be banned. 'Uncurbed and irresponsible attitudes', Leber wrote, 'are incompatible with that external order which assures every man his personal freedom of opinion to a high degree. Strong authority on the part of the State must here engrave boundaries to popular thought, but in such a manner as to leave each citizen the sensation of maximum personal freedom.'

Constantine Fitz Gibbon, quoting this passage in his book *The Shirt of Nessus*, considers this statement must sound 'blunt' and even 'foreign' to Anglo-Saxons who 'believe our sensation of maximum freedom to be the reality'. But what Leber was probably getting at was merely that the man in the street should have an awareness of personal freedom, which he had not developed in the past in Germany.

Leber was released from Sachsenhausen concentration camp in 1937 and went to Berlin, where he became a coal-merchant. He was debarred from writing, although he continued to do so privately. In Berlin he came into contact with the Kreisau Circle, and through its members with some of the military leaders of the 1944 conspiracy, Witzleben, Beck and Stauffenberg. In spite of the doubts of Goerdeler and some of the confirmed conservatives in the Opposition, Leber became one of the driving-forces in active planning against Hitler. By early 1944 he had been accepted even by Goerdeler as someone who should hold high office in a post-Nazi government (Goerdeler would have given him the Ministry of the Interior, but Leber would probably have pressed his claims to become at least Vice-Chancellor).

Leber continued to work and plan for the future of his country almost up to the eve of the July 20, 1944, conspiracy. But in the middle of June 1944 he made what turned out to be a fatal mistake. In his efforts to secure the broadest possible front for action against the Nazis he decided to meet representatives of the increasingly active Communist underground, Franz Jacob and Anton Saefkow. For Leber this was a surprising step, since as early as 1924 he had advocated the banning of the Communist Party.

To the meeting Leber took with him Adolf Reichwein, the 'rolling stone' of the Social Democratic Party, a man of great charm and character who had globe-trotted all over the world, had flown his own plane and fought in Spain and China. At the meeting with Jacob and Saefkow, another Communist, a minor character who was in reality a Nazi stool-pigeon, was present for a time. On July 4 and 5 the Gestapo pounced on Social Democratic and Communist cells all over Berlin. Leber was arrested on July 5, tortured for four days and nights, and then made his own confession, in order to avoid implicating his friends. He was sentenced to death in October and executed in January 1945. His last recorded words were: 'For so good and righteous a cause, the cost of one's own life is a fair price. We did all that we could do.'

The failure of the conspiracy of July 20 put paid to further Social Democratic resistance. The leaders—Leber, Haubach, Reichwein—had been murdered by the Nazis. What opposition continued afterwards was more like the activities of the early Christians in the catacombs than political resistance in a modern state. The Social Democrats, moreover, seemed to have been a liability to the more meticulous, security-minded soldiers of July 20. Leber's widow has denied that her husband betrayed a single comrade under the more than usually diabolical tortures to which he was subjected. This is doubtless true, but the fear that he might break down may have rattled the military conspirators during the last days of preparation. Yet the success of July 20 hung on so many threads that it would be wrong to blame Leber, Reichwein and their associates in any way for its failure.

Did the Social Democratic opposition to Hitler fail—in a general sense—in that it achieved too little, left too small a mark on German history and contributed to the mistaken belief held outside Germany that only a handful of brave Germans fought wholeheartedly against tyranny? Well, the Social Democrats certainly produced martyrs enough. According to one set of figures (from the Hammer Archives in Hamburg), 195 members of the Reichstag and of the *Land* Parliaments died during the Nazi era, 88 of them in the concentration camps and 45 after being 'legally' sentenced to death (including 11 after July 20, 1944). Around one-third of those who suffered—one figure given is 62—were Social Democrats.

Another 121 members of the Reichstag and of *Land* Parliaments were driven into exile. In all—and these figures included the names on the death-roll—416 Parliamentarians were imprisoned by the Nazis, 327 of them in concentration camps. It is not possible to assess exactly how many rank-and-file Social Democrats were imprisoned, executed and murdered between 1933 and 1945. The imprisoned, at least, ran into hundreds of thousands.

Did the Social Democratic Opposition to Hitler, then, fail? I asked this question long years after the war to Fritz Erler, whose underground work in *Neu-Beginnen* earned him nearly eight years in concentration camps. This was what he had to say:

'On the face of things it looks as if we missed a big chance at the outset in 1933. But there was plenty to be done after that. We maintained a minimum of organization and continued to train people to be democrats. We managed to keep our illegal literature circulating until late in the war. We went on telling the workers in the factories that they would in due course have responsibilities to discharge.

'Of course, there was a lack of co-ordination with other groups which opposed Hitler. Our contribution to the actual principal conspiracy to overthrow Hitler may not have been a large one. But some of our leaders played their part in that, too, and I am glad. The decision to kill Hitler was the right one, and it was a tragedy that the attempts failed.

'In the final event, perhaps our main achievement was to keep so many people completely clear of all connection with the Nazis and their contagion. These were the "small" people, who helped more active resisters, who sheltered and fed them when the Gestapo was at their heels—and who really disbelieved in Nazism. They were available for the post-war period, to help build up a better Germany.'

This is a fair summing-up. When the war ended a new Germany had to be created. In Western Germany only two formative forces emerged after 1945—although a third, German liberalism, may yet prove itself. These were the Christian Democratic Union, interdenominational and founded on the Christian ethic and its practical application, and the revived Social Democratic Party, the torchbearer of progressive thought and tradition.

Adenauer so dominated the first eighteen years of the post-war period that it has been easy to underrate the part played by Social Democracy. It has been a big one. Of course, there was a lack of leaders, even after the exiles came home. For the concentration camps had taken a terrible toll. What would the post-war Germany not have given for a Leber, a Reichwein, a Mierendorff! Yet the Social Democrats who survived the Nazi era have given post-war Social Democracy continuity, consistency, common sense. The Social Democractic politicians have applied a useful brake to

Adenhauer's paternalism, and the discipline and moderation of organized labour has played a big part in Germany's economic recovery.

Social Democratic opposition to Hitler was not in vain, for these have been the first fruits of it. Nor will the courage of individual Social Democratic resisters, and the sufferings of so many, ever be forgotten. That is as much a lesson for the future as the strictly political failure of the Social Democratic Party in 1933, and the lack of obvious material success achieved by its spasmodic underground struggle during the twelve years following.

seven

The White Rose of German Youth

'I see His blood upon the rose
And in the stars the glory of His eyes.'
JOSEPH MARY PLUNKETT

IN 1962 the *Bundesgerichtshof*, one of the high courts of the West German judiciary, met to consider the appeal of a man for compensation for his sufferings under the Nazi regime as a 'resister' against Hitler. The man had refused to take up arms when called to the colours in 1939. He was sent to a labour unit but ran into fresh trouble later in the war. He refused to lay mines in an extemporized minefield designed to hold up the Allied advance into Germany. This time he was sent to a 'punishment battalion'. His health and, he maintained, his earning capacity and position in the community suffered as a result.

The *Bundesgerichtshof* dismissed his appeal. The court found that 'resistance' was itself only proven when the 'resister' made a coherent effort to 'remove an existing state of illegality and injustice'. This effort, moreover, should be 'decisive'—whatever the august judges of this high court meant by that. One of them, a Dr. Weinkauff, added the rider that 'resistance must have the aim of improving the situation'. The judges agreed, indeed, that it was justifiable for a soldier to take part in a war of 'aggression'. But they decided that the claim put before them gave no clear-cut picture of the claimant's motive.

Possibly this high court in democratic post-war Germany was searching for a formula in order to avoid pronouncing a judgement which could have awkward consequences (the first of them—all German pacifists of the Nazi era would be entitled to claim compensation for deprivation and suffering). The judgement of the *Bundesgerichtshof* had an obvious bearing on German resistance against Nazism. If this resistance were spontaneous, but neither effectual nor exactly formulated, the view of the *Bundesgerichtshof* could be that it never constituted resistance at all.

The resistance of young Germans of that time to Nazism—a comparatively little-known chapter in the story of the German Opposition—would presumably be regarded by this post-war *Bundesgerichtshof* as both incoherent and ineffectual. What organization and what plans did it have? What were its 'effective' achievements? Did it even involve a conscious and calculated attempt to 'improve the situation'? The answers to all of these questions would have to be negative. And so, by singularly German logic, the utterly gallant efforts of young Germans to resist Hitler would not constitute 'resistance' at all.

But young Germans did resist. To Hitler this must have remained totally inexplicable down to the day of his miserable death—poisoned like a rat, in a cellar, instead of dying in battle as recommended to the millions of enthusiastic members of the Hitler Youth. Hitler seemed to offer German youth so much—among other things, hope, pride and an immense self-confidence. The hope was that of building up a strong and happy German nation. The pride sprang from the special role which German youth was called upon to play. The self-confidence blossomed from the marching ranks with their marching songs, and from a carefully instilled sense of purpose, power and progress.

I first met young Germans, individually and in the mass, only two months after Hitler came into power in 1933. Comical in some ways, they were impressive in others. In argument they were quickly and totally lost, and forced to fall back on selected slogans. They were astonishingly ignorant of the world outside Germany, for they were simply not taught about it any longer. They always sought to avoid giving a personal opinion in order to resort to some stock phrase. They tended not only to believe that the Treaty of Versailles was unjust to Germany, but that the world divided itself into Germans and non-Germans, and that the latter loathed and envied them.

And yet, and yet . . . there was something terribly attractive about these young Germans of 1933. They had a tremendous sense of

154

comradeship amongst themselves. They were happy to learn together, play together, march together and even to learn to fight together. They loved the open air and they flung away clothes from them with an abandon which would have horrified the Victorian generation. Nudity, under the sun, was to them a state of animal comfort, and they thought nothing of bicycling ten miles before breakfast to a river, swimming in the nude and dashing back to begin a working day. They were taught to love the countryside, and everything in it. It was their countryside, their Germany. Their animal energy was gigantic.

Young Germans were taught to be hard, Spartan. This has been much scoffed at by critics of Nazism, although these same critics would regard Leonidas' stand with his 300 Spartans, at Thermopylae, as a military epic. But young Germans were taught, too, to work hard, to believe in recognizable ideals and to become (in the conformist Nazi State) good citizens. Learning became more than an object in itself—it could contribute to a great and powerful Reich, which would regain the 'rights' taken away at Versailles. The ideals were all too obvious: Germany should take back its rightful place in the European Order, build a bridge between East and West, fulfil a cultural mission which had first been shouldered by the Teutonic Knights but which had deeper roots in Charlemagne's Empire. Good citizenship meant carrying out 'labour service' after leaving school, and military service after that, supporting the Party, contributing to the welfare and prosperity of the State.

Nazi youth was indoctrinated with the ideal of service, and one of the most aimless myths about Nazism still is that it was necessary to dragoon and bully youth in order to achieve this. Youth, in any country, is very ready to serve if told that its service is needed. The young German (Werner Gerhardt of Zeitz, in 1932) who told his mother: 'Mummy, don't cry; because I know that I am ready to die for Hitler,' was no freak. Werner, like other young Germans, had been told, among other things, that Germany's future lay in the hands of German youth. The vast responsibility which this implied was an incentive and a challenge. Before 1933 twenty-one members of the Hitler Youth died in order to bring Hitler to power; after 1933 the death-roll ran into millions. In an animal sense happy, physically fit, tanned by the sun and the wind, secure in their share of the future, young Germans continued to serve their Fuehrer with invariable courage and extraordinary devotion down to the last days of the doomed Third Reich. On those last, dreadful days fourteen- and fifteen-year-olds went out to fight Russian tanks, often armed with nothing more lethal than a hand-grenade or a home-made 'Molotov cocktail'.

Two other things should be noted, in passing, about Nazi youth. The first is that it inherited a nationalistic tradition. German students' associations were showing a strongly anti-Semitic tendency as far back as 1816 when books written by Jews were burnt publicly à la Goebbels. In 1819 a student secret society was formed in the universities with the aim of driving the Jews out of Germany. The students' duelling societies—which organized pitched battles with blunted swords, designed to score 'scars of honour' on chin and cheekbone—multiplied during the nineteenth century. Post-1919 youth groups did not need to be 'brown' (or Nazi) in order to be violently nationalistic and militaristic. There was a 'Scharnhost League' and a 'Bismarck Youth', both of which preached Germany's military greatness. There was a *Stahlhelm*, whose iron discipline and esprit de corps were eagerly copied by the Nazis. Even the more traditional *Kyffhaueser* youth, priding itself on its political neutrality, cancelled out this neutrality by its starkly nationalist aims and its inevitable support of political parties which propagated them.

The second point of interest about Nazi youth was its degree of organization. In 1929 a mere 2,000 members of the Hitler Youth took part in the Nuremberg Party rally, but in the same year the 'Nazi school league' was formed, enabling Nazi cells to be organized in every school, and a start was made with the regimentation of young girls into what later became the *Bund Deutscher Maedel*. By the end of 1932 there were 107,000 members of the Hitler Youth, 69 per cent of them young workers and trainees. Very soon six- to ten-year-olds were being organized as *Hitler Pimpfe*, the most junior of all party members, and the ten- to fourteen-year-olds into the *Jungvolk*, whose infused blend of patriotism and pagan joy in living made them into the willing cannon-fodder of World War II.

But it was their seniors who organized, as the 'Battle Committee of the Berlin Students', the twentieth-century bonfires of May 11, 1933, when once again the works of distinguished authors were cast upon the flames with concise accompanying orations. Those of Heinrich Mann and Erich Kaestner were hurled in to shouts of 'Down with decadence and moral perversion!', those of Emil Ludwig to the cry of 'Down with the falsification of history and the slandering of our great ones!', and those of Erich Maria Remarque to that of 'Literary treason against our soldiers!' German youth approved. It was not merely patriotic; it was becoming rabid, ripe for war.

One last question must be considered before going on to look at the performance of German youth in opposition to Hitler. Many, even most, German parents quickly made their terms with Nazism, or decided to support it openly and more or less whole-heartedly. What of the German teaching profession? Teachers, one must always feel and even believe, should be people cast in the image of Gamaliel, dedicated to the truth and proof against the cancerous grip of ideology. A pretty thought, but German teachers had fallen far short of it long before Hitler came to power. Even before 1914 the German teaching profession was nationalist, conservative and liked to regard itself as essentially 'Germanic'.

Schoolmasters flocked to join the National Socialist Teachers League after 1933. They readily accepted the removal of all Jews from their profession. They gladly had themselves classified as civil servants and took the oath of loyalty to Hitler. The professor of economics, Wilhelm Roepke, called this 'a scene of prostitution which has stained the honourable history of German learning'. The violent nationalism of the teaching profession was one of the biggest factors which restricted the growth of a truly liberal spirit in pre-1914 Germany and encouraged its final withering, which is barely understood and totally unlamented even today.

In the circumstances it would scarcely be surprising if resistance to Hitler, on the part of German youth, were spasmodic, individual and largely fortuitous. Most of it was; young people who opposed the Nazis were regarded as fools or knaves by their fellows—who looked forward to the millennium of Hitler's 1,000-year Reich in which they would come into their own heritage of responsibility, co-partnership and power. Yet individualism, even in a race which a British field marshal, Sir William Slim, designated as 'bloodthirsty sheep', had a way of showing itself.

There was the case, for instance, of Helmut Huebener, who was guillotined in Hamburg in October 1942 at the callow age of seventeen and a half. Huebener joined the *Jungvolk* in 1938, aged thirteen, and became an apparently enthusiastic member of the Hitler Youth one year later. He was intelligent, efficient, a model pupil who became a trainee for the civil service as soon as he left school. He was typical of the best, not only of German youth, but of youth anywhere in the world: a boy of charm, determination and individuality.

His individuality began to become unorthodox when Hitler's Stukas dive-bombed the civilian populations of Warsaw and Rotterdam. In 1941 Huebener began listening regularly to B.B.C. broadcasts and decided that the time had come for him to act. Aged still only sixteen, he began to produce his own leaflets on a duplicating machine and distribute them in his native city of Hamburg. The early leaflets concentrated on Hitler's blood-guiltiness for starting the war and pursuing it by brutal methods. The Nazi attack on the Soviet Union brought a change in his leaflets; Huebener printed more and more facts gleaned from the B.B.C. and supplemented them with his own explanation of military and political events. From June 1941 until his arrest in the summer of 1942 Huebener produced at least twenty leaflets.

Huebener was denounced for listening to enemy broadcasts, and his judges—glum executors of a gross tyranny—regarded this alone as grounds for sentencing him to death. In addition, he had preached 'sedition' in 'red' Hamburg, the traditional stronghold of German social democracy which was still evidently not rid of 'Marxism'. With unintentional irony his judges paid tribute to his leaflets—to his diction, his grasp of political and military issues and his soaring vision. In passing sentence they stated that his matureness of mind was such that he had to be treated 'like an adult'. Two other members of the Hitler Youth, Wobbe and Schnibbe, were executed at the same time.

Another such youthful resister against Hitler was Jonathan Stark, who refused in 1943 at the age of seventeen to take the oath to Hitler, or to carry out his military service. Jonathan and his family were Jehovah's Witnesses, who were liable to persecution for their non-conformist views by the Nazis (it is no coincidence that the post-war East German dictatorship, too, has persecuted this sect). He was sent to Sachsenhausen concentration camp and was hanged there in

October 1944. His 'crime' lay in continuing to speak his mind about the evils of war and dictatorship, and his courage was such that the hangman, a convicted criminal, hesitated over his duty. The camp commandant, a man of singular brutality, stood silent and gave no order. It had to come from Jonathan himself, in the memorable words: 'What are you waiting for? Stand up for Jehovah and Gideon!'

His example was typical of the Jehovah's Witnesses of Germany. According to one estimate, they numbered just over 6,000 when Hitler came to power. In all, 5,911 of them were arrested and imprisoned, and more than 2,000 were murdered by the Nazis.

Yet another young man who refused to keep silent was the twenty-six-year-old Michael Kitzelmann, who was sentenced to death by a military court in the Russian town of Orel in April 1942. Kitzelmann had seen enough of war to hate it, and he had seen enough of Nazi methods of conducting war in Russia to realize that they were inhuman and monstrous. He died a convinced pacifist— tortured, as his diary showed, by grief, uncertainty and homesickness, but thanking God for the help given him at the end by an Army chaplain.

More spectacular was the death years earlier of the twenty-four-year-old Anton Schmaus, a young Social Democrat who came to the help of his mother when she was dragged from her bed by brown-shirted Storm Troopers and beaten up. Schmaus shot and killed four of his assailants before he was shot down in his turn.

Here and there in Nazi Germany little groups of anti-Nazi youth formed, were broken up by the untiring Nazi spies and informers, and sometimes re-formed. The biggest group of this kind was the *Edelweiss*, formed originally in Bavaria out of remnants of the dissolved and banned Catholic Young Men's associations and spreading to all parts of Catholic Germany. At one period nearly a quarter of the members of the Hitler Youth in the Rhineland town of Krefeld were believed to belong to the *Edelweiss* group, whose main purpose was to meet clandestinely, discuss events, share information, and reaffirm their largely religious objections to Nazism.

A small but more active group was that of Berlin students led by Werner Steinbrink. This group, which circulated anti-Nazi literature, was infiltrated and broken up in the summer of 1942. According to

Steinbrink's mother, ten of its members were executed on August 18. One small, isolated group was organized by a young musician and schoolmaster, Alfred Schmidt-Sas. Its few members distributed leaflets and pasted up broadsheets. In October 1942 six young people were tried by the People's Court. Four boys of nineteen to twenty-one years of age were executed in December 1942, and one girl sent to prison for seven years.

Other groups whose names have survived were the *Die Meute* in Leipzig and the *Kittelbach-Piraten* in the Ruhr. Later in the war young Bavarians were among those who joined the 'O7' group in Munich and the *Anti-Nationalsozialistische Verband* in the foothills of the Alps. After July 20, 1944, five professors of Freiburg University were arrested and imprisoned in Berlin, but survived the war. They had listened to a lecture by Dietrich Bonhoeffer in the fall of 1942. From then on they were ready to criticize the regime.

The anti-Nazi activities of German youth were serious and substantial enough to warrant the organization of a separate youth department of the *Reichshauptsichterheitsamt* (the State Security headquarters) in the Prinz Albrechtstrasse in Berlin, and the opening of a 'concentration camp for youth' in the Rhineland town of Neuwied, where only boys of under twenty years of age were imprisoned.

For young Germans who opposed the regime, as for older people, the principal question was: what is there we can do to show our contempt and hatred of Nazism? Huebener showed one way, Stark another. Hundreds of young men and women looked in vain for leaders with a formula and a plan. For what plan could there be? It is a paradox of the Nazi era that young people who were asked to surrender their souls to an authoritarian creed, and who could be conscripted to burn down Russian villages and round up the cringing inhabitants of Polish ghettoes, were mostly imbued with ideals and made themselves the willing tools of their masters out of a spirit of self-sacrifice and devotion to duty. To murder their Nazi overlords was something which the young resisters did not contemplate. To take up arms against them was impracticable. It was left to one group, which formed round the Scholl family, to demonstrate the best way of combating oppression. This was by their willing martyrdom, by treading the same path as Christ trod to Calvary.

The Scholls were, to outward appearances, a very ordinary family. The father was mayor of a small Württemberg village in the valley of the Kocher, before the family moved to the town of Ulm. He was a protestant Evangelical, with liberal, rationalistic political and social views. The mother had been trained as a *Diakonisse*, an Evangelical Sister. Their eldest child, Hans, was born on Armistice Day, November 11, 1918. Closest to him in the family of five were his sisters Sophie, three years younger, and Inge. By 1933 all five children were in one or other branch of the Hitler Youth. Their father did not try to stop them joining, although he spoke his mind freely whenever political topics were discussed in his household. The young Scholls fell for the fervour and patriotism of the Nazi movement, for the marching ranks and songs, for the excursions to the idyllic slopes of the Schwaebischer Alb and the wooded winding valley of the Danube. They were typical of their generation.

Who should blame them? Inge Scholl, who with her sister Elisabeth survived the Nazi era, has described their feelings: 'We loved our homeland, its forests and the river Danube . . . we thought of the smell of heathland, of damp earth and fragrant apples when we thought of our homeland. . . . And Hitler, so we were told everywhere, wanted to give this homeland greatness, happiness and prosperity . . . he wanted to ensure that everyone had work and bread; he would not rest until every German was free and happy in the Fatherland.'

Today Inge Scholl talks apologetically about 'our childish enthusiasm at that time'. But was it so childish? One of the main attractions of Nazism to young people was that it made demands on them. It asked them to shoulder responsibilities, in a spirit of comradeship to help in the building of a new and more beautiful Germany. It gave them the sense of being treated as grown-ups. In short, it flattered. The young Scholls could not understand their father for doubting Hitler and mischievously comparing him to the Pied Piper. Hans was angry with him when he said that they were not being taught history right in their schools—his retort, according to Inge, was 'You never learnt it right yourself, Daddy'.

Hans was the first of the young Scholls to find fault with the Nazis. His local Hitler Youth leader told him that it was 'wrong' to sing foreign as well as German songs (Hans played a guitar and sang to his own accompaniment). Hans next had a stand-up fight with another youth leader. He was disgusted with the Nuremberg Party Rally, which he attended as a standard-bearer of the Hitler Youth. His view was that there too much high-flown talk of honour and loyalty but that nobody took the trouble to lay down genuine principles of conduct. Officious party members next 'supervised' Hans's reading-matter, confiscated first a book by Stefan Zweig and then one by Thomas Mann. At sixteen years of age Hans had formed his own views; he knew that Nazi talk of such books being 'decadent' and 'un-German' was nonsensical.

In 1934 the Scholls heard the story of a young teacher, who had been invited to join the Nazi Party, who had refused and had then been put into a concentration camp. Boys and girls of fifteen and sixteen years of age take an interest in their teachers, and the young Scholls asked their father for his view. His answer was: 'This is a state of war during a time of peace, and it is happening in the heart of our country.' The young people wanted to hear more from him. He told them that even Hitler's social and economic successes were illusory; unemployment was only being eliminated by starting an arms-race in Europe which would surely lead to war.

In 1935 Hans and Inge went to Hitler's much vaunted exhibition of art in the Haus der Kunst in Munich. They were deeply depressed (they both had artistic leanings and since the war Inge has run a school of industrial design in Ulm) by much of the rubbish which was being exhibited. But close to the exhibition was a small pavilion which housed Hitler's idea of the obverse of 'true' art—an exhibition of '*entartete*' or decadent art. Hans and Inge were delighted with what they saw there and stayed for hours (the Nazis later had to close down this exhibition, precisely because it attracted far more genuine interest than the absurd display which they themselves were sponsoring).

In January 1937 Hans was among a number of young people who were arrested, for indulging in 'loose' talk, in two groups in Ulm and Stuttgart. He spent six to seven weeks in gaol, and his 'crime' of talking too much was treated as a minor peccadillo. But his private letters were censored from then on, and he was warned that the consequences of a further 'deviation' would be serious.

In fact, Hans had by now decided to deviate, and to some purpose.

His first thought was that the Nazi regime would not last (this was shared by many of its German opponents and by a great number of contemporary European statesmen). He therefore formed a group which joined the highly unofficial 'D. J. One-Eleven' (the name stood for 'German Youth of November the First', the date of the death in the previous year, while climbing, of a young member). The 'D.J. One-Eleven' was non-political, composed of nature-lovers and young people of aesthetic tastes and interests, pledged to regard life as an adventure and to enjoy every phase of it. This may seem a misty sort of concept, but these young people wanted to read books, play games, hitch-hike the length and breadth of their country, think, sing, breathe. Under Nazi regimentation it was becoming increasingly difficult to do all of these things, and remain a free man.

In 1939, shortly before war broke out, the ideas of the Scholl group had moved far enough towards active resistance to the regime for its members to start producing their own, privately circulated, 'news-letter'. This was a small enough undertaking, designed only for a few close friends. Hans had become a medical student at Munich University and had made some firm friends there—Christoph Probst, in his early twenties but already married, Alexander Schmorell, the soft-spoken pipe-smoking son of a Munich doctor. The Scholl news-letter was far less concerned with active resistance to Hitler than with the maintenance of some sort of freedom of thought for its readers. Even the Gestapo would have regarded it as relatively harmless.

The war took Hans, as a medical orderly, to France, but he was allowed to return in the autumn of 1940 to Munich to continue with his university studies. It was about this time that he met Karl Muth, the editor of *Hochland*, a periodical which tried to maintain some kind of independence of outlook, and Theodor Haecker, the Catholic essayist and philosopher. Haecker told Hans that the Germans would never prosper as long as they lacked humility, and almost certainly showed him the anti-Nazi diary which he kept. By now Hans was a violent anti-Nazi himself, but unable to focus on any clear line of anti-Nazi action.

Six months of Nazi labour service had confirmed his sister Sophie likewise in her anti-Nazi opinions. In the labour camp close to the Swiss frontier she tired of the martial chatter of the other girls—

plenty of whom had a kittenish 'crush' on the unmarriageable Fuehrer—and spent her spare time walking to the little chapel in Blumberg. Both Hans and Sophie decided to become Catholics at this time, and a strong sense of the Christian ethic found its way into their view of Hitler and his works.

Shortly after Sophie joined Hans in Munich in order to study philosophy at the University, an event took place which transformed their opposition from discussion and mere endurance into positive action. Someone thrust a leaflet into the letter-box of the family home in Ulm. It contained the address of the Bishop of Muenster, Clemens Count von Galen, protesting against the confiscation of property of the Jesuit Order and the eviction of Jesuit priests from the diocese. The confiscation had been ordered by the Nazi Gauleiter of Westphalia, and Bishop von Galen called upon his flock from the pulpit to stand firm in face of injustice and persecution.

Hans's first reaction to von Galen's sermon, which also contained an outspoken attack on the Nazi euthanasia programme for the disposal of mental defectives, was 'Thank God someone has at last had the courage to speak out'. His second reaction was to buy a duplicating machine and set to work composing leaflets under the romantic heading of the 'White Rose', with the help of the gay and witty Alexander Schmorell and the more earnest Christoph Probst.

Hans would have kept Sophie clear of this underground work, for he was perfectly aware that it constituted treason and that all who took part would be mercilessly punished if they were discovered. But Sophie stumbled on the secret of their nightly conferences quite by chance. Within six weeks of her arrival in Munich she saw a copy of the first of the 'White Rose' leaflets in Hans's room (the little group's security was not watertight). It urged resistance 'before we are overtaken by Nemesis'. This was a quotation from Schiller, and Sophie found a book of Schiller's writings lying open in the room, with this particular passage marked in pencil. Sophie was duly initiated in the secrets of the group. It was to mean her death little more than a year later.

What did the 'White Rose' group think it could achieve with its leaflets, laboriously produced in the dark hours by an increasingly shaky duplicating machine? Inge Scholl, as survivor, has this to say: 'We were desperately anxious to achieve *something*. We had no political training, but the political element had entered into the spirit of the group's resistance. We realized that there was a big gap between intent and effectiveness. The point was to say what we honestly thought and wanted. What we wanted, at least, was clear enough—the end of the war, even if it only came about by the gradual restriction of fighting and of the war effort. To work towards this objective we had to be careful, to lie low, to survive. This kept the group small, and limited its activities.'

Hans Scholl, Probst and Schmorell carried on therefore with their normal work by day. The evening was their own, and as soon as they had eaten frugally at home or had met for a glass of Chianti at the Italian restaurant, 'I Lombardi', the illegal side of their life took over. The first leaflet was distributed in May 1942. It was necessarily in the nature of a 'trial run', but it made good sense. It warned Germans that they degenerated into 'a sickly and aimless herd rushing madly to its destruction'—an obvious reference to the Gadarene swine—and it asked: 'Is not every decent German ashamed today of his Government?' This was not a bad start, and the group's work was given a significant lift in June when its members were invited to the home of a Frau Dr. Mertens to meet one of Munich University's most outspoken and most brilliant professors, Kurt Huber.

Huber was born in the Swiss town of Chur in 1893. His parents were German and most of his youth was spent in Stuttgart and other parts of Württemberg, the province which produced the Scholls and of which the peaceable Swiss themselves say: 'The Württembergers (and Badeners) are our cousins, up to the river Neckar.' Huber did not serve in World War I, as he suffered from a slight limp. He completed his own studies and lectured at Munich University from 1917 to 1937. After that came a short spell at the Humboldt University in Berlin; then back to Munich. A Nazi Party report on him in 1938 said that he was 'dangerously' close to Roman Catholic circles and had criticized Nazism's chief exponent of racial ideology, Alfred Rosenberg. Under pressure from his family and university colleagues, Huber joined the Nazi Party in April 1940.

Huber was a conservative in his political outlook and exercised a restraining influence on the young men of the 'White Rose' (ironically, Hans worried about Huber's personal safety and wanted to organize a safe hideout for him, preferably in the Bavarian Alps). Huber did not believe, as the young men did, that Prussia had been a purely baneful influence in German history. But he had much to contribute to the 'White Rose' movement—a wise, old head, a clarity of thought and diction, a matureness of mind.

The second 'White Rose' leaflet, circulated in June 1942, showed his influence. It concentrated on the moral delinquency of the Nazis, on their slaughter of Jews and Polish patriots after the successful Polish campaign, on other Nazi excesses in Eastern Europe and on the guilt shared by the whole German people for condoning Nazi crime and serving the Nazi war-machine.

There were 'White Rose' leaflets in July and August 1942. The July leaflet urged passive resistance to Hitler, as a priority even to the combating of Bolshevism. It called for the sabotaging of arms production and war propaganda, and urged readers to refuse to contribute to collections of money, clothing, old metal and so forth for the war effort. The August leaflet descended for a moment into histrionics, for which Professor Huber could hardly have been responsible! Hitler's mouth was described as a 'stench-ridden cavern of hell'. But the leaflet went on to point out, in a more matter-of-fact tone, that the German military advances in Russia and Africa were not real victories. How true; Stalingrad and Alamein were only a few months away.

In August 1942 Hans Scholl, Probst and Schmorell were sent to the Russian front, once again serving as medical orderlies. Hans travelled by train through Poland, saw Jews and Poles being insulted and maltreated. One can imagine the frame of mind of this strong but sensitive young man when he saw what the Nazis were doing to mere human beings. He jumped off one train to give his chocolate and cigarette ration to members of a brutalized chain-gang. He ostentatiously shook hands with an old Jew while he was being hustled through a railway station. He gave a single flower to a Jewish girl. How little could such actions achieve, and how much they meant! Each one of them was a courageous act.

While he was in Russia Hans heard that his father had been sent to prison for the second time, this time for four months for making disparaging remarks about Hitler. He told another medical orderly: 'For me this is an honour. . . .' Sophie was at the same time hearing the story of the gassing of spastic children in the Württemberg town of Schwaebisch-Hall by the S.S. An Evangelical *Diakonisse* visited her family in Ulm and told them how it was done: 'When the children asked where the black vans of the S.S. would go, they were told "to heaven", and so they jumped in, happy and singing.' In Russia, meanwhile, Hans met Willi Graf, who had opposed Nazism as an ex-member of a Catholic Youth organization in Saarbruecken, who had been imprisoned for a short time in 1938, and who now promised his help.

Hans, Graf and his friends came back to Germany in November 1942. Hans's first act was to borrow money. A fifty-year-old Württemberger, Eugen Grimminger, gave him 500 marks, and plenty of others helped. The money was for a new leaflet campaign. Leaflets were distributed on a much wider scale during December and January, with Graf acting as a long-distance courier and making train journeys to south and central German towns with a suitcase stuffed with leaflets.

Just how dangerous this was can only be appreciated by someone who lived through the Nazi era. Travellers were subjected in wartime to endless checks, by the ordinary police, by railway police, by the Gestapo and even by the Home Guard. Examination of baggage was quite usual—not, of course, primarily in order to discover leaflets, but to search for food and other goods which might be either sold or bought on the Black Market.

Hans and his friends began, too, at this time to chalk up anti-Nazi inscriptions on walls and hoardings. In a single night, while the battle of Stalingrad was raging, they chalked up 'Down with Hitler!' and other slogans at seventy different places along the Ludwigstrasse and Leopoldstrasse in the middle of Munich. Friends in Freiburg, Saarbruecken and Berlin were doing the same thing.

In January 1943 the Scholls and their friends produced what turned out to be the last of the regular 'White Rose' leaflets. Professor Huber was this time asked not only for general ideas, but for his help in framing the wording of the leaflet. Possibly Huber was responsible for the passages in the leaflet which dealt with long-term aims—the establishment of democratic freedoms, the restoration of social justice, the decentralization of the *Einheitsstaat* into a federal Germany with some of the characteristics of the Swiss Confederation.

'Hitler cannot win the war', the leaflets proclaimed. 'He can only prolong it. The German people sees nothing . . . hears nothing'.

The leaflet concluded with a stirring appeal: 'The German name will remain for ever dishonoured unless German youth rises at last, to punish and atone, to crush its torturers and to build a new, spiritual Europe.' Once again thousands of leaflets were distributed with infinite care in Munich and other large towns.

Early in February an event occurred which drove the Scholls into open rebellion. The uncouth and brutally stupid Nazi Gauleiter of Bavaria, Paul Giesler, gave an address on the prosecution of the war to the students of Munich University. After recounting their war-time duties to the boys, Giesler had this to say to the female students:

'As for girls . . . they have healthy bodies; let them bear children. That is an automatic process which, once started, continues without requiring the least attention. There is no reason why every girl student should not for each of her years at the University present an annual testimonial in the form of a son.

'I realize,' Giesler went on with a lecherous leer, 'that a certain amount of co-operation is required and if some of the girls lack sufficient charm to find a mate I will assign to each of them one of my adjutants, whose antecedents I can vouch for; and I can promise her a thoroughly enjoyable experience.'

The Munich students did not pause to consider that this disgusting passage was, in fact, no more than orthodox Nazi policy. The *Lebensborn* experiment of human stud-farms had already begun, and young and physically attractive S.S. men were being coupled with 'suitable' mates in order to step up the birth-rate and produce a Germanic population for the great areas of Poland and Russia whose people were to be ruthlessly decimated. This was the basis of Heinrich Himmler's weird plan for the creation of German villages 'from the Gulf of Finland to the Sea of Azof'. But in the university square Giesler was howled down by the bitterly offended students, many of whom rushed out into the streets to demonstrate. Giesler's infamous proposals were bruited abroad, and other, minor, demonstrations took place in Stuttgart, Mannheim, Frankfurt and the Ruhr.

The Scholls decided on a far more open act of defiance. Stalingrad was falling and it seemed to them that this—combined with Giesler's gutter-talk—required a big gesture from them. A broadsheet was produced in double-quick time. It called for self-determination for the German people, free elections and the removal of the Nazi Party: 'There can be only one cry; fight the Party!' The production of the broadsheet led, unfortunately, to disagreement between Huber and the youngsters. Huber wanted a phrase inserted: 'Stand by our glorious Army!' The pacifist-minded Scholls refused to include it, and Huber stalked off in a huff. He never saw the Scholls again.

For on the morning of February 18 Hans and Sophie Scholl set off for the University with suitcases packed tight with copies of the final broadsheet. It was a beautiful morning and one can guess what sort of thoughts passed through the minds of these two young people, aged twenty-five and twenty-two, as they trudged down the Leopoldstrasse under a blue sky. This time there was to be no clandestine insertion of leaflets into letter-boxes; Hans and Sophie dropped copies of the broadsheet in the lecture rooms and along the corridors of the university buildings, then went up to the top floor of the main building and poured out their fluttering pieces of paper into the university square and over the entrance hall. The whole performance was the reverse of surreptitious, and at one point Sophie told a busy *Putzfrau* (cleaning woman) not to clear up the leaflets which were lying everywhere—'they are meant to be read'.

The doorkeeper at the main gate was alerted (possibly some of the broadsheets fluttered straight down to him). He closed and locked the gates, telephoned the police. Police cars screamed through the streets of Munich bringing a squad of Gestapo.

Nazi security procedure was undeniably efficient. But Hans and Sophie, it seems, made no attempt to escape or to hide themselves. Why? Hans Rothfels, author of *The German Opposition to Hitler*, wrote: 'The Munich students can hardly have believed that a spontaneous rising on their part could alone alter the course of events. They were, on the other hand, firmly convinced of something else, of the necessity of bearing witness to their faith and clearing themselves as well as the name of God.'

Inge Scholl is not so definite. Hans had been warned a few days earlier by a friend, Ott Aicher (he subsequently married Inge Scholl), that the Nazis suspected him of underground activities. But this knowledge, although it may have hastened the action which he planned, would not of itself have projected an apparent act of suicide. Hans had told Inge: 'We must go on working; it is our duty to survive.' This argues against the theory that the two young people knew that they were going to their deaths. And yet, Inge is no longer sure. Nor does she agree entirely with Rothfels; she has since come to the conclusion that Hans and Sophie thought that their open act of defiance would produce a spontaneous demonstration which would ring through the length and breadth of Germany.

In the event, very little happened. The Munich students were caught unprepared and were merely stunned by the arrests, first of Hans, Sophie and Probst, then of the other ring-leaders of the revolt. Indeed, some of them took on the work of chalking up anti-Nazi slogans. Others collected money for the legal defence of the imprisoned members of the group. Hundreds of students pocketed copies of the broadsheet and dropped them all over Munich. Here and there a new inscription appeared on the walls: '*Ihr Geist lebt weiter*' ('Their spirit lives on'). But that was all.

Hans and Sophie were taken to Gestapo headquarters in the Wittelsbach Palace. Probst was arrested in Innsbruck and brought to Munich by express train. This was a particularly bitter blow to Sophie, who adored the whole Probst family (there were three small children, the third only a few weeks old). Their interrogation began. It lasted, on and off, for three days.

Gestapo interrogations were always tough and generally terrifying. The Gestapo regarded the use of torture as an absolutely normal method of extracting information. The ripping out of toenails and fingernails, the crushing of genitals, the application of electrodes to the most sensitive parts of the body—these were, indeed, perfectly 'normal' by the Gestapo standards. Along with such methods went the withholding of food and drink, the lighting of cells at night, unending interrogation in which physical violence was mixed with infinite patience and 'reasonability', so that the prisoner came to realize that his captors would not give up until they had learnt the whole truth.

The two Scholls and Probst seem to have come off comparatively lightly. They were ruthlessly interrogated, but they were not tortured. (The story of Sophie limping into the courtroom with a broken leg was incorrect.) This was partly because they did not conform to the ordinary pattern of 'plotter'; their rooms must have yielded up a treasure-trove to the Gestapo, containing letters, lists of names and leaflets. The Munich Gestapo, it was learned long afterwards, had been watching the 'White Rose' campaign for at least six months. The Scholls' lack of security precautions, inevitable in the circumstances, meant that the Gestapo were able to round up the other important members of the group during the next few days.

But there were two other reasons for not torturing the three young people. Hans and Sophie fully and freely admitted their 'guilt', and tried to take all responsibility for the 'White Rose' campaign. Above all, they tried to shield Probst. This was mildly disconcerting to their captors. But, in addition, even the thugs of the S.S. found their courage and essential decency impressive. Inge, coming to the building to inquire about her brother and sister, was told by junior officials that they were being 'wonderfully brave'. The Gestapo tended to be organized on a local basis, especially in Bavaria. Hans and Sophie were being interrogated by people who did not forget that they were all South Germans together (the *Reichshauptsicherheitsamt* in Berlin later complained that the Munich Gestapo should have been able to extract a great deal more information from the Scholls and had proceeded far too decorously about their business).

Hans firmly declined to give the names of accomplices. He insisted that the leaflets were his own work, and one of the prison warders later testified to his resolution (so did a temporary cell-mate, Helmut Fietz, who had been imprisoned for getting up on a beer-barrel in a village public house and comparing Hitler disadvantageously with pigs and other farmyard animals). On his cell wall Hans wrote. '*Allen Gewalt zum Trotz sich erhalten*'—'Uphold yourself in face of every pressure'.

Sophie had one interrogation which went on for seventeen hours. This lasted until eight o'clock on the morning of February 19. Other prisoners recall her arriving back in her cell, looking tired but composed, and saying loudly that the Allied invasion would come in April and Germany would be rid of her tyrannical rulers. The Gestapo may even have been discomfited by Sophie's assurance, allied to her youth and sweetness of manner. She was asked: 'Miss Scholl, if you had been given the chance beforehand to hear all that

I have explained to you, then surely you would not have involved yourself in this affair?' Her answer was uncompromising: 'On the contrary, I would have acted in exactly the same manner. It is you, and not I, who have the wrong outlook.'

Sophie pleaded to be given the same treatment as her brother: 'For I am as responsible as he.' It may be remembered that St. Peter, given the immense honour of knowing Him, denied his Master. Sophie denied nothing; for she only knew that she loved liberty and was prepared to praise it and, if necessary, to die for it.

On her last night in gaol, according to Inge, Sophie dreamt that she was carrying a child in a white dress to be baptized at the altar. She had to climb a steep hill to the church with the babe in her arms. Suddenly there was a great chasm yawning in front of her and she had only time to thrust the child back into safety. Then she dropped into bottomless darkness. . . . Her own explanation, given to her parents, was that the child was the idea of freedom. It, at least, would survive.

At nine o'clock on the morning of February 22, 1943, Hans and Sophie Scholl and Christoph Probst were taken to the Munich Law Courts. Trying them was the Nazi People's Court, presided over by Roland Freisler. This monstrous court constituted the ultimate Nazi perversion of the principles of justice; it functioned only in order to sentence Hitler's enemies. It did not need to invoke any law of the land; it could exact the penalty of death under any of the very many 'emergency' ordinances.

The court's case against the three was straightforward; they had 'foretold Germany's defeat' and had depicted their opposition to Hitler as a struggle for freedom. Nor did they show the slightest signs of 'repentance'. Sophie told the court: 'You all really agree with what we have said and written, but you are afraid of saying so.' Hans was equally uncompromising when castigated for 'ingratitude' to the Nazi State. His only moment of weakness—if it could possibly be described as such—was to ask for clemency for Probst, because he had a young wife and three small children. Freisler chipped in: 'If you have nothing to say for yourself you can be silent.' Sophie refused to speak the 'last word' which the three were surprisingly allowed in court.

Equally surprisingly the Scholl parents were allowed to see them at four o'clock in the afternoon after they had been sentenced to death by beheading. Hans, whose face was described as having 'gone very small and strained, as after some desperate battle', as a result of the endless interrogations, showed no other signs of worry. His father told him: 'You will be a part of history, for we shall still have justice.' Hans answered: 'I have no feeling of hate.' He refused a sweet which was offered to him, but Sophie ate one, relaxed and smiling. She told her parents: 'We have taken responsibility for everything.' The two Scholls hoped, and may have believed up to the last, that none of their other friends would suffer too.

Probst was allowed to write a letter to his mother. He wrote: 'Thank you for bringing me into this world. When I reflect on the matter I know there is one road to God. I am treading it just ahead of you, in order to prepare a splendid reception for you.'

The three were taken to Stadelheim prison, where they were to be executed and buried. Contrary to all orders and at considerable risk to themselves, their S.S. guards allowed them out of their cells to meet together for a few brief minutes for the last time. Probst was alleged to have said then: 'I never knew how easy it would be to die. I can die without any feeling of hate. In a few minutes' time we shall meet in the hereafter.' They were taken out one by one to the block. Hans called out 'Long live liberty!' before the axe fell. As far as is known the two others said nothing.

Some months later several members of the S.S. were executed in Stadelheim gaol. Their crimes, their trials and everything to do with them, were kept rigidly secret. For these were members of the Nazi élite who had offended their own masters, superior animals who had to be dispatched out of sight of the rabble. What were their crimes? Were any of them young men who took note of the high courage of the 'White Rose' group, and drew their own conclusions? Unfortunately the secret of their acts and motives has been kept.

On February 23 the Nazis spread the word round Munich that Hitler's personal pardon had been on the way to Stadelheim when the Scholls and Probst were executed, but that it 'unfortunately' had not arrived in time. But the Nazis acted at the same time with their usual speed and ruthlessness in order to break the spirit of the resistance. The other members of the Scholl family were arrested and placed in *Sippenhaft*. This word did not exist in the German language before Hitler came to power. It means a state of arrest for all members of a family, and all kinsmen. The nineteen-year-old Elisabeth Scholl was two months in gaol and was released when it was seen that she was not only gravely ill but was utterly harmless. Inge was in gaol for six months. So was her mother. Her father was released just before the end of the war, after serving a two-year sentence, but he was almost certainly let out by mistake. He was known to have been an anti-Nazi for years past and had already been in prison because of it. Would a man like this, whose son and daughter had led a revolt against the regime, have been intentionally spared? He slipped through the Nazis' fingers.

Other members of the 'White Rose' group were relentlessly rounded up. Willi Graf was caught in his rooms in Munich. Alexander Schmorell, a man of action as well as a budding philosopher, took to the mountains. But he had been born in the great plains of Russia and had spent much of his youth there. In the mountains he felt trapped. He came back to Munich and was caught in an air-raid shelter, during a periodic police check of its occupants. Members of the group were arrested in Hamburg, Freiburg, Berlin and other towns. According to Inge Scholl, there were between eighty and one hundred arrests in all of members of the group and their sympathizers.

Freisler and the People's Court prepared a second trial, which took place on April 19. In the dock this time were three more 'chief offenders'—Graf, Schmorell and Professor Huber—along with eleven others. Freisler's 'court' consisted of himself, one S.S. *Gruppenfuehrer*, two S.A. *Gruppenleiters* and one Nazi lawyer. Such was the basis for the dispensation of German justice!

Schmorell and Graf were singled out for special attack by the prosecution, because they had shown no gratitude to the Fuehrer for paying for their medical studies and for enabling them to reach the 'honourable' rank of sergeant in the armed forces. Huber was accused of systematic academic perversion of the young and of failing to help them to 'become fighters ready to sacrifice themselves for our people'. Huber had wanted 'the Wehrmacht to act against the Nazi Party'. He had sown doubt in the minds of his pupils.

Perhaps it was unwise of the People's Court to let Huber appear in the dock at all. The purpose had been to 'expose' him publicly and so discourage further acts of overt resistance. Huber defended himself, and the 'White Rose' movement, with clarity and courage. He exonerated his pupils and claimed that they had done nothing illegal and not carried out or advocated any act of force. On the contrary, they had stood by the rule of law: 'They asked . . . for the return to clear moral principles, to the rule of law, to mutual trust among all men—this was not illegal but . . . a restoration of legality.'

Huber attacked Nazism: 'During the past ten years the Party has destroyed every sense of moral obligation, as well as freedom in the next generation; the entire educational system has been bolshevized.' History, he added, 'will charge Hitler with full responsibility for Stalingrad'—a point which was not lost even on his judges and the packed courtroom. Another telling phrase: 'Every morally responsible citizen should raise his voice against the threatening tyranny of might over right, of capriciousness over free will.'

The trial dragged on for weeks, to the point when, in his final speech, Huber cried in a great voice: 'History will judge my actions and intentions. . . . I appeal for the return of its freedom to the German people.' No argument, no appeal to mercy, would have helped, anyway, and Huber's attitude was that of Bishop Latimer, who said to Bishop Ridley, before going to the stake 400 years ago: 'Come, Master Ridley, today we shall light such a light . . .'

Huber, Graf and Schmorell were sentenced to death and met it with the same exemplary courage as the Scholls and Christoph Probst. Graf's last words were 'Death is something good. I am not afraid of it'; and Schmorell wrote to his mother from the death-cell that 'This blow is harder for you than for me', and that his death was no more dreadful than that of thousands who fell on the field of battle. Huber and Schmorell were executed on July 13, Graf not until the beginning of October.

The eleven others who sat in the dock at the same time as these three were given a total of thirty-seven years' imprisonment. In Hamburg two girls were sentenced to death, as 'White Rose' sympathizers who had involved themselves with other resistance groups as well (their executions were fortuitously postponed until the British Army marched into Hamburg). Here and there in Germany other young people who had been in touch with the Scholls were sent to prison too. The last member of the 'inner circle' of the group to be arrested was Hans-Karl Leipelt, on October 8, 1943. He was executed only on January 29, 1945.

Thousands upon thousands of Germans knew about the 'White Rose' movement. For Schmorell had distributed leaflets as far afield to the south as Linz and Vienna, and Graf as far to the north as the industrial Ruhr. Millions more Germans learned at least something of the 'White Rose' when the trials took place and were reported in the Nazi press. Some Germans, at least, would have picked up leaflets dropped by British planes late in 1943 (the story of the 'White Rose' reached Britain via Count Moltke and the Norwegian Bishop Bergraf).

Millions of Germans had become accustomed to reading between the lines, in a country where every printed word was supposed to be censored but in which a certain amount of oblique and veiled criticism continued to escape the censor's eye. To most of these Germans the story of the 'White Rose' suggested an epic of courage and idealism.

Could the young people of the 'White Rose' have achieved more? Could they have raised the standard of revolt, or at least worked with other, more materially powerful opponents of Hitler? Since the war Inge Scholl has told me: 'We never ceased wondering what more we could do. We did believe that the Allied invasion in the West was coming sooner, and that Churchill—that rock in whom we always put our trust—would be ready by the summer of 1943, or at least when, in his own words, "the leaves would begin to fall". We tried to get into touch with the men of the 20th of July [Hans did establish contact with the left-winger, von Harnack]. We tried to get in touch with resistance groups in Nazi-occupied countries. We may seem, in retrospect, to have been ineffectual. But our real purpose, after all, was to let the truth be known, to tell the youth of Germany that it was being misused by the Nazis, and to give hope to the persecuted. For we had no material power, and we never expected to gain it.'

In an article written for the Social Democratic weekly, *Vorwaerts*, in July 1961, Inge Scholl said that the 'White Rose' students 'did indeed tread a lonely path', but 'always with an eye on society as a whole, which they felt they belonged to, and which they felt

The three leaders of the White Rose youth movement: *left* to *right*, Hans Scholl, Sophie Scholl, Christoph Probst

Carl Goerdeler, a representative of the old, conservative Germany
and the leading Conservative civilian who opposed Hitler

responsible for'. Her friends, she wrote, 'were not heroes, who courted death. . . . They loved life, for they were on the side of life.'

Long years after the event Inge Scholl saw the revolt of the Munich students as a protest not only against dictatorship but against the cult of brute force. 'Don't let it come to the test again,' she wrote. 'Let us study force and the use of it. Let us stop brute force at the earliest possible moment. Let us recognize force, when it threatens the humblest individual and his liberty. If we fight against it, then our way of life is safe.'

There can be no clear-cut, precise summing-up of the part played by youth in resisting Hitler. Speaking at the unveiling of a memorial to the Munich students, Dr. Karl Vossler, a history professor, said: 'It is the privilege of young people to dare the impossible and to shun no danger.' Well, yes, it is easy for an old man to use such brave words, in a free country and in time of peace. The Scholls and their friends fought against a cruel and efficient dictatorship, in time of war, when their motives and actions would be misunderstood by the bulk of their compatriots.

Their path was indeed a lonely one, for they seemed to be traitors to their age group, they were condemned as traitors to their country and died a traitor's death. And 'country' meant, to the German of the day, his Fatherland, and something holy. These young people were not able to say, with inward assurance, 'our kingdom is not of this world'. For they dearly wanted to put their dedicated youth, their bounding vitality and their wealth of ideas at the service of their people.

There is an overwhelming bitterness in failure. The men who opposed Hitler did so because their consciences told them it was right, and only reached their crucial decisions in dark and silent hours of communion with themselves. The consequences of failure were bitter too. One may be allowed the reflection that those famous artists who depicted the Crucifixion as a dramatic, almost colourful affair of great crowds, interest, emotion, pity and the gathering storm-clouds of God's displeasure, were doing Christianity a grave disservice. The ultimate form of sacrifice is that of a traitor's death, utterly alone.

The influence of the Scholls and their friends has lived on long after their death. For they exemplified the rightness of independence of mind. There was no characteristic more badly needed by German youth, after the regimentation and the real and bogus enthusiasms of the Nazi era. One of Western Germany's leading essayists, Friedrich Sieburg, has written that the 'new sceptical generation' in Germany is uncritical and defenceless. The West Berlin periodical, *Der Monat*, wrote that post-war West German youth 'is neither nationalist nor European, neither anti-Semitic nor anti-Nazi, neither pacifist nor militarist, idealistic nor realist. . . . It is nothing at all, and I find it horrible.'

This is a trite and possibly immature judgement. Why should the new German youth conform to any one pattern? If it did, that would be far worse than *Der Monat*'s unintentionally apt summing up of German youth's extreme and understandable diffidence and restraint. The Scholls would probably be not too displeased by present-day West German youth. For it has independence of mind, and that is a beginning. The vibrant enthusiasm, which all youth should have but which seems almost to have disappeared throughout Europe, may follow. The Scholls would not have expected more than this. The very breath of freedom, which has blown through Western Germany since 1945, would have refreshed them.

A final reflection, to relate the past of the 'White Rose' to the German present and future. Young Germans since 1945 have been disconcerted and depressed by the fact that their fathers can offer them no knowledge, no judgement, no advice about how they should view the past. One young West German author, Christian Geissler, gave his central character these lines in his book *Die Anfrage* (*The Inquiry*): 'We are in search of fathers, and that is not a nice business; we are looking for fathers who will tell the truth, who are repentant, who will think about the way that they went, and the way we have to go in the future.' There had to be an almost total lack of such German fathers in the first decades after 1945. Geissler's conclusion is that the break with the past has to be complete, for the young German of today.

That is not the whole truth. The Scholls and most of their friends died too young to have had children. They are the elder brothers and sisters of every generation of young Germans, ever since. They are the lasting emblem of German youth. So German youth need not worry about 'a break with the past'. For it is inextricably linked with the only past that matters.

eight

The Road to Rastenburg

'*Die Tat ist alles, nicht der Ruhm.*' ('The deed is everything, not the fame of it.')

JOHANN WOLFGANG VON GOETHE

IT HAS been necessary in this book, in order to give the story of the German Opposition some sort of coherence, to leave the conservative and military opponents of Hitler at that crucial point—September 1938—while recounting in the meanwhile the efforts of Roman Catholics, Evangelicals, socialists and students to resist in their own more passive ways. More passive because, with the exception of the very few churchmen and socialists who were ready to go to any lengths in their opposition to Hitler, the rest of the members of these sections of German society were trying exclusively to stand up for what they believed to be right. The essential value of their opposition lay in their example and sense of sacrifice. This was, in itself, a considerable contribution to society; but it had nothing to do with getting rid of Hitler and the Nazis by force.

Churchmen like Bonhoeffer and Bethge, socialists like Leber and Haubach, necessarily made only a minor contribution to the plans of those who were scheming to remove and, after the outbreak of war, to kill Hitler. This is not to minimize their courage and resolution, but conservatives and soldiers were bound to continue to play the main part in concrete plans which had to provide for the seizure of effective control throughout Germany and the organization of a new regime, as well as the disposal of Hitler and his lieutenants.

It might have been supposed that there were plenty of opportunities for the conservative and military opposition to have taken action against Hitler between the Munich Agreement and the outbreak of the Second World War—in fact between September 1938 and September 1939. The main reason why nothing was done was that, after the Munich Agreement, Hitler stood at the very apex of his popularity and power. 'The genius of the Fuehrer', General Alfred Jodl wrote in his diary on September 29, 1938, 'and his determination not to shun even a world war have again achieved victory without the use of force. One hopes that the incredulous, the weak and the doubters have been converted, and will remain so.' The Fuehrer had, indeed, won a signal victory over the doubters, especially in the Army. They had assumed French and British military intervention to save Czechoslovakia, and had prophesied woe and destruction for Germany. Hitler had proved them utterly wrong. The confidence of men like Beck and Witzleben in their own judgement must have been reduced to zero.

And plenty of anti-Nazi conservatives, especially in the Foreign Ministry, drew the conclusion from Munich that the situation would now stabilize itself. Hitler had been brought to the conference table by the Western Powers and had drawn back from his ultimate threat of achieving his objectives by war. What, after all, had come out of Munich? The 'return' (Germans used the unjustified phrase of '*Heim ins Reich*' of Sudetenlanders who had never belonged to the post-1870 Germany, but had been Austrian citizens up to 1918) of 3,000,000 people of German extraction to the Fatherland! What could be wrong with that? The mass of the German people, who had thoroughly disliked the idea of war, both approved and heaved a sigh of relief.

Hitler utilized his immense prestige and popularity in the months after Munich to carry out policies which might have caused grave alarm before September 1938 but now aroused hardly a flicker of resistance. On November 9, 1938, he launched his all-out offensive on German Jewry, in the terrible pogrom of the 'Reich Crystal Night' when 20,000 Jews were arrested and 267 synagogues burnt to the ground. Around forty Jews were murdered in their homes or on the streets. This was followed by the imposition of a collective fine of 1,000,000,000 marks (then about £80,000,000) on the Jewish communities. In March 1939 Hitler entered Prague and proceeded to carry out the dismemberment of the Czech state which he hated so bitterly.

Meanwhile, he shifted generals inimical to him from positions where they could have been dangerous. Witzleben was transferred from Berlin to Kassel. Adam, the general who doubted the strength of the Siegfried Line, was retired. Beck was already in retirement and Halder evidently gave up all thought of active resistance about this time. Men like Keitel and Jodl, who belonged heart and soul to Hitler, were promoted. Along with Grand Admiral Raeder, Marshal of the *Luftwaffe* Goering and the Army Commander-in-Chief von Brauchitsch, these men constituted the higher command of the formidable military machine which Hitler was welding for World War II.

In May 1939 Hitler told his generals that he was preparing to attack Poland at the first opportunity. He told them, too, that Dutch and Belgian neutrality would certainly be violated if war had to be waged against Britain and France. The details of 'Operation White', for the invasion of Poland, were perfected. The Hitler-Stalin Pact was signed. The outbreak of war, on September 1, 1939, was rendered inevitable, for Hitler intended to have Danzig, the Polish Corridor, Upper Silesia, and much besides, and the Poles were prouder and more resolute than the Czechs and certainly not disposed to give way to threats.

During the year between Munich and the outbreak of World War II there had been plenty of activity among the conservative and military opponents of Nazism. Beck and Oster decided to warn the British Government that Hitler was utterly determined to attack Poland. They did so, in March 1939, through an unusual but well-chosen sort of intermediary, Mr. Ian Colvin, the Berlin correspondent of the *News Chronicle*. Mr. Colvin saw both Lord Halifax, the British Foreign Secretary, and Mr. Neville Chamberlain. The information which he produced may well have pushed the hesitant Chamberlain over the brink of giving Poland a guarantee of military support in the event of a German invasion. The guarantee might just have averted war, had Hitler not already made up his mind and had he not been so clearly influenced by the Czech fiasco into believing the British move to be a piece of bluff.

Similar warnings were conveyed to the British Government by von Hassell, although they were transmitted to the weak and physically ailing British Ambassador in Berlin, Sir Nevile Henderson,

Von Hassell, the Kordt brothers and von Kessel were among others who urged their British friends to 'stand firm' as the sole means of preventing Hitler from blundering into war. Von Kessel's final warning to Henderson, on August 24 in Hitler's *Berghof*, had a touch of comedy about it. He did not notice that an official German interpreter was standing behind Henderson, who accepted his agitated and hurried words with a quizzical stare. As it happened, the interpreter was an anti-Nazi.

At the head of the Abwehr, Admiral Wilhelm Canaris was equally active. Early in September he learnt of Hitler's plans for physically annihilating Poland, quite apart from defeating her armies in the field. He obtained an interview with Hitler, but failed completely to dissuade him with the somewhat improbable argument that the persecution of the Poles could lead to the French mounting a serious offensive in the West.

It may have been about this time that Canaris first warned the Ruler of Hungary, Admiral Horthy, of Hitler's true intentions, and first established the contacts with Franco which he allegedly used in order to help to keep Spain out of the war. The fact that Canaris's widow was given a pension by the Spanish Government after the war is suggestive. Early in 1940, certainly, he told the Swiss Government of the draft plan for marching through northern Switzerland in order to bypass the Maginot Line to the south. Canaris was, however, a supremely patriotic and emotional man. He was to irritate Hitler later with his memorandums, advising against invasions of Denmark and Greece. In the interests of his country, it seems, he was inclined to concentrate on first preventing war and then stopping it from spreading, rather than in actively opposing Hitler.

Carl Goerdeler, now working for the Robert Bosch electrical firm in Stuttgart, was extremely active too, in his own way. The failure of the 1938 conspiracy to be transmitted into action had depressed him immeasurably. His opposition to Hitler took to an increasing degree the form of feverish literary activity, in which he drew up plans for a future German Government, for the reorganization of German society and the German economy, and for peace terms between Germany and her potential enemies which could lead to a sweeping adjustment of the whole map of Europe.

In April 1939, for instance, Goerdeler produced a memorandum which showed very plainly how much German conservatives had been affected by Hitler's easily won successes up to that point. Goerdeler wanted the problem of the Polish Corridor 'solved' by the return of territories which had been German up to 1918. He wanted Germany to be given 'a colonial domain as great and as potentially capable of development as possible', and Germans should in addition be allowed to settle in British and French colonies. The annexation of the Sudetenland by Germany should be formally guaranteed, and Germany should be granted a loan of 4,000,000,000–6,000,000,000 gold marks in order to 'protect her currency'. In return for all these concessions Germany would give a vague promise of military help to 'restore the economic position' of the Western Powers in the Far East.

Goerdeler's biographer, Gerhard Ritter, discusses this memorandum in all seriousness. His comment: 'That he was a German patriot who desired the best for Germany and not her humiliation seems as clear to me as that he thought of the Reich of the future, not as the eternal plague and tyrant of Europe, but as a genuine peace-power embedded in a European community.' It should, needless to say, be equally clear that Goerdeler was at this stage beginning to lose touch with reality. This fact was recognized by, among others, Hjalmar Schacht, who was amazed by Goerdeler's wildly optimistic view that the Nazi regime would crumble to pieces if a European war broke out. Schacht believed, on the contrary, that the West should be warned of Germany's increasing military strength. Schacht was perfectly right.

The oubreak of war made the task of Hitler's opponents, on the whole, more difficult than before—certainly with regard to securing popular support for any action against the Nazi regime. For however unpopular war may have been, it helped to unite the German people with their leaders. Hitler had powerful and seemingly conclusive arguments for having embarked on war. The French and Polish guarantees to Poland were reviled as examples of that enemy, *Einkreisungspolitik*—the policy of 'encirclement'—which Kaiser Wilhelm II invoked as the best reason of all for waging World War I. War would wipe away the injustices of Versailles. It would give the German people then sufficient *'Lebensraum'* (living space) which had been denied to it.

In addition, Poland was by nature and history an inferior, 'subject' race, while the Western democracies were weak and decadent. Even the Pact with Communist Russia—denounced in *Mein Kampf* as Germany's arch-enemy—could be explained away to the mystified as a necessary means of avoiding the dreaded 'war on two fronts'. And behind all these arguments lurked those old, dangerous dreams of a 'Greater German Reich'—dreams which Hitler, like the legendary *Kyffhaeuser* Emperor come to life, could translate into reality. What German patriot could fail to be moved by the brilliantly successful Polish campaign, and by the later, even more astounding, victory in the West? Once more Germany was united from 'the Maas to Memel' and from 'the Etsch to the Belt', as the old National Anthem had it. The dreams of a Greater German Reich seemed really to be coming true.

The conservative and military Opposition did, admittedly, derive some benefits from the outbreak of war. One was the recall from retirement of General Kurt von Hammerstein, who tried unavailingly to lure Hitler to his Army headquarters in Cologne, where he proposed to arrest and court-martial him. This advantage was temporary, for von Hammerstein was first transferred to Silesia and then once again placed in retirement. Courageous and intelligent, he needed only more energy to have become the leader of the military opposition.

Certainly, the military conspirators now had greater opportunities for cloaking their activities and for opening up new centres of resistance. But war brought one obviously greater disadvantage—the liability of leading members of the Opposition to be transferred at any moment from one post to another, on purely military grounds. This may have enabled more people gradually to be inducted into the ranks of the Opposition; but it made the planning of broadly based action against Hitler much harder.

This may have been the salient reason why military and conservative opposition, in particular, tended to pursue two particular lines of activity during the first three years of the war—the informing and sounding of Germany's enemies in order to find out what sort of peace could be won after Hitler's removal, and the concerting of hard and fast plans for his removal by comparatively small groups of men. Here were the seeds of the actual attempts to remove Hitler, which were made in 1943 and 1944.

First, the informing and sounding of Germany's enemies by Hitler's opponents. Both the Foreign Ministry and the Abwehr were active. Theo Kordt had been appointed to the German Legation in Berne, where in November he met Mr. Philip Conwell-Evans, sent by Sir Horace Wilson, the chief industrial adviser to the British Government and the bearer of vaguely encouraging verbal assurances. A little later von Hassell met a British agent, Mr. Lonsdale Bryans, in the Swiss mountain resort of Arosa, and asked that the British Government should automatically recognize a post-Nazi German regime, and should accept the 1914 German frontiers as well as Hitler's annexation of Austria and the Sudetenland.

Although these terms—which, by implication, would have included the dismemberment of Czechoslovakia—may seem fantastic, it must be remembered that the conspirators always hoped to secure the support of the German people. They felt they could not afford to forfeit that support by renouncing 'German' Austria and Bohemia. In February 1940, moreover, when von Hassell was in Arosa, a great many Germans were becoming aware of the military weakness of Britain and the miserable morale of the much-lauded French Army. Von Hassell's 'terms' would have looked no more than barely acceptable to them.

The Abwehr sent a Bavarian lawyer, Dr. Josef Mueller, to the Vatican to open a new channel of communication with London. He established contact with Mr. D'Arcy Osborne, the British Minister to the Vatican, and attracted the personal interest of Pope Pius XI. The Pope showed keen interest in the 'Abwehr Peace Plan' which included removal of the Nazi regime and Western recognition of its successor, an armistice on the Western Front, and the restoration of Germany's 1914 frontiers in the East.

Both von Brauchitsch and Halder were approached, on the basis of this Peace Plan. Both were reminded of Chamberlain's September 4 speech, when he said: 'In this war we are not fighting against you, the German people, for whom we have no bitter feeling, but against a tyrannous and forsworn regime which has betrayed not only its own people but the whole of Western civilization.' But both Brauchitsch and Halder declined to take or support action against Hitler; their reasons were that their country was at war, and that they were bound, more than ever before, by their oath to their Fuehrer and Fatherland.

To von Hassell, Halder added fatuously that Hitler should be given 'the chance to deliver the German people from the slavery of English capitalism'.

Far more spectacular than Mueller's cool and calculated attempt to give the generals an adequate reason for acting against Hitler were the personal activities of Hans Oster at this time. He had sent Schlabrendorff to London shortly before war broke out, and Schlabrendorff was able to confirm to Mr. Winston Churchill and Lord Lloyd that Hitler was determined to invade Poland. After the Polish campaign was over, Oster made contact with the Dutch Military Attaché in Berlin, Colonel J. G. Sas. Oster now went far beyond mere mildly 'treasonable' activities; he readily betrayed military secrets of the utmost importance. Sas was warned, successively, of the November 12, 1939, German plan to invade the Low Countries (it was cancelled late in the day), of the April 1940 invasions of Denmark and Norway, and of the finally selected date for the invasions of Holland and Belgium. But the British were not alone in being impervious to timely warnings; the Dutch and their friends did nothing—a heart-rending state of affairs when it is realized what risks Oster and his friends ran.

The German invasion of the Low Countries and France, by reason of its spectacular success, was a heavy blow to Hitler's opponents. When the numbers of German troops are considered—rather than their superiority in tanks, aircraft and other equipment—this German campaign might be regarded as one of the greatest military victories in the history of war. Its planning showed all the marks of genius, its execution was a miracle of flair, speed and savage efficiency. The German troops who marched to Dunkirk and the Somme, and on to Paris and Bordeaux, were imbued—as anyone who saw them will testify—with unbounded confidence and a rooted belief that all serious fighting was over. This was their ideal war—cleanly fought under brilliant blue skies, under commanders who matched those of the days of Friedrich the Great and Bismarck. They were invincible. Between bouts of fighting they were gay, as they strode through a land of sunshine, wine and attractive women, a land of plenty.

On May 29, 1940, von Hassell recorded in his diary: 'Among the upper strata in Berlin, I found some who were indulging in unrestrained triumph, accompanied by plans for dividing up the world in great style.' On the other hand: 'The masses of the people take everything with an astonishingly stolid indifference; deafened, I suppose, by seven years of listening to loud-speakers.' Von Hassell might have added—perhaps he did not do so because he had begun to avoid senior Army officers like the plague—that the morale of the armed forces was tremendous. Indeed, less than a year later we find von Hassell writing: 'Speedy and great success in the Balkans. The Army is an incredibly brilliant instrument, with all the stronger characteristics of the German people, and filled with absolute self-confidence. It is tragic! With this magnificent instrument the destruction of Europe is being accomplished to perfection.'

Military success does not go to German heads only. But the invasions of Denmark, Norway, the Low Countries, France, Jugoslavia, the Greek mainland and Crete, comprised a magnificent tapestry of blood-stirring event and achievement. It is hardly surprising that there was no effort worth the name during this period to kill or otherwise remove Hitler. The only attempts of any kind were the Burgerbraukeller bomb episode of November 1939, which may have been a Nazi 'plant', and a mysterious 'attempt' by the diplomat, Erich Kordt, who was to have been given a bomb with which to blow up Hitler. For reasons which have never been made clear, the bomb was not delivered to him. Kordt, at all events, was not by nature a man of action.

The invasion of the Soviet Union in June 1941 brought considerable changes in the attitudes of the military and conservative conspirators. Paradoxically, Hitler's greatest gamble of all brought the German people as a whole more unitedly on to his side. The Hitler-Stalin Pact had been looked upon by most of them as a curious politico-strategic expedient which had never been fully explained to them. After all, the Nazis had never previously ceased to denounce Communism as the greatest evil and enemy of all. The German Communist Party had been ruthlessly and totally suppressed, and to the observant German it was significant that the Pact brought no change in the Nazis' attitude towards German Communists. They remained in exile or in the concentration camps. Nazi propaganda, moreover, was still effective. It was easier to sell the lie in 1941 that Stalin was about to tear up the Pact and was mobilizing millions of men on his western frontiers, than it had been in 1939 to convince German citizens that Poland was about to invade them.

Plenty of Germans liked or at least 'went along with' the idea of a 'crusade' against Soviet Communism. And the spoils from such a crusade could be immense—the strategically valuable Baltic seaboard, the huge grain reserves of the Ukraine, the oil of the Caucasus, and the metals and coal of the Don and Donetz basins. Himmler began to draw up his plans for the systematic depopulation of the whole of southern and western Russia and its resettlement by German 'village-communities'. Goebbels talked of a new birthrate-drive, which would raise the German population from 80,000,000 to 130,000,000 in sixty years. The average 'small' German sustained himself with the comforting thought that his country's legions would be regarded as the defenders of Western civilization against Eastern 'barbarism'.

Historians have almost unanimously depicted Hitler's Russian campaign as wild, senseless and doomed in advance to failure. It is usually forgotten how nearly it succeeded. Had Hitler left strategic planning to commanders of the calibre of Erich von Manstein and Heinz Guderian, it is perfectly possible that the Russian armies would have been pulverized in a series of great enveloping actions, that European Russia would have been overrun and its population expertly decimated, and that the whole of Continental Europe would have been ground under Hitler's heel.

Up to the battle of Stalingrad, at the end of 1942, men like Manstein and Guderian continued to envisage this possibility. After Stalingrad they decided that it was their duty to go on fighting for their country in what was becoming a desperate struggle for survival. There was too little time—it seemed to them—to join the Opposition to Hitler. Albrecht von Kessel's view of their reactions to proposals that they should help overthrow Hitler is apt: 'They either answered that they were busy stabilizing their sector of the front, or they pointed out that they were just about to launch a new offensive.' Manstein, in one sense, was unequivocal; he wanted to get on with the war in which he, as a highly skilled professional soldier, was deeply absorbed. The story of him may well be true that at only one stage did he seriously consider joining Hitler's opponents, and then decided that it would be much more rewarding to take the fortress of Sevastopol first.

Early in 1942 Field Marshal von Witzleben was once again in the forefront of plans for overthrowing Hitler. He was Commander-in-Chief of German forces in the West, and he proposed to move an armoured corps from France to Germany in order to seize power. The plan would have been very difficult to carry out, for an armoured corps can hardly be moved 500 miles in secrecy and the Nazis would have had ample time for counteraction. Witzleben, as it happened, had to drop his plan when in March he was operated on in hospital —Wheeler-Bennett says for haemorrhoids, but according to German historians it was for cancer of the stomach.

General Alexander von Falkenhausen might have been considered as an alternative to Witzleben. He was Military Governor of Belgium but he had no troops worth the name under his command. For men to carry out the direct action against Hitler, which was becoming a matter of increasing urgency, the Opposition began to look to the German armies in Russia.

They did not look there in vain. In the headquarters of Army Group Centre, commanded by Field Marshal Fedor von Bock, was a senior officer who possessed all the attributes needed to organize and carry out an attempt on Hitler's life. Major-General Henning von Tresckow was born in Magdeburg in 1901. He came of a military family and von Tresckows had served in the Prussian and German armies for 300 years. In many respects he was a typical Prussian Conservative, hard-working, God-fearing, honest and energetic. At the same time he had humour, positive ideas and an individual outlook. Prussian officers were by no means always the sabre-clanking clothes-dummies of caricature.

Tresckow served with distinction through World War I and stayed on in the Reichswehr for two years afterwards. But it is impossible to agree with Wheeeler-Bennett's view that he was 'a very typical example of the Reichswehr officers who at the outset embraced National Socialism enthusiastically'. For one thing, he was not a typically dedicated Reichswehr officer; he left the Army in 1922, took a job on the Berlin stock exchange and earned enough money to save his mortgaged family home and estate at Wartenberg.

In his personal habits Tresckow was distinctly unlike the average

Reichswehr officer. He disliked drill and wore uniform as seldom as possible. He disbelieved utterly in the slogan of blind obedience (*Kadavergehorsam*). Moreover he quickly became closely associated with Beck when he rejoined the Reichswehr in 1931 and must have been proof against the more exaggerated forms of enthusiasm for the Nazi cause. Schlabrendorff, who knew him intimately, says that he was a convinced anti-Nazi long before the war broke out. It is more than likely, although there is no record of it, that Tresckow was one of many who were disgusted and repelled by the barbarism of the Roehm Blood-Bath.

Tresckow had the admirable Schlabrendorff as his A.D.C. when he was appointed to Bock's staff in the summer of 1941. He and Schlabrendorff between them managed to infiltrate two of their friends, Count Hans von Hardenberg and Count Heinrich von Lehndorff, into Bock's headquarters staff. What became almost a 'family circle' of officers conspiring against Hitler was extended to include Colonel Freiherr Rudolf von Gersdorff, Major Ulrich von Oertzen and Colonel Alexander von Voss.

These, moreover, were men of action like Tresckow. They at once began planning, under Tresckow's direction, to take action against Hitler. In August 1941 they were ready to strike, when Hitler paid a visit to Bock's headquarters in Borisov. That nothing came of this plan reflects no discredit on Tresckow. Hitler was superlatively well guarded by his S.S. men. The Borisov visit was a trial run rather than a misfire; it gave Tresckow first-hand knowledge of the obstacles which he was up against.

During the winter of 1941 Tresckow strove to win over Bock to his plans. When Bock was replaced by Guenther von Kluge, Tresckow concentrated his fire on him and kept cajoling him throughout 1942. He had good reason to do so; had the Commander-in-Chief of a whole Army Group been won over, the Eastern front could have been stabilized after a strategic line-shortening retreat, just as soon as Hitler had been dealt with. And the accession of an Army Group commander to the Opposition would have given it prestige as well as striking-force. But Bock had his eyes firmly fixed on the capture of Moscow, while Kluge was too slippery for Tresckow, too inclined to put off a decision and wait to see if a better situation might not arise.

Tresckow was in close touch with Beck and Goerdeler. The latter, indeed, travelled to Russia where, under the closest secrecy, he met Kluge in November 1942 in the Forest of Smolensk. According to Schlabrendorff, Goerdeler almost won Kluge over then into taking his key place in the ranks of the Opposition. Yet Kluge shifted his ground the moment Goerdeler had returned to Germany, even though he was being blackmailed politely at the time by Tresckow and Schlabrendorff for having accepted a cheque for 250,000 marks and a building-permit from Hitler on the occasion of his sixtieth birthday (October 30, 1942).

Tresckow put it to him that he had been bribed by Hitler and must 'wipe the slate clean'. The acceptance of money might just have been considered consonant with the honour of a German officer—presents of money have, after all, been made to military commanders by the governments of other countries. But the building-permit, since all building by private persons was strictly controlled in war-time, was manifestly an 'under-the-table' gift.

The battle of Stalingrad was at this moment approaching its climax. Historians have pointed to this bloodiest of all World War II battles as being the arch-example of the catastrophic results of Hitler's personal interference in the conduct of the war. This is doubtless correct; the German armies in Russia were forced to dissipate their strength by being called upon to launch almost simultaneous offensives against Leningrad in the north, against Stalingrad, and into the Caucasus in the far south. Yet those who are wise after the event have not hesitated to castigate Hitler for attacking Stalingrad at all, and the suggestion has been made by more than one responsible historian that he did it primarily because he attached some 'mystic significance' to the city which bore Stalin's name.

In reality, Stalingrad was an obvious military target in the summer of 1942 for the German armies. Its strategical importance was immense—a fact which was recognized twenty-five years earlier by both 'Reds' and 'Whites' when fighting their biggest and most bitter battle of the Russian Revolutionary War there. At Stalingrad the Volga bends sharply right-handed and southwards on its way to the Caspian. Possession of Stalingrad would have given the German armies interior lines of communication on a long and vital sector of the front. North-south communications to the east of the Volga, moreover, were very bad in 1942; and had the Germans captured Stalingrad they could have held the line of the river with little difficulty and with a huge saving of man-power which was needed elsewhere.

Hitler's mistake, of course, did not lie in attacking Stalingrad, but in allowing the offensive in the Caucasus to continue at the same time. Had he fought a containing action in the Caucasus (which would have been easy enough to do), he could probably have withdrawn sufficient divisions from there to ensure that he took Stalingrad. Even as things were, he came desperately near to success.

In November 1942 the Russians had built up sufficient strength to launch their tremendous counter-offensive in the Stalingrad sector and gradually surround the 100,000 troops under General Friedrich Paulus which already held three-quarters of the city. Hitler refused to let the garrison fight its way out, and this refusal led to a minor conspiracy among the garrison. Generals Walther von Seydlitz and Freiherr Alexander von Daniels wanted Paulus to countermand Hitler's order, break out to the west and then lead a military rising against the Nazi regime. A *Luftwaffe* pilot flew in with a message from Beck to Paulus, urging that he should issue a manifesto proclaiming Hitler to be a traitor who recklessly squandered German lives.

Paulus did none of these things. He fought doggedly on until Stalingrad fell on January 30, 1943, and he formally surrendered to the enemy. For this extreme example of wooden obedience he was, on the day following, awarded a Field Marshal's baton. In captivity, Paulus was to be brain-washed by the Russians into deserting his Fuehrer and putting himself at the disposal of the anti-Nazi 'National Committee for a Free Germany'. Von Seydlitz and von Daniels joined much more readily in this unsuccessful project.

One week before Stalingrad fell, the heads of the British and American governments, Mr. Winston Churchill and President Franklin D. Roosevelt, met in the Moroccan town of Casablanca and issued a joint statement demanding the unconditional surrender of the Axis Powers. There can be little doubt that this baldly uncompromising statement was a blow to Hitler's German opponents. They had angled for so long for a clear-cut assurance from the Western Allies that a post-Nazi German Government would be given some consideration and peace-terms acceptable to the German people. The

Count von Stauffenberg, the mainspring of the 1944 conspiracy
to destroy Hitler

Dietrich Bonhoeffer, who saw in Hitler the arch-enemy of his own
Evangelical faith and of all Christianity

formula of 'unconditional surrender' seemed to knock all such hopes on the head, and it is not surprising to find hardly a German living today who does not denounce the Casablanca declaration.

Schlabrendorff attributed it to Roosevelt's lack of knowledge of conditions inside Germany and lack of understanding of German psychology. Gerstenmaier has stated that Casablanca meant that 'from then on the foreign-political efforts of the German Opposition to Hitler were terribly difficult, in fact hopeless'. Kessel asks indignantly why Roosevelt and Churchill failed to make it clear that they wanted the unconditional surrender of the Axis regimes, rather than the 'enslavement' of their subjects.

Hitler's opponents agreed at the time—and they still agree on this —that Casablanca merely fortified the Fuehrer in his determination to fight on to the bitter end. It is idle to point out to them that the two primary purposes of the unconditional surrender formula were to reaffirm the Western Allies' intention of fighting on until final victory had been won; and to reassure the Russians, who had been waiting so impatiently for the opening of the 'Second Front' on the European mainland and who had been fobbed off with the North African landings.

Since Stalingrad and Casablanca so nearly coincided, it is not really possible to distinguish their respective impacts on Hitler's opponents at the time. The fable that active Opposition to Hitler began only after Stalingrad should already have been exploded by what I have written in previous chapters. It seems, however, that the theory that Casablanca sabotaged the efforts of the Opposition is at least equally untenable. The efforts of Tresckow and his friends were certainly not lamed; on the contrary, they were pushed ahead with greater energy than before. And their increased vigour was matched by greater readiness in Germany itself to work out plans for exploiting successful action against Hitler's person. There, Oster and the commander of the Wehrmachtamt, General Friedrich Olbricht, were ready to act as the executive arms of Beck and Goerdeler.

Schlabrendorff told me in 1963 that the plans for 'Operation Flash' —the revolt which was to have followed the disposal of Hitler by Tresckow—were detailed and thorough. They were destroyed by the conspirators themselves, when the attempts on Hitler's life organized by Trescknow and his friends had failed. They involved military *coups* in three capital cities—Berlin, Paris and Vienna—and the mobilization on the side of the revolt of troops in Munich, Cologne and other German towns.

The Commander-in-Chief of the Home Army, General Friedrich Fromm, teetered on the very brink of the conspiracy. Olbricht believed that he would be won over the moment that Hitler was dead and 'Operation Flash' went into action. Beck and Goerdeler, it need scarcely be said, were ready to take their appointed places in the temporary regime which would be set up, Beck as co-ordinator of all military and police action and planning, and Goerdeler as head of the civil political administration. The first obvious steps of the emergency government would have been to round up all prominent Nazis, disband the armed S.S., establish internal order, invite the Western Allies to propose peace-terms, and organize a fighting retreat on the Russian front which would leave the German armies in strong defensive positions in Poland and Lithuania.

Schlabrendorff had more to say about the thinking of the conspirators at this time. The spring of 1943, they believed, was an ideal time for 'Operation Flash'. The German people had been badly shaken by Stalingrad and by the final rout of Field Marshal Erwin Rommel's army in North Africa. Whatever conclusions Hitler and his advisers had drawn from Casablanca, the German people as a whole was not envisaging a 'war to the death' and was inwardly growing ever readier for peace.

'Nineteen-forty-three was the time for action,' Schlabrendorff told me. 'For the Russians were tired then and would not have pressed our armies. Of course, Hitler's death would not have avoided some sort of reverse for Germany. Much would have had to be given up, but this would have been far preferable to leaving the Nazis to lead us into final catastrophe. I believe Churchill would have used his influence in favour of a feasible peace and that Germany would have been allowed to go on existing as an entity. We should have lost Austria, of course, but as a Prussian I regarded Austria only as a liability.

'A successful *coup* would necessarily have been followed by a phase of military direction of government. Germans like to be given orders, and they function best when their orders are clear and definite. The alternative to temporary military control, anyway, would have been chaos. Our purpose was to organize normal civil government as soon as possible, and Goerdeler would have played a leading part there. He had great experience in administration. And a peace treaty? Something reasonable could have been obtained—remember, our armies still had immense fighting capacity in 1943. And everyone, in all countries, wanted peace.'

Schlabrendorff has told the story of the 1943 attempts on Hitler's life in his book *Officers Against Hitler*. The following passages of the book constitute the clearest and fullest account of those attempts:

'At the last meeting between Olbricht and Tresckow, towards the end of 1942, Olbricht asked for eight more weeks to perfect the plans for seizing power in Berlin, Cologne, Munich and Vienna. At the expiration of this period, that is by the end of February 1943, I was charged by Tresckow to have another talk with Olbricht, and it was then that he spoke the memorable words: "We are ready; it is time for the flash."

'To elucidate all details and avoid any possible friction in the sequence of events, one more meeting was imperative between our circle at the eastern front and our confederates in Berlin. This time the talks did not, as before, take place in Berlin, but in Smolensk at the headquarters of the Central Army Group on the Russian front. For that purpose Admiral Canaris organized a service flight from Berlin to Smolensk. He arrived at our headquarters accompanied by many officers of his staff. To cover his real intentions, he had summoned a large meeting of intelligence officers.

'The decisive talk, however, took place far from the bustle, in a modest room used by an officer in charge of the war diary. Here, at a late hour of the night, Tresckow, Dohnanyi and I met, and Tresckow informed Dohnanyi of our intention to attempt the assassination of Hitler in the near future. He made sure of the state of preparations in Berlin, and we explored and co-ordinated ways and means of communication, agreeing on a code that only those immediately concerned could understand. Then we separated.

'In the meantime Tresckow had redoubled his efforts with the Commander of our Army Group, Field Marshal von Kluge, to win him over to the idea of doing away with Hitler. It seemed essential that Kluge, as Commander-in-Chief, should support the insurrection from the outset, as thus he might exercise decisive pressure upon hesitant commanding generals at the front, as well as upon those of our home army.

'At the same time, Tresckow was busy preparing "Operation Flash". This required that Hitler should leave his headquarters in East Prussia for a visit to the staff of our Army Group, which was then quartered in a forest camp near Smolensk. We wanted to lure Hitler to unfamiliar surroundings, where we would have the advantage over him. To induce Hitler to pay such a visit was a most difficult undertaking, as he lived in an atmosphere of deep suspicion and refused to leave his heavily guarded headquarters except in answer to impulses of his own.

'For this purpose Tresckow made use of a long-standing acquaintance with Hitler's chief aide-de-camp, General Schmundt. He suggested to him that he should persuade Hitler to visit our headquarters. Schmundt was a firm believer in Hitler, but he was not intelligent enough to perceive that Tresckow's request was a trap.

'So it came about that Hitler announced his intention to visit Kluge in Smolensk early in March 1943. But Hitler ran true to form and cancelled his visit shortly before the date fixed. The visit, in fact, had been arranged and postponed several times before Hitler at last arrived by air, on the 13th of March, 1943. Had the Field Marshal [Kluge] then been ready to take action, the tyrant would have been destroyed. With Kluge's assent the assassination of Hitler would have been easier, particularly as Lieutenant-Colonel Freiherr von Boeselager, the commander of a cavalry regiment stationed at the headquarters of our Army Group, was in the plot. The officers of this regiment had been carefully selected for our purpose, and Boeselager combined in his person soldierly efficiency and boundless audacity.

'But Kluge, although he recognized the right course, had not the strength of will to follow it. He kept raising objections, saying that neither the German people nor the German soldier would understand such an act at that time and that we ought to wait until unfavourable military developments made the elimination of Hitler an evident necessity.

'Kluge's attitude made it impossible for us to use for our revolt the channels of the military command, which the Central Army Group provided. For this reason Tresckow and I decided to take matters into our own hands. We hoped that, once the deed was done, Kluge would accept a *fait accompli* and follow his fundamentally sound convictions. To make it easier for him and for the Army Group Command, Trescknow and I planned the following course: we would not shoot Hitler, but would eliminate him during a flight by smuggling a delayed-action bomb into his aeroplane. The appearance of an air accident would avoid the political disadvantages of a murder; for in those days Hitler still had many adherents who, in the event of his assassination, would have put up a forceful resistance to our revolt.'

Lieutenant-Colonel Freiherr von Boeselager, it should be noted at this point in Schlabrendorff's narrative, was prepared to use his cavalry regiment to surround and seize Hitler. He would have no part in his assassination, and he would have acted only at the command of Kluge. He was an interesting amalgam of the gallant and the hidebound. Tresckow, however, had been fully prepared to kill Hitler himself, if the 'Boeselager plan' had worked. He regarded it as far too dangerous to allow Hitler to go on living, and he had made it clear to Olbricht that certain of the Nazi leaders at home—one assumes that Goebbels and Himmler would have headed the list—would have to be killed too, without compunction.

Tresckow and Schlabrendorff took immense trouble over the selection and preparation of the right kind of bomb for the attempt on Hitler's life. They decided to use two bombs and to pack them in a parcel, which would represent and resemble two bottles of brandy. These would ostensibly be on their way, as a gift, to Tresckow's friend and (but only somewhat later) fellow-conspirator, General Helmuth Stieff, Chief of the Organization Branch at Army headquarters at Rastenburg, in East Prussia. On March 13 the bomb-parcel was prepared, ready for its fuse to be set in motion by hand, and the code-word signalling that the attempt was about to be made on Hitler's life was transmitted to Berlin. There it was received by telephone, by Captain Ludwig Gehre, of the Abwehr. He passed it on at once to Oster and Olbricht.

After arriving at Smolensk Hitler drove to Kluge's headquarters, where a lengthy meeting took place at which Tresckow was present. He and Schlabrendorff had considered whether, after all, this might not be the best time to kill Hitler. They decided against action in the conference chamber on the grounds that Kluge and his Army commanders would be blown up too. They were needed, however, for implementing the conspirators' plans—for Tresckow was still convinced that Kluge would join the conspiracy the moment that Hitler was out of the way.

After the conference Hitler lunched with Kluge and his officers, and impressed Schlabrendorff with the disgusting nature of his table-manners. His vegetable-mess, looking like the sort of dog's-dinner which any self-respecting dog would refuse, was prepared for him. He then, like an animal, put his face down to his food, and not the food to his face. After lunch he was due to leave at once on the return flight to Rastenburg.

Schlabrendorff's narrative goes on:

'During lunch Tresckow approached Colonel Brandt, one of Hitler's staff-officers, and asked him whether he would oblige him by taking back to headquarters a small parcel containing two bottles of brandy for one of Tresckow's friends, General Helmuth Stieff. Colonel Brandt agreed.

'After lunch, Hitler, accompanied by Kluge and Tresckow, returned by car to his aircraft, while I took the time-bomb and drove with it in another car to the airfield. Hitler and his escort had used two big aeroplanes for their trip. Hitler sat in one with the persons belonging to his immediate entourage, while in the other the rest of his escort were accommodated. The two aeroplanes were accompanied by several fighter aircraft.

'Having arrived at the airfield, I waited until Hitler had dismissed the assembled officers of the Central Army Group, and when I saw he was boarding the plane I started the fuse of the bomb. The detonator was set, as it were, in the neck of the bottles and the parcel had been so wrapped that I could get hold of it through a small chink in the paper. To make sure that the pressure on the fuse would be strong enough I kept a key hidden in my hand, and with it I dinted the fuse. The bomb was timed to explode within half an hour. At a sign from Tresckow, I handed the parcel to Colonel Brandt, the officer of Hitler's Staff who had promised to take it with him to supreme headquarters. It required some self-control to remain calm at that moment.'

Some self-control! The understatement is typical of the cool-headed, eminently modest Schlabrendorff. He and Tresckow were jubilant when Hitler's plane, accompanied by escorting fighters, took off from the Smolensk military airfield. The bomb was believed to be fully effective and its explosion was certain to wreck the plane and bring it down to earth in flaming fragments. The flight from Smolensk to Rastenburg would normally take two hours, so that there was an ample margin of time for the bomb to work.

The moment Hitler's plane took off, Schlabrendorff telephoned Gehre in Berlin and gave him the second code-word. The third would have followed the moment that Smolensk or Rastenburg was informed that Hitler's plane had crashed. This would have happened automatically, by one of the escorting fighters sending a radio-signal. This was not a part of the conspiracy, but a part of their normal training.

But Hitler's plane did not crash, and Hitler landed safely at Rastenburg. Schlabrendorff at once flew on another plane to Rastenburg and collected the bomb-parcel, which was reposing in Colonel Brandt's office. He made the excuse that the wrong bottles of drink had been sent and he brought two genuine bottles of brandy to replace them. With considerable courage, Schlabrendorff, who had found some excuse for travelling on by train to Berlin, dismantled the bomb-parcel in his sleeping compartment that night:

'Having stripped the cover I could see that both explosive charges were unaltered. With care I dismantled the bomb and took out the detonator. When I examined it, I found to my great surprise what had happened. The fuse had worked; the glass globule had broken; the corrosive fluid had consumed the retainer wire; the striker had operated; but—the detonator-cap had not reacted.

'I felt both disappointment and relief, disappointment that a singular mischance had frustrated our attempt; relief because I could hope that we had managed to avoid discovery of our conspiracy.'

Tresckow must have been cruelly disappointed, but within a few days he made another attempt to have Hitler killed, this time by Major (later Major-General) Freiherr Rudolf von Gersdorff, Kluge's G.S.O. II. The occasion selected was the opening of an exhibition of war pictures on March 21, at the *Zeughaus*, or Arsenal, in Berlin. The opening of the exhibition by Hitler was a part of the annual commemorative ceremony for the dead of World War I. Hitler was to make a short speech and then spend half an hour at the exhibition. Finally, he would take the salute at a march-past of a guard of honour.

Gersdorff, whom Tresckow had initiated into his plans only a short time before but who had for a long time been a confirmed anti-Nazi, managed to get his name on to the short-list of those accompanying Hitler through the *Zeughaus*. In addition, he learnt that the time of the inspection and the ceremony would be altered by several hours only just before it was due to begin—a security precaution typical of Hitler, who not only wore a bullet-proof cap, took his own cook everywhere to taste his food, and surrounded himself with a phalanx of S.S. bodyguards, but who made a point of frequently changing his time-table at the last possible moment.

On March 21 Gersdorff prepared himself—melodramatic though this may sound—for his own death. He was armed with two bombs, one in each of his overcoat pockets. Both were fitted with ten-minute fuses and Gersdorff's intention was to remain at Hitler's heels wherever he went in the *Zeughaus*. But after Hitler had entered the building, and before Gersdorff had started the fuses of the bombs, one of the Fuehrer's adjutants told him that Hitler would stay, in all, only eight to ten minutes in the building. In the event, he stayed less than eight minutes, which Tresckow and friends—listening to a broadcast of the ceremony on the Russian front—heard with horror and bitter disappointment.

There was some further talk in Smolensk about inviting Hitler there for another visit, and using the honest but hyper-correct Boeselager to capture him and his entourage. But this talk was desultory; Tresckow and his friends were already beginning to wonder if Hitler would not have to be killed in his own head-quarters. The bomb would then be brought to him, and not he to the bomb.

Tresckow therefore backed to the full the first plan of this kind which could be made. In November 1943 it was proposed that Hitler should be blown up when he was inspecting new uniforms and over-coats, modelled by upstanding young officers, in Rastenburg. The uniforms and overcoats were to be for the use of the troops on the Russian front. Among the officers in the squad showing them off was the Freiherr Axel von dem Bussche, a twenty-four-year-old captain serving in Tresckow's old regiment, the 9th Infantry (formerly 1st Foot Guards).

Bussche had become an active conspirator after seeing Jews being slaughtered in large batches—around 1,600 in all in a single afternoon —in September 1942. He was horrified and enraged. Like Gersdorff, he was prepared if necessary to die himself, if he could kill Hitler at the same time. The new uniforms were to have been inspected by Hitler around November 25, and Bussche was 'on duty' at Rastenburg for the show from November 23 onwards.

Now taking part in active opposition to Hitler, General Helmuth Stieff would have helped in this attempt on Hitler's life. He was to infiltrate Bussche into the squad. Bussche was to carry a hand-grenade with a $4\frac{1}{2}$-second fuse. The intention of Bussche was to grapple with Hitler at the propitious moment chosen for starting the fuse. Himmler and Goering were to have been present at the inspection, offering a unique opportunity of removing two of his most dangerous lieutenants along with the Fuehrer.

By incredibly bad luck the new equipment was destroyed in a Berlin railway-yard before being brought to Rastenburg. The inspection was postponed until Christmas, and then—with all preparations made for the second time—Hitler cancelled his plans and decided to spend Christmas in Bavaria with his mistress, Eva Braun.

Bussche was badly wounded in Russia in January and dropped out of the picture (indeed, his severe war-wounds resulted in his surviving the war). His place was taken by Ewald von Kleist, the son of Schlabrendorff's conservative landowning friend, von Kleist-Schmenzin. Once again a date was fixed, February 11, 1944. This time the demonstration was apparently cancelled by Stieff, ostensibly because Himmler would not be accompanying Hitler but possibly because his nerve failed him.

It is questionable whether the Bussche and Kleist plans belong to the 'Tresckow phase' of conspiracy to kill Hitler, or whether they should be regarded as part of the prelude to the July 1944 plot which was the culminating-point of all conservative and military resistance. For towards the end of 1943 Colonel Claus Schenk, Count von Stauffenberg, was emerging as the dominating figure in the conservative and military Opposition. Stauffenberg, indeed, helped and advised both Bussche and Kleist.

Tresckow was to be only one of a great many high-ranking officers involved in the July 1944 plot. But his contribution as an active conspirator remains second only to that of Stauffenberg. Two of the attempts, at least, which he organized on Hitler's life came far closer to success than anything else done up to that time. Tresckow laid down the two conditions essential to success in overthrowing the Nazi regime—that Hitler must first be killed, and that no risk was too great to take in order to achieve this. The nobility of Tresckow's character, first and foremost, but the staunchness and ready spirit of self-sacrifice of Gersdorff, Bussche and Kleist, constitute one of the most lasting memorials of the Opposition.

Tresckow and his friends failed by only a narrow margin. Had they succeeded, Europe might be a very different place today. The Poles, Czechs and others might have been able to regain true freedom and independence. The Communist advance would certainly not have reached the Elbe, and Berlin would not today be a source of bitter discord between East and West. Since bad Germans brought war and woe on Europe and the world in 1939, it was tragic that good Germans like Tresckow were deprived by ill-fortune of the chance of redeeming their country and their people.

nine

The Communist Interlude

'Were pity priced
So low, how spare true misery a tear?
What though you bear the cross of Antichrist?
It is in very truth a cross you bear!'

ROBERT NICHOLS, *Lines from the Sea*

IN HIS memoirs Walter Schellenberg, Hitler's war-time secret-service chief, maintains that Stalin instructed the German Communists—years before the Nazi seizure of power—to regard the Social Democrats, rather than the Nazis themselves, as their principal enemy. Schellenberg's explanation of this curious tactic—for in countries like France and Italy, Communists and Social Democrats made common cause in 'popular fronts'—was that Stalin wanted democratic government wrecked in Germany, in order 'to mobilize Germany against the West'.

Stalin's enemies in Germany, Schellenberg goes on, were the 'bourgeoisie' and the non-Communist working class. According to Schellenberg, Colonel Nicolai, once the head of the Kaiser's military intelligence service, advised General von Schleicher, then German Chancellor, to advance Hitler 42,000,000 marks in 1932. This was done on Soviet prompting. Stalin believed that the Nazis could be built up to the necessary strength to destroy the Weimar Republic, but that Hitler would turn to the Soviet Union afterwards, as a fellow-conspirator against Western democracy, as a huge and expanding market for German industrial products, and—even—as a lasting ally.

Schellenberg is a somewhat unreliable witness and interpreter of events, as his memoirs clearly show. But his reading of Stalin's long-term aims may, in this case, have been accurate. The German

Communists dissociated themselves very largely from Hitler's other opponents before he came to power, and almost completely afterwards. They took their orders from Moscow. Their attitude to the other groups of Germans who opposed Hitler was mainly one of contempt and innate distrust. It was revealingly expressed in an article which appeared (unsigned) in the West German Communist newspaper *Freies Volk* in September 1955.

Freies Volk admitted that 'Nobody can of course deny that a bourgeois resistance to Hitler existed.' But, the paper went on, its character was ordained by class prejudices, and its members were the tools of German capitalists. Carl Goerdeler, for instance, was a 'bad patriot', who wanted a separate Prussian State in 1919, and advised President Hindenburg to have all workers' wages reduced in 1932. Goerdeler was the friend of the 'capitalists' Goering, Schacht and Robert Bosch (the Stuttgart industrialist). Goerdeler, furthermore, was backed by 'the City of London and Wall Street' (how glad poor Goerdeler would have been to have had any backing whatever from either!), and he was a rabid anti-Communist who was ready to intrigue with 'Hitler-Generals' in order to keep the Soviet Union out of Europe.

'The same capitalistic forces which brought Hitler to power', the *Freies Volk* proclaimed, 'tried to separate themselves from him when catastrophe loomed. . . . The whole policy of these imperialists had nothing to do with the national interests of the German people.' *Freies Volk* called the July 20 conspiracy against Hitler the 'Officers' *Putsch*' and described its chief purpose as being to consolidate German militarism and imperialism.

So much for the Communist view of other resistance groups, which—as with so much Communist propaganda—was an ingenious blending of truth and fiction. *Freies Volk*, of course, wrote nothing about the basic reason for Communist collaboration with these groups being impossible—which was the need to take orders from Moscow and subordinate German to Russian interests. *Freies Volk*, again, could say nothing about the very real failures of the Communist resistance, nor begin to explain these failures. Thanks to Stalin's personal amalgam of guile and gullibility, these failures were very great.

One year before the Nazis came to power the Communist Party

was able to collect 5,000,000 votes and return one hundred members to the Reichstag. It had 360,000 members, and an estimated 10,000 to 12,000 cells in the factories. It was a major and growing force in German politics, and its members still retained much of the idealism and humanitarianism which actuated their earliest leaders, Karl Liebknecht and Rosa Luxemburg.

But the German Communists made one mistake after another in 1932–3. They refused alliance with the Social Democrats (one or two purely declamatory 'offers' in 1933 were not genuine and were not taken seriously). They underestimated the strength of the Nazis. They began to lose their own rank and file in the working class to the Nazis (Gerhard Ritter, in his biography of Goerdeler, asserts that 70 per cent of the Communist Party members joined the Nazis during that period, but this is almost certainly a wild exaggeration). Like the Social Democrats, the Communists thought that the Nazi movement would 'fall apart' and failed to realize that the bulk of the working class had already made their private peace with Hitler. So seriously did they underestimate the Nazis, that in November 1932 they combined with them in a general transport strike designed to bring down the right-wing government of Franz von Papen.

Communist propaganda, during the first years of the Nazi era, was totally unrealistic. The international Communist congress held in Brussels in 1935 prophesied mass unemployment for Germany, near-starvation and the beggary of a working class which would have to foot the whole bill for German rearmament. In reality, unemployment had been cut by 75 per cent in under three years by the Nazis, there was no food shortage at all, and the working class was living an enchanted life in a springtime of more jobs, more new homes, the cheap holidays and excursions of the 'Strength through Joy' movement, and a jingoistic atmosphere of false patriotism and promised revenge for the Versailles Treaty.

At the Moscow eighth congress of the Communist International in August, admittedly, there was an urgent appeal for a united struggle against Fascism, and Communists were encouraged to join the International Brigade in Spain. And in Germany itself the Nazi seizure of power left the Communists in no further doubt as to the seriousness of the situation. The Communist members of the Reichstag were arrested on March 21 and 22 and prevented from attending the crucial Reichstag session, in which the Nazis passed the Enabling Act. They were beaten up, tortured and thrust into concentration camps and unnamed prisons. Hundreds of other leading members of the party went into hiding—becoming so-called 'submarines', who lived without valid documents, without jobs, and were kept supplied by means of collections of money made by fellow-members (even in the concentration camps!). A great many more Communists went into exile.

At the same time, the organization of a Communist underground began as soon as the Reichstag Fire Trial (September 1933) showed that Nazi tyranny was being consolidated and Stalin's old hopes of a Nazi-Communist *rapprochement* were unfounded. Instructions went out to build 'anti-fascist', or 'Antifa', cells and to infiltrate Nazi Party organizations. The underground workers were told to believe in the 'coming Red October'—in fact, in revolution organized by Moscow and carried out by the working class. The production of leaflets began on a big scale (the Nazis claimed that they 'captured', on an average, one million Communist leaflets each year). The leaflets were largely crude stuff (what German worker, for instance, would be impressed by vague ranting about world revolution and the creation of a Marxist Europe?). But no one would deny that an all-out effort was being made.

The Communists have since claimed—especially in the *History of the German Anti-Fascist Resistance Movement* published by the East German Ministry of Defence in 1958—that Nazi reprisals were on a huge scale. Allegedly, 340,000 Communists were sentenced to, in all, over 1,000,000 years' imprisonment during the first six years of the Nazi era. More than 600 were sentenced at both Wuppertal and Duisburg-Hamborn in mass-trials. There were other mass-trials of Communists in Hamburg, Luebeck and at the Zeiss optics factory and Leuna chemical works. Sentences of up to six years' imprisonment were imposed for listening to foreign broadcasts and distributing 'seditious' information. At least fifty-seven Communist members of the Reichstag and of *Land* Parliaments died or were executed or murdered in Nazi gaols.

Early in 1939 an international Communist congress at Berne in Switzerland confirmed that a basic Communist aim was the destruction of the Nazi regime. Then came, like a bolt from the blue, the signing of the Russo-German Pact of September 1939. The ground was cut from under the feet of the Communist resisters in Germany. They had just issued a stirring call against war. They were becoming expert in the arts of the go-slow in the factories, the sit-down strike and the industrial sabotage which they hoped to practise if Hitler dared to go to war. Communist accounts of the Communist underground, indeed, have outlined all of this laudable activity.

These accounts come to a sudden, blank end the moment that the 'Robbers' Pact' was signed. It was not beyond Communist propagandists to produce some specious explanation of why the Pact was 'necessary' (such as that the Western Powers were not prepared to fight, Nazi Germany would have got the whole of Poland if Stalin had not made terms with Hitler, the Soviet Union had to 'consolidate its borders' by absorbing the Baltic States and Bessarabia before the Nazis had the chance to march in).

But Communist propagandists simply did not attempt to explain what was the Pact's effect on their own Communist resisters inside Germany. Only a few minor Communist prisoners were amnestied. The *History of the German Anti-Fascist Resistance Movement* writes ingenuously: 'After their release from concentration camps in 1939, comrades of the Communist Party joined together again to form resistance groups against Hitler's dictatorship.' How? When? Why? No Communist can answer these questions with a clear conscience. For in actual fact all Communist resistance to Hitler in Germany ended in September 1939 and had no faintest possibility of restarting until Hitler invaded the Soviet Union in May 1941.

During this 'close season' for Communist resisters there is at least one interesting pointer to official German Communist thinking on its role in an Old World dominated by its two foremost mass-murderers, Stalin and Hitler. The Communists in exile were at least as bewildered as the Comrades who had stayed on in Germany. In countries like France, Sweden and Switzerland they took counsel amongst themselves, and mostly decided to lie low. It was otherwise in Moscow, where the biggest group of exiled German Communists had to applaud sycophantically at their host's collaboration with their own worst enemy. The sycophantic applause was led by Walter Ulbricht, since the war the acknowledged dictator of Eastern Germany and nicknamed 'Comrade Cell' because of his gifts of organizational ability and of turning himself, whenever necessary, into the Kremlin's ventriloquist's dummy.

Ulbricht decided at a very early stage in his career as an active Communist that his role was to be that of Stalin's stooge. Between 1924 and 1926 he was trained, intermittently, in a Comintern school in Moscow. A year later, aged thirty-four, he was party general-secretary in Berlin, master of the details of an organization which included 4,500 officials and 130,000 members. Before the Nazis came to power he built up the powerful 'Red Front Fighters' League', an organization whose members were highly skilled in street-fighting but always uneasily aware that the hand of the police and every uncommitted bystander would be against them, rather than against their Nazi or Social Democratic opponents. Ulbricht continued to fight the Nazis after 1933, going underground when elected a member of the Reichstag in 1933, building up 'resistance cells' of a dozen members each and only escaping from Germany to Moscow at the last possible moment.

Ulbricht had probably already begun, before then, to carry out orders from Moscow which had nothing to do with the aims and interests of the German Communists. On March 3, 1933, the idealistic, basically stupid but patriotic leader of the German Communist Party, Ernst Thaelmann, was arrested in Berlin by the Nazis. He was actually in hiding when a courier arrived with a message from Ulbricht. The courier was caught by the Nazis too, but was released later and may well have been a Nazi stool-pigeon. Ulbricht, perhaps significantly, was not caught.

After Ulbricht reached Moscow, a plan was evolved for the rescue of Thaelmann. A warder who had access to Thaelmann's cell in the Moabit prison in central Berlin had duplicate keys made for his cell door. The turnkey, a man named Moritz, intended to leave spare keys with Thaelmann. But the night before this plan was to have been put into execution, Moritz was told by the Communist underground that there would be no escape. He lost his head and committed suicide. Ulbricht may not have transmitted the relevant order to Moritz. Even if he did, he may simply have decided that Thaelmann —a man of immense physique but limited intellect—was required to be a Communist martyr.

After the signing of the Robbers' Pact in 1939 no effort was made by the Soviet Government, or by the Communist exiles in Moscow, to save Ernst Thaelmann. He was left to rot in a series of concentration-camps and was eventually murdered in August 1944 in Buchenwald. Since the war, Communist guides (Buchenwald is in the East German Republic) have proudly pointed out the place where he was martyred; but not the fact that he was done to death because Stalin intended, through Ulbricht, to decimate the ranks of the old-guard Communists who would no longer trust him or the Soviet Union's brand of imperialistic Bolshevism.

Ulbricht was the most powerful and unscrupulous executor of Stalin's plan. In August 1933 Max Hölz, the founder of the short-lived People's Republic in Saxony in 1920, was mysteriously drowned in the river Moskawa. In 1937 Willi Muenzenberg, who had travelled with Lenin in the sealed railway carriage which the Germans sent through to a Russia in the throes of revolution in 1917, was disgraced; he was murdered in Southern France in 1940. Hans Beimler, who escaped from Dachau concentration camp and reached Republican Spain in 1938, was shot in the back 'by mistake' in Catalonia a few months later. He had protested against the internal Communist purges in Spain, which were carried out by Ulbricht from his head-quarters in Albacete. A dozen other leading old-guard Communists disappeared in Russia between 1933 and 1941, and the mysteries of their deaths have never been explained.

Ulbricht had no difficulty, in Moscow, in going into reverse in 1939. He hailed the Robbers' Pact as the expression of solidarity and friendship between the Russian and German peoples, and between their working-class populations. He complacently described the Czech and Polish nations as 'peoples affiliated with the German National State'. Consider what sort of hideous hypocrisy this was! Hitler had imposed the infamous 'Protectorate' of Bohemia-Moravia on the Czechs, and had set up a puppet, utterly helpless Slovak State. In Poland he had embarked on the programme of persecution and mass-murder which lasted for five years, and had created the 'Polish ghetto-state' of the so-called 'General-Gouvernement'. Ulbricht underwrote these monstrous injustices, readily and blandly.

And Ulbricht went into reverse, once again, when Hitler invaded Russia, in June 1941. Hitler had 'betrayed' the German workers. German Fascism, he proclaimed, would be fought with every possible means, and beaten. The German people would be brought back to the true path of Russo-German understanding, the path chosen by Bismarck, General Hans von Yorck and the Reichswehr, the path of true friendship between the German and Russian peoples. The official Communist *History of the German Anti-Fascist Resistance Movement* commented, with utterly undisguised and possibly involuntary cynicism: 'As a result of the entry into the war of the Soviet Union, they [the German Communists] became convinced that it was necessary to restart with their Communist work.'

Restart they did. The pattern of resistance was now fixed on the concept of the *troika*, the three-man team which worked in perfect trust and with iron efficiency (in Jugoslavia, the early *troika* teams began to chalk-up formidable tallies of German soldiers, shot in the back while they strolled at night in the streets of Belgrade, Zagreb and Sarajevo). 'Red' Hamburg was one of the first places in Germany where a fully functioning Communist underground was reorganized. The shipbuilding firm of Blohm and Voss is believed to have been one of the earliest of the new Communist strong-points. In Hamburg Bernhard Baestlein, who worked in a precision-tool firm, emerged as a natural leader, a man of dogged courage and pertinacity who deserved better of his Communist masters in Moscow. Along with him, and looking after propaganda, was Franz Jacob, a locksmith. Their group was to advance beyond the concept of merely taking Russian orders, and was to strive, and fail, to build a 'popular front' with the Social Democrats in 1944.

The business of Communist resistance was even tougher than that of resisting Nazism with any other group. For almost every man's hand was against the Communists. Conservative resisters could turn to their personal friends, to people of 'family' or with land and possessions, to the aristocracy and the Army, with every chance of finding someone who would help. The Social Democrats were innately 'respectable' and were recognized as being such; they, too, could find sympathizers in many quarters. The Army was a fraternity, and one of the outstanding features of the military resistance to Hitler was that any particular anti-Nazi Army officer could talk to another, pro-Nazi, officer with astonishing candour. And he would not be betrayed. The Communists anticipated, and found, enemies everywhere. Baestlein was caught in October 1942, but escaped early in 1944 from the Berlin-Ploetzensee prison. Jacob had to move to Berlin and went completely underground there, living without papers, ration cards or livelihood. The Hamburg group was thrown into a state of disorganization when Baestlein and Jacob left and was virtually dispersed.

But before the Hamburg group dispersed it had established close contact with Communists in a dozen other cities, including Hanover, Mannheim, Duesseldorf, Breslau, Munich and, of course, Berlin. In all of these cities it built up cells, many of which survived its 1942 collapse. There were thirty cells of the group in Berlin alone in 1943, mainly concentrated in the factories but also infiltrating the *Wehrmacht* and the municipal services. In Berlin Anton Saefkow, first a long-distance lorry-driver and then a metal-worker, emerged as the principal leader and managed to give some continuity to Communist resistance there. He remained active until the middle of 1944 and was remarkably successful in circulating propaganda in the Wehrmacht.

In Mannheim at least fifty-four people were tried between February and October 1942 and about half of them were executed, including an old lady of sixty-five, Frau Wagner. Valuable links were established with the Georg Schumann group in Saxony and the Theodor Neubauer group in Thuringia. The Schumann group was especially active. Its newspaper, *Widerstand*, was printed in Leipzig and its leadership *troika* (Schumann, Otto Engert and Kurt Kresse) established contact with Goerdeler and met him at his Leipzig home at the end of 1943. Goerdeler (who should blame him?) told them that there was no place for Communists in his 'new order' which should rule Germany after the Nazis had been dealt with. Goerdeler knew that these men were in continuous contact with Moscow.

The maintenance of contact with Moscow was another of the remarkable achievements of the Communist underground. Contact was latterly very largely by radio transmission, using low-wave frequencies and sending messages in code. Earlier it was mainly through neutral countries, particularly Sweden (for a time Herbert Wehner, postwar Deputy Chairman of the West German Social Democratic Party, played a big part in the Stockholm 'liaison office'). The German Communists were very much aware of the need to keep in touch with their Russian masters, and this was always one of their major purposes. In this sense, other German resistance groups were less fortunate. This clandestine contact with foreign countries was especially repulsive to the Nazis and they worked hard to uncover it. As early as August 1942 they pounced on four radio transmission sets, whose operators were communicating direct with the Soviet Union and with Communist resisters in European countries occupied by the Nazis.

Untiring and in its fashion dedicated, the Communist resistance produced one group which is remembered above all others. The '*Rote Kapelle*' ('Red Orchestra') had a romantic name and a remarkable history. This group, according to official Communist sources, was formed in 1935. Its strongest cells were in firms like A.E.G., Shell and Borsig, and it was particularly active in Berlin, where it infiltrated the Ministry of Posts and the *Reichsbahn* (German Railway Directorate) with its agents. It had its own underground printing-press, poured out illegal leaflets and produced its own newspaper, the *Innere Front*.

The leader of the '*Rote Kapelle*' was a young man, Harro Schulze-Boysen, whose exhibitionist behaviour suggested that he was a Hitler Youth *manqué* but who, in reality, possessed tremendous courage and a genuine belief in Communist ideals. Schulze-Boysen was one of the last people one might have expected to find in the Communist resistance. His father was an admiral, his mother a friend of Goering. Good-looking and gay, he wore his blond hair in a wild mane, set it off with a black sweater, and cultivated friends in the artistic world. He was an anti-Nazi as early as 1931, when he founded an extreme left-wing newspaper, *Der Gegner*. He readily took part in street fights with the brown-shirts and showed a furious courage. According to the fanciful Walter Schellenberg, on one occasion he threatened a Communist agent in the street with his revolver for neglecting his Communist propaganda work. He was arrested in 1933 and held in gaol for several days, when he was beaten up as a 'lesson'.

Schulze-Boysen married Libertas Haas-Heye, the daughter of Countess Eulenburg, another friend of the Nazis. Thanks to the Eulenburg connection, he was given a job in Goering's own intelligence service, known as the *Luftwaffe* Research Office. This was at the very beginning of the war and there is just a chance that Schulze-

Boysen was at the time disillusioned by the Hitler-Stalin Pact and by what he must have regarded as an unholy alliance. It is hardly possible to guess what Goering was thinking about. The most likely explanation is that he was assured that Schulze-Boysen was a 'drawing-room Communist' and therefore comparatively harmless. He was raised to the rank of captain.

Meanwhile active resistance began again in the '*Rote Kapelle*' as soon as Hitler attacked the Soviet Union. The orientation of the group was plainly indicated by one of its members, Hans Coppi, who said that it was 'better to die for the Soviet Union than to live for Fascism'. Schulze-Boysen and his accomplices intended serving Russian, not German, interests. They envisaged the destruction of Nazism by the victorious Red Army and Germany's conversion into a Communist satellite state. This is why postwar German historians of the resistance to Hitler have regarded the members of the '*Rote Kapelle*' and other Communist groups quite simply as traitors, whose names do not deserve to be mentioned in the same breath as those of Stauffenberg, Beck, Leber and the rest.

This may be unfair in one respect; the act of resistance in itself demands certain qualities of courage, idealism and strength of mind. These German Communists cannot be totally identified with Soviet 'Communist-imperialism'; they could not know, at the time, what the Soviet Union would do to Germany, or that the yoke of Stalin could become almost as hard to bear as the yoke of Hitler had been. Schulze-Boysen roped in some surprising allies. One was Arvid Harnack, who worked in the American section of the Ministry of Economics and who had married an American student, Mildred Fish, after working at Wisconsin University. Mildred was Jewish, and this must have had an influence on Harnack, who had had close connections with the Soviet trade delegations in Berlin and, as one of the officials responsible for the allocation of raw materials, probably believed in the economic virtues of a Russo-German *entente*.

Another fellow-conspirator was Dolf von Scheliha, who had been Counsellor at the German Legation in Warsaw. Von Scheliha came of an old and esteemed Prussian family, with estates in Silesia and a record of service to the Kaiser and attachment to the traditions of the Wilhelminian era. It has been unkindly suggested that von Scheliha became a Russian agent in order to pay his debts. But his relatives could have done that for him. It is more likely that this was the case of an errant disciple of General von Seeckt, who, while building up and dominating the post-1919 Reichswehr, believed that Germany's 'mission' was to be the 'civilizing partner' in a Russo-German alliance.

Schulze-Boysen established other, worthwhile governmental contacts. There was Horst Heilmann in the Foreign Broadcasts Monitoring Service, Countess Erika von Brockdorff and Frau Schumacher in the Ministry of Labour. The '*Rote Kapelle*', moreover, had contact with other European countries; according to Schellenberg, it had radio transmitters in Marseilles, Utrecht and Brussels. It had links with foreign workers inside Germany, and the 'Baerenschenke' tavern in the Friedrichstrasse in Berlin became a collecting-point for them. Instructions were sometimes carried from Russia by agents who were parachuted into Germany. Some of them were never caught and the identities of two of the leaders outside Germany, '*Grand Chef*' and '*Petit Chef*', are still the undisclosed secret of the Russian secret service.

By 1942 the '*Rote Kapelle*' had become such an important source of information to the Soviet Union that Admiral Canaris stated that the organization had 'cost the lives of 200,000 German soldiers' (probably a wild exaggeration). By then Schulze-Boysen was working out plans for large-scale sabotage aimed at paralysing German armaments industries. Other activities included the production of illegal newspapers (*Der Vortrupp*, the *21 Seiten Blatt* and the *Innere Front*), the collection of money and food for Jews who were being hunted by the Nazis, the collection of arms and ammunition and the hiding of all enemies of the Nazis. When the Nazi exhibition '*Das Soviet Paradies*' was opened in Berlin, the group stuck posters all over the premises in the Tauentzienstrasse, with '*Das Nazi Paradies —Krieg* [war]*—Hunger—Terror—Elend* [misery]*—wie lang noch* [how much longer]*?*' on them.

The '*Rote Kapelle*' conspiracy was uncovered almost by chance. A Russian agent who had parachuted into Germany in August 1942 was caught by Canaris's Abwehr and turned over to the Gestapo. Under torture he betrayed members of the '*Rote Kapelle*'. For once the two rival intelligence organizations of the Abwehr and the S.D. (*Sicherheitsdienst*) under Schellenberg seem to have co-operated successfully and readily. Four radio-transmitters were discovered. Around one hundred people were arrested, many of them intellectuals, artists and civil servants. Only a dozen or so were workers. So good had been the internal security of the '*Rote Kapelle*', that most of its members knew only one or two others.

Some of the conspirators, including Schulze-Boysen, were tortured in the most brutal manner imaginable. With Communists, whom they regarded as the worst of all enemies of their country, the Gestapo were utterly merciless. Schulze-Boysen showed incredible courage, and even Dr. Manfred Roeder—known as 'Hitler's bloodhound'—who was put in charge of preparations for the trial, affirmed that he 'died like a man'. Around fifty members were sentenced and executed in August and another fifty after a second trial in December. In the second trial Hitler personally demanded death-sentences, but Roeder dissented and took no further part in the proceedings. Another judge was appointed President of the special court, and awarded only prison sentences to some of the prisoners, including Mildred Harnack and Erika von Brockdorff. But Hitler again intervened. The two women were executed, like the others being slowly strangled to death by a rope hung from a hook.

The trials were, of course, farcical. The accused were not allowed to consult their lawyers, who were themselves appointed and instructed by the court. Nor could the accused exchange a word with the lawyers in court. The lawyers, for their part, took next to no interest in proceedings which were for them a mere formality. Often they did not even take the trouble to read up their client's case.

The '*Rote Kapelle*' was probably the best-organized, large-scale spy network in Nazi Germany. With its collapse—and the subsequent collapse of the Saefkow and other groups—Communist resistance became increasingly concentrated on two unusual types of organization. The first was in the concentration camps, the second among prisoners-of-war in the Soviet Union. It could be held that these two complexes should come outside the boundaries of 'orthodox' resistance to Hitler. Yet both have a special interest.

In the concentration camps the Communists, partly by reason of long service by many of their number but much more as a result of their superior organization, became the most effective resisters of authority. Some Communists became '*Kapos*', or trusties acting under the orders of their S.S. guards. They were often as brutal as the S.S. themselves, and pitiless in their extortions against other, weaker prisoners. Kapos stole food, personal belongings, clothes and even the gold from the teeth of weaker, usually utterly helpless, prisoners. They used their loot to buy more food for themselves or treat themselves to visits to the camp brothels.

But all Kapos were not Communists, and Communist Kapos were not always like this. In many camps, but especially in Buchenwald, they organized the 'illegal committees' which helped to save the lives of other prisoners and even collected arms and ammunition for the day of deliverance. Other committees which achieved a high degree of organization were in Auschwitz, Neuengamme, Dachau and Mauthausen. The Dachau committee smuggled out two Catholic priests, with instructions to get to the advancing Americans and urge them to bring succour quickly.

In some camps the Communists fought their private battles for power against convicts who had been imprisoned for criminal offences. In Buchenwald, for instance, a convict on one occasion reported the Communist committee to the S.S. for listening to foreign broadcasts on a radio set which was kept hidden in the sewers. When the S.S. failed to find the radio set they took fifty Communists to the quarries and slaughtered them there. The Communists gained control of the prisoners' illegal committees in Buchenwald only in the middle of 1942.

There are plenty of stories of Communists saving the lives of Frenchmen, Englishmen and other foreigners, usually by hiding and feeding them when the S.S. were searching for them to murder them, and Jewish and other children. Plenty of the Communists were idealists who bore little resemblance to the Moscow-true indoctrinates of post-war Communist parties. One story illustrates the humanity of some of them. In one prison camp an Austrian count was placed in a cell with two Communist 'comrades'. Their first action was to insist that he use the single bench in the cell, while they slept on the floor. On the first Sunday there was a church service in a hut just across the yard from the cell window, but the Count was not allowed to attend it.

His presence in the cell was known about, and the door of the hut was left open so that—by pushing the bench up to the window and standing on tiptoe—he could hear the prayers and the singing. At one stage during the service one of his cell mates broke into a flow of relatively harmless blasphemy. 'Shut up!' his companion told him. 'Can't you see that the Count is in church?'

At Buchenwald the Communists were politically organized. They carried out acts of sabotage when sent out on work parties. They had their most trusted agents in the camp hospital, stealing medicine and extra food in order to save the lives of the sick. In camp offices they deliberately muddled up official forms, delayed orders and even prevented executions from taking place. They organized go-slows among the slave labourers and even strikes (according to the Gestapo there were often more than 8,000 slave labourers on strike in a single month). During an air raid on the nearby town of Weimar in August 1944 they began to steal arms, although they never collected enough to fight their S.S. guards before the liberation.

Nor were they strong enough to prevent most of the murders carried out by the S.S. On April 6, 1944, they even 'selected' victims for the transports to the death camp of Theresienstadt from among the most helpless Jewish and Gentile prisoners. There was no room for sentiment among the inmates of Buchenwald. The cause which the Communist resisters in the concentration camps most propagated was that of survival. But much of their resistance work—even when incidental—was memorable.

Of a very different nature was the 'external resistance' organized by the Russians in prisoner-of-war camps after the fall of Stalingrad. Before the battle of Stalingrad the Russians had probably captured no more than 30,000 German soldiers in more than eighteen months of hard fighting. These were unfortunates, members of a victorious army. Most of them still believed implicitly that Hitler would win the war. Stalingrad, on the other hand, was a gigantic disaster for German arms and around 100,000 men fell into Russian hands. The Stalingrad army totalled nearly a quarter of a million men, and not more than 50,000 were evacuated during the course of the battle. Those who fought to the last were evidently aware of a sense of betrayal, for this was the first major defeat for German arms since the war began and it must have been plain to most officers and N.C.O.s that a tactical retreat could have been organized during the early stages of the battle.

The sense of betrayal was certainly not apparent while the Stalingrad army fought bravely on, believing that Field Marshal von Manstein's armoured columns would thrust their way to their relief. In his book *The Shadow of Stalingrad* Count Heinrich von Einsiedel wrote: 'I have known only five or ten people in Germany who do not believe in a victory for Hitler, and my comrades used to laugh at me when I doubted it.' Einsiedel was probably being wise after the event, but he was certainly right about his comrades' belief in total German victory in Russia. It was a belief founded on a sense of alleged racial superiority, and the supposition that the Soviet people was so 'backward' that it could not fight on—any more than it had done in World War I. The men of Stalingrad were aware of betrayal when their immense prisoner-of-war columns were formed up on February 1, 1943, and marched away from the battlefield; when they were paraded through the streets of Moscow on a Red-Roman holiday; and when they were deposited in prison camps from which only one in every three of them was to emerge alive.

The Russians believed that they would organize an effective 'external resistance' to Nazism from among the officers and senior N.C.O.s of the Stalingrad prisoners. The morale of these German prisoners was broken by underfeeding, occasional ill-treatment and careful interrogation. Einsiedel, for instance, was asked: 'Your war is a just one? You have justly bombarded Stalingrad, Voronesh, Rotterdam, Belgium and London? Justly you murder the Jews, Poles, Ukrainians, Frenchmen, Jugoslavs?' And Einsiedel, according to his own account, answered: 'No—the war is one thing, the murders another.' A great many Germans had a sense of guilt in February 1943.

The Stalingrad officers and N.C.O.s were bribed with better rations and the promise of better treatment—even of better jobs after the war ended—if they would merely listen to Russian propaganda. At the same time they were reminded of the long tradition of Russo-German co-operation, dating back to General Yorck and, long after, to Bismarck and von Seeckt. They were asked to be angry about Hitler's 'desertion' of them when they were fighting an epic defensive battle, and to be war-weary in their need for peace. German Communists were sent along to give them the feeling of 'being at home' with people of their own nationality. Many of the senior officers were allowed to keep their own clothes and equipment, were given clean bed-linen once a week and good food (although doled out in small quantities always).

They were given a 'movement' (and Germans longed for 'inspiration'), and the Manifesto of the National Committee for a Free Germany was founded on the spurious material advantages of Russo-German collaboration and the dimly remembered precepts, demanding German freedom and unity, of Yorck, Clausewitz and Ernst Moritz Arndt ('It has to be a Germany, united and one'). They were even given the old German National black, white and red colours and not the black, red and gold of the Weimar Republic. The oath to Hitler was denounced as immoral, as it meant wrecking the German community in the interests of a crazy dictator.

Some of the Stalingrad officers argued that Soviet Communism was still in a 'formative' stage, and that its further development would open the way to the best and most progressive sort of Russo-German *entente*. Many relied on Stalin's pronouncement that Nazism must be destroyed but the German people would 'live on'. A few of the Stalingrad generals, in an atmosphere engendered with specious talk, vodka and Crimean wine, cooked up an 'agreement' under which the Soviet Union would guarantee Germany's pre-1914 frontiers, in return for the promise of alliance (the Russians, naturally, paid not the slightest attention to this curious document, which bore the signatures of ten of the most senior German officers whom the Russians had captured). The National Committee of Germans suffered from being kept totally isolated from outside events.

After the July 20, 1944, conspiracy had failed they were told by Rudolf Herrnstadt (later a leading East German Communist who was disgraced in 1953) that 'The *Putsch* was nothing but an attempt by the ruling classes in Germany to free themselves from the Praetorian Guard. In order to avoid the revolution which was imminent they had once called in these men and had then become their prisoners. Now, under the orders of the heavy-industrialists, the Generals were to overthrow Hitler and clear the way for a capitalist democracy.' Herrnstadt was not an inaccurate prophet when he added that the failure of the *Putsch* would benefit Communism—which now had a better chance of destroying all of its enemies in Europe.

The members of the National Committee swore an oath, ending:

'If I should break this oath and thereby become a traitor to my people, my family and my Fatherland—my life shall be forfeit.' This weird oath illustrated the small degree of trust which the Russians placed in the officers of the National Committee. Rightly so. They produced some leaflets, broadcasts and occasional pieces of advice—delivered by loudspeaker in the front line—to German soldiers to desert. A very few National Committee men were dropped by parachute inside Germany, before the war ended. A proportion of the men of the National Committee were so far indoctrinated that they genuinely doubted the intentions of the Western Allies and decided that a Soviet victory in Central Europe offered the German people its best chance of survival. Some of the National Committee men after the war took leading positions in the Communist East German State. Einsiedel, for a time, was one of them. He fled to the West in 1949.

The National Committee, with its curious confrontation of old-guard fanatical German Communists with German Army officers, with their eye-glasses and collar-badges, their prejudices and inhibitions, is no more than a random postscript to the story of Communist resistance against Hitler. The Communist underground in Germany was as a whole too much dependent on Moscow, and too little on individual belief and individual daring, to leave a big mark in German history. Because of that, its essential significance is less that it could have been.

For the Communist resisters worked for the collapse of all law and order in Germany, as well as for the end of Hitler's Reich. A huge gap separated them from the Social Democrats, who were patriots seeking the reconstruction of a democratic German State. The Communists were prepared to make war, if told to do so, on other resisters. In Eastern Germany Social Democratic opponents of Hitler were carted off to Soviet concentration camps after the war. So were conservative resisters like Justus Delbrueck and the Freiherr von Sell. The German Communists were nearest to those very few ultra-nationalists who preferred a power-minded and power-hungry Russo-German *entente* to the thought of any sort of dependence on a 'decadent' West. Yet courage is unforgettable. The German Communist resisters, too, had that. They should not be completely forgotten.

ten

Operation Valkyrie

'The tree of liberty must be refreshed from time to time with the blood of patriots and tyrants. It is its natural manure.'

THOMAS JEFFERSON

IN THEIR struggle against Hitler the various groups of the German Opposition necessarily required ideas to sustain them. The Social Democrats—even more than the opportunist Communists—fell back on a political creed. Churchmen of all denominations had their religious faith, and the Munich students were young enough to be imbued with a tremendous enthusiasm for the abstract ideals of freedom and justice.

It is inescapable that many of the soldiers and conservatives who opposed Hitler wanted something like a restoration. Von Tresckow, according to Schlabrendorff, 'wished to prolong the Victorian-Wilhelminian era for as long as possible', although he, and his younger followers even more so, had plenty of progressive ideas. Whatever political progress might be needed in the future, as Tresckow saw it, could be born out of a re-established, pre-Weimar state of society, animated by veneration of tradition and the ideal of service. Men like Tresckow visualized the 'new' Germany shaping itself in that spirit of personal 'wantlessness' which may have been the chief of the Prussian virtues. Thus, it would continue to be very like the old Germany.

There were plenty of monarchists among Hitler's conservative and military enemies, and others who would have been prepared to give a monarchy another chance. The monarchists—chief among them von Hassell and Schacht—were mainly among the older members of the Opposition. They were confronted with one very difficult problem

221

—that of deciding on a candidate. Kaiser Wilhelm II, who would in any case scarcely have been considered, died in exile in Holland on June 5, 1941. His eldest son, the titular Crown Prince, was unsuitable —although at one time he drafted a lengthy declaration for the conspirators which would have been used if they wished to place him on the throne, and in which he expressed his willingness to serve the German people as a liberal monarch.

Crown Prince Rupprecht of Bavaria was a man of immensely greater character and popularity—but only, of course, in his native Bavaria. Possibly the most suitable candidate would have been the Kaiser's eldest grandson, Prince Wilhelm. But he died, from wounds received three days earlier, in a field hospital in France on May 26, 1940. A huge crowd, estimated at over 50,000, attended his funeral in Potsdam. After this, his younger brother, Prince Louis Ferdinand, became the most favoured candidate of the monarchists. He had worked in the United States for five years, was intelligent and able, with a charm of manner and a wider knowledge of the world than that of any other descendant of Kaiser Wilhelm II.

If Hitler had been overthrown there would have been a strong attempt on the part of the monarchists to push Prince Louis Ferdinand's claims, but the likelihood is that it would have been unsuccessful. The principle of monarchy was emphatically not one which basically animated the Opposition, and the lack of post-war interest in a royalist restoration has shown how little popular support there would have been before 1945.

For inspiration the soldiers and conservatives were able to turn instead to a source created by younger members of the aristocracy and the intelligentsia, who began in 1940 to organize one of the most formative groups of thinkers in the history of Germany during the last hundred years. This group became known as the 'Kreisau Circle', taking its name from the Silesian estate of Count Helmuth James von Moltke, a great-grand-nephew of the Field Marshal who played the major part in winning the Franco-Prussian war of 1870.

Moltke's mother was English, the daughter of a Chief Justice in the Transvaal. Born in 1907, Moltke was trained as a lawyer and early on in his life cultivated enlightened and liberal views of society. He split up a large part of his estate—his father died when he was very young—into independent farm-holdings, worked voluntarily in youth labour camps before the Nazis came to power, travelled extensively and acquired a cosmopolitan as well as a progressive view of life.

The English editors of his letters, Mr. Lionel Curtis and Mr. Michael Balfour, described him as realistic, dryly humorous, a man who loved the simple joys of life but who was something of a Puritan in his rejection of many of life's good things. The Oxford scholar, A. L. Rowse, of All Souls, was as much struck by the rapier-like quality of his brain as by his imposing appearance—he was six feet seven inches tall, slim, ascetic, wiry and full of nervous energy. He had the German genius for hard work and a truly Prussian integrity. But, unlike some fellow-Prussians, he was the very reverse of an automaton, investing everything he did with his restless personality and spirit of inquiry.

Moltke was never a Nazi. He refused persistently to give the Hitler salute and once prevented swastika flags from being hoisted on his office building in Berlin, where he worked as an expert on international law. The occasion was a visit to the capital by Mussolini.

Moltke gave every assistance to Jewish clients who wanted to leave the country, and he intervened after the outbreak of war, when he was attached to the High Command of the Armed Forces, on behalf of prisoners-of-war and the civilian populations of occupied territories. He warned Norwegians and Danes who were intended victims of the Nazis, and in 1942 managed to inform the Western Powers that Hitler was proposing to butcher all Frenchmen who fell into German hands when fighting for the Allies. Moltke never ceased to be a patriot, but he was always on the side of humanity.

In the summer of 1940 he began to group around him men of like views, mostly conservatives and landholders to begin with, but gradually forming a wider circle which included liberals, socialists and Trade Unionists. It is necessary to mention only a few of the early members of the Kreisau Circle. One was Count Peter Yorck von Wartenburg, a relation by marriage and the descendant of the General Yorck who joined the Russians in 1812 in defiance of the King of Prussia's orders and played an outstanding part in the War of Liberation against Napoleon. Three years older than Moltke, Yorck too was a lawyer and a deeply religious man.

Two years younger than Moltke was Adam von Trott zu Solz, a

former Rhodes scholar at Oxford University, a diplomat, philosopher and restless, questing genius. Like Moltke, Trott had valuable contacts in Britain, but he was not altogether trusted by them. More was the pity, for from his own Foreign Ministry Trott learned a great deal about what was going on, and he had the right kind of 'political mind' to utilize his information. He was desperately keen to secure support in the United States and Britain for the German Opposition.

A. L. Rowse considered Trott supremely attractive but elusive: 'With him black was never black, and white white; black was always in the process of becoming white, white of becoming black. Nothing was clearly defined from anything else.' Here one can see the influence on Trott of Oxford, where one was taught to see both sides of every question. But Rowse's real difficulty seemed to be to understand that an opponent of Hitler could remain a German patriot. It was, indeed, the tragedy of Hitler's opponents that few people outside Germany could bring themselves to trust them entirely.

Trott and Yorck were natural associates for Moltke, in that they were contemporaries, came from the same section of society, were intellectuals and had broadly similar tastes and outlooks on life. But all sorts of other people were drawn into the Kreisau Circle. They included Prussian conservatives like Count Friedrich Detlev von der Schulenburg, Count Ulrich von Schwerin-Schwanenfeld, Horst von Einsiedel and Hans Bernd von Haeften; Catholic priests like Fathers Delp and Roesch; the Social Democrats Leber, Reichwein and Haubach; Eugen Gerstenmaier and Harald Poelchau from the Evangelical Churches, and Jakob Kaiser from the Christian Trade Unions. All these men turned to Moltke, as the natural focus of a sort of debating society, whose primary purpose was to plan for the post-Nazi future of Germany. It is a measure of Nazi totalitarianism and tyranny that these men were to be regarded and treated as traitors, and their talk as plain treason. Nearly all of them were to be murdered by the Nazis.

The Kreisau Circle held three big meetings, in the spring of 1942, the autumn of 1942 and the spring of 1943. These meetings were important in that a handful of men set out at them to grapple with the essential problems of Germany's and Europe's future. Probably there were never more than forty members of the Circle, but every one of them had friends and associates outside it whom they influenced. The effect was that of a snowball, or better, of a stone dropped into a stagnant pool, with the ripples running outwards and onwards, and a feeling of stir and movement at the very fringes of sentient society. Whereas the generals had to organize action against Hitler, Kreisau produced the moral and intellectual ideas which gave them faith and sense of purpose.

It was, on the whole, beside the point for the American columnist, Dorothy Thompson, to send messages during the war to Moltke, calling on him to take up arms against the Nazis, in her series of broadcasts entitled, 'Listen, Hans.' It endangered Moltke. It could even be regarded as an impertinence. For Moltke had a totally different task to discharge, and he never wavered in carrying it out. No man was less in need of 'outside' encouragement.

Moltke and his associates who were nearest to him in thought were intimately concerned with the fate of the individual. Planning for Europe after the war, Moltke wrote to a friend in England in 1942: 'is less a matter of frontiers and soldiers, or of grand plans and top-heavy organizations. The real question which Europe will have to face after the war is how the picture of the human being as such can be re-established in our hearts.' The basis of individual existence and happiness, Moltke believed, was belief in God, and his insistence on this point won over even Social Democrats like Haubach and Mierendorff, who had never regarded Christianity as necessary for them.

The Christian ethic meant, to Moltke, 'Thou shalt not kill', and for that reason he refused to have anything to do with plans to assassinate Hitler. From this premise he deduced that Nazism would have to run its course and that internal revolt would only confuse issues. An intellectually convinced and morally aware Opposition, under Hitler, would play its part later. It should be preserved for that purpose.

It is interesting to note that Moltke and his friends flatly rejected traditional German nationalism, and would not consider German interests as distinct from those of Europe as a whole. They had none of the arrogance so often associated with Germans, and they did not believe that a moral and intellectual renaissance could or should be restricted to their country. Moltke was enheartened by contact with

Christian resistance groups in European countries occupied by the Nazis (it is interesting that only in France he found no opposition based on deep-rooted moral grounds, presaging the post-war growth of rabid materialism in that country).

There were all sorts of nuances of views among members of the Circle. Gerstenmaier, for instance, saw its primary task as that of concentrating on the salvation of Germany. He called the Opposition to Hitler 'the biggest and most self-sacrificing attempt at German self-help', and he added: 'Our sole theme was—the rescue of Germany.' Gerstenmaier regarded it as a main aim to protect the Reich from a collapse which would result in the loss of millions of lives and homes, and he was rather regretful that there was so little understanding of the Opposition outside Germany. But, he agreed, how should there have been—when its objectives were totally unconnected with Allied war-aims and war-plans? Others than Gerstenmaier may not always have appreciated this.

Gerstenmaier's views, again, differed from those of Moltke in that he believed that Hitler, the tyrant, must be struck down, if Germany were to secure her own salvation and rescue her dignity and honour. At the end, many of the members of the Circle thought and acted as he did. But the *coup d'état* never became the objective of the Circle as such. 'The men of Kreisau', Gerstenmaier wrote later, 'occupied themselves almost exclusively with political, cultural, economic and legal problems—the problems which would confront a new, post-Hitler government. Military matters were not their concern. They were neither Army leaders, nor did they have at their disposal any organized power. Their field was of thought; their task the drafting of a new order for a state based on law. Their intention, the overthrow of the ideology of the total state. Their aim, the rebuilding of Germany in the spirit of Christianity and of social justice, and its incorporation in a united Europe. . . .'

It was inevitable that the Kreisauers should move away from all traditional, preconceived ideas, save those of the Christian faith. They envisaged a synthesis of conservatism and socialism, under the roof of a Federal State. They wanted the end of class warfare and of the rivalry of Christian denominations. Social reform was regarded as vital, perhaps taking such forms as the nationalization of heavy industry, the reorientation towards the land of the industrial worker, the 'humanization' of technocrats, the merging of the individual with the State which represented rather than ruled him, and the diffusion everywhere of the sense of citizenship and personal liberty.

The Circle thrashed out such complex subjects as a new federal constitution, the curtailment of industrial cartels, the reform of existing systems of land-tenure, the liberalization of education, the jurisdiction of international courts over war-criminals. The Kreisauers wanted, in fact, a new form of society.

Their greatest achievement was to make themselves, and others, think. In this way they supplied much of the intellectual content of the Opposition during 1942, 1943 and 1944. Plenty of Germans have since criticized the 'Gandhi element' in the Kreisau Circle, and Moltke's rejection of direct resistance at his trial—he used the phrase 'I had nothing to do with the Goerdeler *Mist* [trash]'—has been much misunderstood. More apposite was this passage in one of his last letters: 'I stood before Freisler [the President of the Nazi People's Court] not as a Protestant, not as a landowner, nobleman or Prussian, not even as a German—but as a Christian and nothing else.' The force of example of the Kreisauers has lingered on after the war. The calibre of their thought has guaranteed their contribution to post-war Germany.

The more immediate impact of their ideas lay in the inspiration which they gave to Hitler's opponents in 1944. It is just possible that, without this inspiration, opposition might have tailed off after the Tresckow-Schlabrendorff bomb failed to explode in March 1943. For Hitler's opponents had a long run of misfortunes in 1943 and 1944— misfortunes which indicated the growing awareness on the part of the Nazis of the enemies in their midst, and the growing efficiency of the Nazi security forces under Himmler and Walter Schellenberg.

Himmler's biggest *coup* against the conspirators was somewhat fortuitous. In April 1943 he arrested Dietrich Bonhoeffer, Joseph Mueller and Hans von Dohnanyi. This was the result of disclosures made by one of their minor associates who was being charged with smuggling foreign currency across the German frontier. The man, Schmidthuber by name, tried to buy himself off, by disclosing to the Nazis all that he knew about Hitler's enemies in the Abwehr.

Apart from the three arrests, suspicion fell at long last on Hans Oster. He was kept under close scrutiny by the Gestapo, and in

December 1943 was transferred from active service to the Reserve. This was a severe blow to the Opposition. Meanwhile, Beck had undergone a serious operation, for cancer of the stomach, and General von Hammerstein had died. The Opposition thus lost two of its leading figures, while the third, Beck, never recovered his original determination and confidence.

Schellenberg's initial success appeared to be quite incidental. He penetrated one of the many opposition discussion-groups where the ideas of the Kreisauers and others were debated—sometimes with a lack of discretion. This particular group centred on Frau Hanna Solf, the widow of a former German Colonial Minister and Ambassador to Japan, and their daughter, Countess Lagi von Ballestrem.

Both ladies were lively and gallant but voluble, and it was not altogether surprising that Schellenberg managed to infiltrate into the group of Dr. Reckzeh, who worked at the Charité Hospital in Berlin and was an agent of his. This happened in September 1943 and the Gestapo waited until January 1944 until deciding that the activities of the 'Solf Circle' were potentially dangerous. But when they struck, Moltke was among the dozen people arrested. All were executed, save Frau Solf and her daughter, who owed their lives to the intercession of the Japanese Ambassador in Berlin.

Schellenberg's next success was the indirect result of the destruction of the Solf Circle. Erich Vehmehren and his wife Elizabeth were living in Istanbul at this time, where Vehmehren was working for the Abwehr. He had close friends in the Solf Circle and had just heard of their arrest when he was suddenly ordered to return to Berlin. Fearing the worst, he took refuge in the British Embassy in Ankara. This brought one unforeseen result. Admiral Canaris, who had headed the Abwehr for the past nine years, was sacked on February 18, 1944. The 'cover' which he had provided for the conspirators had been invaluable. Although his nominal successor, Colonel Georg Hansen, was an anti-Nazi who had played a minor part in the 1943 attempt on Hitler's life, effective cover was now no longer possible. For the Abwehr was now placed under the direct control, and the sharp eyes, of the Nazi security services.

The loss of Mueller, Dohnanyi and Bonhoeffer could be borne, although this meant the loss of Mueller's contact with the Western Allies through the Vatican and of Bonhoeffer's with them through

Stockholm. The loss of Hammerstein, although he had taken little direct part in Opposition plans since 1940, was more serious. For Hammerstein would have acted without hesitation or compunction if and when an attempt had been made to overthrow Hitler, and in view of Beck's ill-health would have had a key role to play.

The retirement of Canaris and Oster were irreparable reverses. Although they remained in the conspiracy, they had been deprived of their unique sources of information. With the failures of Tresckow, Schlabrendorff, Bussche and Kleist to dispose of Hitler, this meant that the Opposition had to make a virtually new start in their plans to kill him.

That it was able to do so was due most of all to the somewhat earlier appearance in its ranks of Count Claus Schenk von Stauffenberg. He was a South German, born in 1907. His father had been Chamberlain to the last King of Württemberg, and his mother was descended from General Yorck and from the Prussian Army reformer of the 1807–20 period, Count Neithardt von Gneisnau. In 1926 Stauffenberg joined the 17th Bamberg Cavalry Regiment (the so-called '*Bamberger Reiter*'). When the Nazis came to power he was one of many Army officers who initially accepted them as a lesser evil than the crumbling Weimar regime or a possible Communist dictatorship.

In 1936 he was at the War Academy in Berlin and in 1938 he joined the élite (it had only had 187 members) of the reformed General Staff. That summer he joined the staff of General Erich Hoepner, commanding the 1st Light Division in Wuppertal. This was the division which was to have been diverted on its way through Thuringia to the Czech border, for use by the conspirators of the 'Generals' Plot' of September 1938.

During the war Stauffenberg saw active service in France, Russia and North Africa and held various staff appointments. On April 7, 1942, he was very severely wounded in Tunis, losing his left eye, his right arm and two fingers of his left hand. Yet he reported back for service as soon as his wounds healed and in the summer of 1943 became Chief of Staff, as a lieutenant-colonel, to General Friedrich Olbricht.

All those who knew Stauffenberg personally have joined in praising him as a man of compelling charm and intense, surging vitality. He was a devout Roman Catholic, and out of his religious beliefs sprang a romanticism of outlook which matched his candour and gaiety. Among his surviving friends, Bussche recalls that Stauffenberg seemed to be nearly always laughing—even after he had involved himself in the desperate business of planning Hitler's downfall. At the same time he radiated optimism and inspiration, and he laughed so often quite simply because he loved and enjoyed life. He loved his family and friends, too, horses and the countryside, poetry and the arts, and action of every kind. He was beloved in return by all who knew him and he exercised a powerful magnetism over them. Walter Goerlitz, in his *History of the German General Staff*, wrote simply that Stauffenberg 'had power over men'.

As a young man Stauffenberg had fallen under the influence of the poet Stefan George, who believed in an aristocracy of talent and surrounded himself with young men whom he wanted to form into a cadre of the elect. Reading gave Stauffenberg a depth of character —he might otherwise have developed into a more conventional Teutonic Apollo. At the War Academy he wrote a paper on 'The Defence Against Enemy Parachute Attack' which won him a prize. In his spare moments he studied history, music, architecture. But he remained physically very tough, with great powers of endurance which he fostered without any foolish thought of mortifying the flesh.

So much has already been written about Stauffenberg that it is necessary here only to give the briefest account of his path to leadership of the 1944 conspiracy. He certainly came into touch with anti-Nazis in 1938, and he was disgusted by the Nazis' anti-Semitic campaign which first became fully apparent in November of that year. Early in 1939 he was approached by a former party member who had become a leading anti-Nazi, Count Friedrick Detlev von der Schulenburg, who told him that it was his duty to oppose Hitler in any way that he could. Schulenburg suggested that he should try to get the job of A.D.C. to the Commander-in-Chief, Brauchitsch, and bring his influence to bear on him.

Stauffenberg was unwilling to do this—according to some writers because he did not believe that the German Army would act against Hitler. It may well be, however, that Stauffenberg was to some extent susceptible at this time to the atmosphere among younger officers of overheated enthusiasm that the hated Treaty of Versailles was being torn to shreds.

This did not mean that he wanted war. He was reported to have said of Hitler in 1939: 'The fool is going to make war,' and to have expressed the view that this would be fatal for Germany. But there was nothing exceptional about that. Stauffenberg's anti-Nazism would seem not to have matured or found a focus at this stage. In any case he was extremely busy a few months later, fighting for his country. For a brave soldier, the Polish and French campaigns brought glamour and excitement as well as hard work and hard fighting.

In the summer of 1941 Stauffenberg met Tresckow and Schlabrendorff on the Russian front. He was certainly aware by then of some of the details of the conspiracies being hatched against Hitler. But according to Ritter he had a certain contempt for the older opponents of the Nazis. At the time Beck was more than usually racked by indecision, Hammerstein was sick and growing old, and Goerdeler was burying himself in his paper-plans. Tresckow and Schlabrendorff were different; they were tired of talking and determined to act. Schlabrendorff said that it took only one or two meetings with Stauffenberg to convince both Tresckow and himself that here was a man who could lead the Opposition. What impressed them most was his supreme audacity.

Why then did Stauffenberg do next to nothing, in the way of active opposition, in the next year and a half? The only answer would seem to be that war is always an absorbing affair for the born soldier, and that World War II was a titanic struggle which put matters of apparently lesser importance out of mind. In Russia Stauffenberg was preoccupied with the raising and drilling of anti-Communist Russian units. Hitler may have seemed eminently undesirable by then, but the Soviet Union was a mighty and implacable foe. Stauffenberg may have confused his order of priorities although Bussche believes he was merely biding his time. Why, he may have argued, should Soviet Communism not first be destroyed, and Hitler dealt with afterwards?

What lent this line of thought added weight was the ease with which the Germans found Russian recruits who were ready to fight against Stalin. Another anti-Nazi officer, Goelo von dem Knesebeck, has told me how quickly Russian prisoners responded to decent treatment and how they developed a feudal loyalty to German officers who took trouble with them. The Germans were able to recruit over 800,000 Russians for the so-called 'Vlassov Army'—and this in spite of a total lack of understanding on the part of the Nazi hierarchy and the most appalling cruelties practised by the Nazi security forces in occupied Russia.

In October 1942 Stauffenberg was boldly criticizing Hitler's Eastern policies at a seminar held for staff officers in the Ukrainian town of Winniza. In December he was urging Manstein to join Hitler's opponents. Like others who tried their hand at convincing Manstein, Stauffenberg found him elusive and noncommittal. Early in 1943 Stauffenberg asked to return to active service, and was only then sent as a result to Tunis. This suggests that he had temporarily lost interest in the conspiracy. Only after being badly wounded in Tunis, and in the darkness of his hospital-bed—both his eyes were bandaged for some time—did he come to the conclusion that action must be taken against Hitler and that he must play a leading part in it. Around May 1943 he told his wife: 'You know, I feel I must do something now, to save Germany. We General Staff officers must all accept our share of responsibility.' From this decision he never turned back.

Stauffenberg was first to carry a bomb into Hitler's headquarters at Rastenburg in December 1943, but he had no chance of using it then. He was closely consulted about both the Bussche and Kleist attempts on Hitler's life. He made a point of meeting all the leaders among Hitler's opponents. In talks with them his brother, Berthold, acted as his helper and confidant. Berthold was closer than brothers usually are, and Eberhard Zeller, in his book *The Spirit of Freedom*, quotes an unnamed witness as saying of the brothers:

'We argued, endured, thought, believed, fell silent and so on. We all reacted, according to our strength, shouting or murmuring our answer to the inescapable which we both saw and foresaw. Sometimes, it is true, to judge by their remarks, the Stauffenberg brothers seemed to share the opinions and feelings of the rest of us; and yet one was surprised to discover that in their inner being they were really quite unaffected by it all. They lived, thought, acted, not as men answering a challenge or driven by an external force, but as men following a curious inner certitude . . . They were not at all the victims of compulsion; without this compulsion they would still have fulfilled their destiny.'

This unnamed witness was presumably talking of some time early in 1944, some months at least after Stauffenberg joined General Olbricht at the German Army Office in Berlin. But long before this Olbricht, who had fallen completely under his spell, proposed Stauffenberg as, in effect, 'Chief of Operations' for the final plan to assassinate Hitler and overthrow the Nazi regime. In June 1943 Stauffenberg—then on convalescent leave—was entrusted by Beck and Goerdeler, with the approval of other leaders, with the task of drawing up a complete plan for the military seizure of Berlin after Hitler's death.

This plan was to be known as 'Operation Valkyrie', and it was given a useful 'cover story' for the event of some of its details leaking out. This was that the Home Army must have a cut and dried plan of action for the event of either a mutiny of the S.S. against Hitler or of a mass rising among the millions of foreign slave-labourers who had been deported from their homes and were working in Germany. 'Operation Valkyrie' was, in fact, nominally an official plan—which could be turned against the Nazis.

Stauffenberg set to work with a will. The S.S.—and one has to remember that Hitler's Germany was the worst of all police states —actually outnumbered the troops in and around Berlin. But of these troops—consisting in the main of the Guard Battalion and contingents at the infantry, cavalry, artillery and tank training schools at Doeberitz, Krampnitz, Jueterbog and Wunsdorf—about three-quarters could be expected to carry out their orders without hesitation. These orders would include the seizure of Government buildings, the Berlin radio stations and newspaper offices, and the rounding-up of the S.S. In this the troops would be helped by the Berlin Police Force, which was still commanded by Count Helldorf, with Count Fritz von der Schulenburg as his deputy. The Commandant of the City of Berlin, General Paul von Hase, was a confirmed anti-Nazi, and men favourable to the conspiracy occupied key posts in all the military units in and round the city.

The conspirators had reason to be confident about the implementation of their plans in Berlin. They knew that many of the troops were sick of the war and loathed the S.S., with their smart uniforms, their superior military equipment, superciliousness and swagger. In Berlin, more than in any other place in Germany, the shock-effect of Allied bombing-raids had induced a longing for peace and an awareness that total defeat should be avoided at all costs.

On the other hand, the conspirators could not count on the support of General Friedrich Fromm, the commander of the Home Army. Yet the orders which they drafted had in any event to go out under his name. Fromm had been sounded and it was clear that he was a 'trimmer', who would join the side which was winning in an all-out struggle between Army and S.S., but who would certainly not commit himself in advance.

'Operation Valkyrie' was complete in all its details by August 1943. At the same time as he was working them out, Stauffenberg was using up some of his inexhaustible stock of surplus energy in completing the chain of 'Opposition contacts' which now ran through the whole Army. Only a few of these need be mentioned. In the Army High Command were the Quartermaster-General, General Eduard Wagner; the head of the Organization Department, General Helmuth Stieff; the head of the Ordnance Department, General Fritz Lindemann; and the head of the Foreign Armies Department, Colonel Alexis Freiherr von Roenne. In the High Command of the Armed Forces there was General Erich Fellgiebel, the head of Communications.

In the West the Opposition could count on General Karl von Stuelpnagel, the Military Commander of Paris, and General Freiherr Alexander von Falkenhausen, the Military Governor of Belgium. Moreover, early in 1944 Field Marshal Erwin Rommel, commanding Army Group B in France, was won over to some degree, in that he was ready if needed to assist in arresting Hitler and, in any event, to 'play his part' afterwards. Von Tresckow and his friends could still be implicitly relied upon in Army Group Centre in Russia, and for a time towards the end of 1943 they seemed at last to have secured the support of Field Marshal von Kluge. Berlin and the Home Army were already taken care of; at this stage Canaris was still in charge of the Abwehr.

'Operation Valkyrie' therefore had every prospect of success at the time of the Bussche and Kleist attempts on Hitler's life, and at the time of Stauffenberg's own attempt, in December 1943 (on that occasion Hitler cancelled an intended appearance at a conference on manpower problems). But after the failure of Kleist's attempt the conspirators found no further opportunity, for the next six months, of carrying out the first part of their plan, Hitler's assassination.

With the departure of Canaris from the Abwehr they lost their chief source of information. Hitler seems, moreover, to have been more than usually unapproachable during this period, and his animal-like prescience for sensing undeclared and unidentified enemies around him led to his living in increasing isolation—guarded be a security staff estimated at nearly 3,000.

Some of the Opposition leaders, again, lapsed during this period into vain hopes that a peace could be negotiated 'over Hitler's head'. Von Hassell, for instance, had already gone down on the record in his diary with: 'We must bring off one remaining achievement, of making either the Russians or the Anglo-Americans understand that an intact Germany lies in their interests. . . . I myself prefer the Western game, but would also accept an understanding with Russia.' Von Trott travelled to Switzerland to contact British and American agents, and to urge them to offer a 'fair' peace to a non-Nazi Germany —ostensibly in order to discourage the Opposition from 'turning East'. In addition, Trott wanted the cessation, as a gesture, of all Allied bombing of Berlin.

The former Ambassador to Moscow, Count Werner von der Schulenburg, simultaneously urged an appeal to Stalin. There was even some wild talk of dropping him by parachute behind the Russian lines. But Schulenburg was virtually alone in looking for a reconciliation with Russia; the men of the Opposition were over-whelmingly 'pro-Western' in outlook.

It is a moot point whether the Western Powers should have made some offer of fair peace-terms to Hitler's enemies. It is not at all clear, for one thing, that peace-terms would have helped them to blow Hitler up, or to carry out a *coup d'état*. Of course, they might have been given added confidence and impetus. On the American side Mr. Allen Dulles has made it clear that the conspirators' idea that they could make common cause with the West—after getting rid of Hitler—and hold a 'defensive front' against the Russians, was a chimera. In Dulles's view this 'obsession', as he called it, discouraged both London and Washington from making any promise to the Opposition.

On the British side Mr. Anthony Eden (since then made Earl of Avon) had explained his government's viewpoint in a speech made eighteen months earlier in Edinburgh. He said then: 'The longer the German people continues to support and tolerate the regime which is leading them to destruction, the heavier grows their own direct responsibility for the damage they are doing to the world. Therefore, if any section of the German people really wants to see a return to a German State which is based on respect for law and for the rights of the individual, they must understand that no one will believe them until they have taken active steps to rid themselves of their present regime.'

This was cold comfort indeed, and it might well be argued that von Trott should have stressed the reality of the Tresckow, Schlabrendorff and other efforts to kill Hitler, instead of conveying veiled threats of a separate approach to the Soviet Union. Trott, indeed, went even further than this; either he or an emissary of his saw Madame Kollontay, the Soviet Ambassadress in Stockholm, early in the summer of 1944. Von Kessel's explanation of this move —and he was a close friend of Trott's—was that it was designed to lull growing Soviet suspicions that a 'deal' might be negotiated between Hitler's opponents and the Western Allies. But did the Russians really suspect the imminence of such a deal? Trott, for one, knew that it simply was not on the cards.

There was another, more practical reason why the Western Allies did not want to make promises to Hitler's opponents. For what sort of peace terms would the latter have contemplated? As their elder statesman, Goerdeler produced a series of draft proposals which he thought could serve as a basis for discussion. His last recorded 'peace plan', in mid-1943, proposed that the Allied bombing of Berlin should cease, the Western Allies should halt their plan for landings in Europe, and there should be no invasion of Germany.

In addition, Germany should be given her 1914 frontiers in the East, should retain Austria and the Sudetenland, and should annex the South Tyrol, which then formed—and still forms—part of the Italian province of the Trentino! Alsace-Lorraine was to have an autonomous government which, Goerdeler refused to realize, its inhabitants simply did not want.

According to Ritter, Stauffenberg had these peace terms transmitted to Britain in the spring of 1944. If so, they could only have made the worst possible impression. For they were totally unacceptable to the Western Allies. As for the cessation of Allied bombing of Berlin, it would have been a humane and in many respects sensible step. But it would, undeniably, have made the Russians smell a rat.

Vague talk about a negotiated peace discouraged the Opposition from pressing ahead with its plans during the first half of 1944. As it happened, this lull gave Goerdeler the opportunity to draw up his final list, of June 1944, of members of the Provisional Government which would have succeeded the Nazi regime. This list has already been published in many books, sometimes with small differences. This is what it looked like:

Regent (*Reichsverweser*) and temporary Commander-in-Chief of the Armed Forces: General Ludwig Beck.

State Secretary to the Regent: Count Ulrich Schwerin-Schwanenfeld.

Chancellor: Dr. Carl Goerdeler.

Vice-Chancellor: Wilhelm Leuschner.

Deputy Vice-Chancellor: Jakob Kaiser.

Minister for War: General Friedrich Olbricht, or General Erich Hoepner.

Secretary of State for War: Count Stauffenberg.

Commander-in-Chief of Wehrmacht: Field Marshal von Witzleben.

Minister of the Interior: Julius Leber.

Minister of Economics: Dr. Paul Lejeune-Jung.

Minister of Finance: Johannes Popitz.

Minister of Justice: Joseph Wirmer, or Dr. Carl Sack.

Minister of Education: Eugen Bolz.

Minister of Agriculture: Andreas Hermes, or Dr. Hans Schlange-Schoeningen.

Minister for Reconstruction: Bernhard Letterhaus.

Minister for Foreign Affairs: Ulrich von Hassell.

Chief of Police: General von Tresckow.

Minister of Information: Theodor Haubach.

Some other of the Ministries had alternative candidates marked into Goerdeler's list. Various names were down more than once in the list. Its special interest is that it shows that Hitler's opponents were determined to create an all-party (barring the Nazis and Communists) administration of 'all the talents', which would command wide popular support. Out of 18 key positions, probably 5 would have gone to acknowledged conservatives, 3 or 4 to Social Democrats and either 2 or 3 to members of the defunct Catholic *Zentrum*.

Probably seven members of the Provisional Government would have been nominally 'non-political', although most of them would have been men of conservative upbringing, with a trend towards liberal, enlightened thinking. In general it can be said that this would have been a well-balanced 'team', with a sufficient number of men of action in it to ensure a power of decision. This would have involved the drawing up of a new constitution and the re-establishment of representative government. There is no suggestion, in Goerdeler's final list, that the Opposition had become divided against itself during the difficult first six months of 1944.

In the first week of June Stauffenberg was appointed Chief of Staff to General Fromm. This was a key position, since the conspirators had to depend on the troops of Fromm's Home Army. Surprisingly, Stauffenberg hesitated before accepting the appointment. There is no logical explanation of this; yet he may have realized that he was going to be saddled with too many responsibilities. As Fromm's Chief of Staff, he would have periodic access to Hitler's headquarters and, therefore, the opportunities for killing him. But as the man who had drawn up the 'Operation Valkyrie' plan, he was the obvious person to execute it. Rastenburg and Berlin were nearly 350 miles apart; and obviously he could not be in two places at once.

There was little question, however, that by now Stauffenberg and his friends were champing for action. Stauffenberg was to take up his appointment under Fromm on July 1 and could expect a chance to kill Hitler soon afterwards. But on June 6 came the British and American landings in Normandy. Within a fortnight it became plain that the German armies in France could not contain the Allies, let alone drive them back into the sea. As a result, two contrary lines of thought emerged among the conspirators. Some argued that there was a better chance than ever before of a 'deal' with the Western Allies. Instead of vague plans for landing Allied troops at Cuxhaven and Bremerhaven and welcoming Allied parachute units in a drop round Berlin, there was the prospect of Rommel 'opening the front' to the Anglo-American armies and letting them race through to the Reich.

The opposite view was that, lacking any assurances from the Western Allies, the assassination of Hitler and seizure of power in the Reich had become immensely more urgent than before. In June Stauffenberg sent his close friend, Count Heinrich von Lehndorff, to East Prussia to ask Tresckow's advice. Tresckow was now Chief of Staff of the Second Army on the Russian front and had been summoned to attend a conference in East Prussia. Schlabrendorff was with Tresckow when they met Lehndorff at the latter's home of Steinort. Tresckow told Lehndorff:

'The assassination must be attempted, at any cost. Even should it fail, the attempt to seize power in the capital must be undertaken. We must prove to the world and to future generations that the men of the German resistance movement dared to take the decisive step and to hazard their lives upon it. Compared with this, nothing else matters.'

This answer was decisive for Stauffenberg. For it underlined a factor which had not played much part in the counsels of the conspirators so far. This was that an attempted *coup d'état*, even if it failed, might secure Germany better peace-terms than would otherwise have been the case. Patriots to a man, the conspirators were now clearly confronted with the prospect of sacrificing a great many lives —and not just the life of a single man who would seek to kill Hitler.

Stauffenberg faced a crucial choice, but there is no indication that he hesitated. From July 1 onwards he was ready to take the first chance of killing Hitler and ordering 'Operation Valkyrie' to begin. On the morning of July 1 he told a junior officer: 'There is no point in beating about the bush. I am employing all the means at my disposal for the purpose of committing high treason.' On July 4 he repeated this thought at a meeting in his house in the Wannsee suburb of Berlin, to a small gathering of close friends.

On July 11, 1944, Stauffenberg had a chance of killing Hitler at a conference at the Obersalzberg in Bavaria. He took a bomb with him which, after careful one-handed practice, he was confident of being able to explode. From the Obersalzberg he rang up Olbricht in Berlin and told him that he was ready to go ahead. With him was an adjutant, Captain Friedrich-Carl Klausing, who was standing by with a car, ready to drive him to the neighbouring airfield of Freilassing the moment that the bomb exploded. But Olbricht, and this was sheer tragedy, advised against the attempt on the grounds that Himmler was not present. On July 12 it was decided at a meeting of the conspirators that in future there would be no question of waiting to kill the 'two birds with one stone'.

Stauffenberg had his next chance on July 15, this time at the Rastenburg headquarters. He flew there with an unsuspecting Fromm (it would have been all to the good if Fromm could be blown up along with Hitler) and Klausing. Stauffenberg sent Olbricht a preliminary message, announcing his safe arrival. Olbricht accordingly issued the 'Valkyrie' order at about 11 a.m., and troops began to move into Berlin. At 1 p.m. the Rastenburg conference began and Stauffenberg left the conference chamber to tell Olbricht that Hitler's death was imminent.

But when he returned to the room he found that Hitler had left it! Once again the Fuehrer's uncanny premonition of danger had saved him. Stauffenberg at once telephoned Olbricht and 'Operation Valkyrie' was called off. To Fromm, on the latter's return from East Prussia, Olbricht was able to explain more or less convincingly that this had only been a training exercise.

On July 18 Stauffenberg learnt that he would attend another conference at Rastenburg on July 20. But in the weeks preceding this the conspirators had suffered three more setbacks, two of which were more obviously dangerous than Stauffenberg's failure to explode his bombs at the Obersalzberg and Rastenburg. On July 4 the prominent Social Democratic opponent of Hitler, Adolf Reichwein, was arrested by the Gestapo after a meeting with members of the Communist underground at which a Nazi informer was present. The Communists were rounded up too, and on July 5 the Gestapo arrested Julius Leber. This was a shocking blow; Leber was in the inner circle of resisters and knew all about the plans for killing Hitler and seizing power.

Furthermore, he was a close personal friend of Stauffenberg's and his arrest could well have impaired the latter's judgement. In the next few days Stauffenberg was heard to say several times: 'We need Leber, we must get him out.' And at any moment Leber might break down under torture or drugs and give the Gestapo bloodhounds some clue as to the size and nature of the conspiracy. To Leber's eternal credit he kept his mouth shut and his captors at bay.

On July 17 Field Marshal Rommel's staff-car was shot up by a British fighter on the Livarot-Vimoutiers road in Northern France. The driver was killed and Rommel was terribly badly wounded and put completely out of action. Only five days before this he had met von Kluge, who had been transferred to France to replace Field Marshal Gerd von Rundstedt as Commander-in-Chief West, and had a most friendly talk with him. Kluge agreed that action against Hitler was now a stark necessity, and on July 15 Rommel sent an ultimatum to the Fuehrer, telling him that the Western Allies were about to break through in France and calling on him to 'draw your own conclusions from this without delay'. Rommel remarked afterwards: 'I have given him his last chance. If he does not take it, we shall act.'

There had been divided views among the conspirators about the wisdom of securing Rommel's support. He was tremendously popular in the Army and something of a national hero. A great many Germans would not have regarded it as treachery if Rommel had sought peace terms from the Western Allies and proclaimed an armistice. Virtually the whole Army (save the fighting units of the *Waffen* S.S.) would have accepted his leadership after Hitler's assassination.

Of course, Rommel was not a true opponent of Nazism, in that he was ready to act only when he judged that Germany's military position was hopeless. But neither was he—as he has often been depicted—a 'Nazi General' and a devoted follower of Hitler's. Although he wanted nothing to do with assassination, he was all in favour of the overthrow of the Nazi regime. He was essentially a patriot, whose intellectual capacity was circumscribed and whose understanding of his country's political problems in no way matched his military genius. His value to Hitler's opponents would have been very great on July 20.

General von Falkenhausen was relieved of his military command on July 15. But this was a matter of minor importance compared with the issuing, on July 17, of an order for Carl Goerdeler's arrest. According to his biographer, Gerhard Ritter, someone betrayed to the Nazis the fact that Goerdeler had been drawing up lists for a provisional government, following the overthrow of the Nazi regime. Goerdeler was, of course, down on his own lists as future Chancellor. Unlike the doughty Leber, Goerdeler was a garrulous man whose courage and integrity would not prevent him from saying too much if he were caught (later events proved the truth of this). In addition, he was quite liable to be carrying on his person one of his many 'peace plans' or lists of conspirators. These plans and lists had been multiplying of late. Goerdeler's descendants have, since the war, come into possession of the ninetieth draft of his declaration to the German people, which was to have been published after a successful *coup d'état*.

As it happened, Goerdeler at first showed something of the ability of a Sinn Feiner in the Irish Civil War to keep 'on the run'. He was sheltered first by a niece in Potsdam, then moved on July 19 to Hersfeld, and from there went to a series of friends in and near Berlin. He had the good sense not to show his face on July 20 and he successfully remained hidden for nearly four weeks in all.

Stauffenberg was in no way deterred by the arrest of Leber, the removal of Rommel from the scenes and the flight of Goerdeler. These reverses merely strengthened his determination. On July 20 he proceeded to carry out his part of the conspiracy with the blend of perceptiveness, efficiency and daring which might have been expected of this remarkable man. The dramatic events of July 20 have been described so often that it is not necessary to give more than an outline of them here.

At 6 a.m. on July 20 Stauffenberg drove out to Rangsdorf airfield, south of Berlin. He had wrapped his bomb in a shirt and placed it in his brief-case. It was the same type of bomb as that used by Tresckow and Schlabrendorff in March 1943, and it was timed to go off within ten minutes of the detonating process being set in motion, and the capsule being broken which would release the acid into the mechanism. The bomb had been prepared by Stauffenberg with the utmost care during the night of July 19-20.

Stauffenberg's plane took off for Rastenburg at 7 a.m. and reached its destination at 10.15 a.m. Accompanying him was an adjutant, Lieutenant Werner von Haeften, who instructed the pilot of the plane to be ready to take off on the return flight to Berlin at any time after midday.

Stauffenberg's first action on arriving at the 'Wolf's Lair' headquarters in Rastenburg was to see Erich Fellgiebel, the general in charge of communications. Fellgiebel's task was to transmit to the conspirators in Berlin the news of Hitler's assassination, and then to block all communications coming to or leaving Rastenburg for as long as possible. This would give the conspirators in Berlin the maximum start over the S.S. and over the Nazi generals at Rastenburg.

The conference which Stauffenberg was attending was put forward from 1 p.m. to 12.30 p.m., because Mussolini was due to arrive for a private meeting with Hitler at 2.30 or 3 p.m. The conference took place in the *Gaestebaracke* (literally, 'guest barrack'), a long, one-storey wooden building. Its walls had been given a casing of concrete during the previous winter to provide protection from incendiary and small high-explosive bombs. The conference chamber was about thirty-five feet long and fifteen feet across. The room had ten windows, all of which were open on the morning of July 20. It was a very hot day.

On his way to the conference chamber Stauffenberg stopped at the telephone exchange in the *Gaestebaracke* and told the sergeant-major in charge that he was expecting a telephone call from Berlin which involved information for the Fuehrer. He should accordingly be informed the moment that the call came through. Stauffenberg thus had a ready-made excuse for leaving the conference chamber after planting the bomb there. He made his arrangements with the sergeant-major in a loud voice in front of Field Marshal Keitel, who would be master-of-ceremonies at the conference. He and Keitel entered the conference chamber together. The time was 12.36 or 12.37 p.m.

Just before this conversation with the sergeant-major Stauffenberg had broken the capsule in the bomb and so set the mechanism working. In the conference chamber he leaned the brief-case against an oak support of the conference table, close to where a staff officer, Colonel Heinz Brandt, was sitting (the same Brandt who had unsuspectingly carried Tresckow's two bombs with him in March 1943 on the flight from Smolensk to Rastenburg). Brandt was sitting only three places away from Hitler, to his right. The brief-case with the bomb was, in fact, resting on the near side to Hitler of the oak support and no more than twelve feet away from him.

Allegedly, Stauffenberg muttered something to Brandt about an incoming telephone call. Keitel did not see him go, but, looking round the conference chamber a moment later, noticed his absence and recalled his conversation with the sergeant-major at the telephone exchange. As a result he suspected nothing, but Brandt, moving about in his seat, kicked the brief-case. It fell or was pushed on to the far side of the oak support against which it was resting. This almost certainly saved Hitler's life.

At 12.42 the bomb exploded with a gigantic crash. Most of the roof of the building fell in and all the windows were blown out. Chaos reigned within. The official stenographer, Berger, was killed. Three officers present, including the unlucky Brandt, died subsequently from their injuries. Two others were badly wounded, and four more rather more lightly. Hitler had his hair set on fire, his right leg badly burned, his right arm temporarily paralysed and both eardrums damaged. But he was alive.

This was something which Stauffenberg could not have foreseen. He saw the building collapsing and he later described the explosion as equivalent to a direct hit by a 150-millimetre shell. Within two minutes of the explosion taking place he and Haeften were on their way to the airfield. They were challenged twice, at the inner and outer barricades, but each time bluffed their way through. At the outer barricade the guard-commander insisted on confirming, with the duty officer, their right to leave. The duty officer happened to be the Deputy Commandant, Colonel von Moellendorf, an anti-Nazi and a friend of Stauffenberg's. He gave the order to let Stauffenberg's car through. By about 1.10 p.m. Stauffenberg's plane was airborne and on its way back to Berlin.

General Fellgiebel had meanwhile telephoned the conspirators in Berlin, who this time—as a result of the confusions of July 15—were waiting for news of the assassination before putting 'Operation Valkyrie' into action. Fellgiebel's call came through shortly after 1 p.m. and was received by the head of the Signals Branch of Army headquarters, General Fritz Thiele. He was with others of the conspirators at the time, in the Defence Ministry in the Bendler-strasse. Fellgiebel told Thiele that the attempt on Hitler's life had been made, but indicated that he was still alive.

For fear of Gestapo tapping of telephone-lines, Fellgiebel wrapped up his information in guarded language, and some uncertainty lingered in the minds of the conspirators present, Olbricht and Hoepner. They waited for further confirmation of what had happened at Rastenburg. But this was precisely what they would not get. For Fellgiebel was now carrying out the second part of his instructions, which was to block all communications in and out of Rastenburg. He was doing this with such remarkable success that Hitler's head-quarters were isolated from the rest of the world for around two and a half hours.

The first failure on July 20 was to kill Hitler. Nobody could be blamed for that. It could only be classified as an 'Act of God', although it is not possible to think of any reason why the Almighty should have preserved Hitler's life. But the second failure, to order 'Operation Valkyrie' to begin as soon as Fellgiebel gave the word, was culpable. Not only did Olbricht and Hoepner do nothing, but Beck did not arrive at the Bendlerstrasse until nearly four o'clock in the afternoon. He was dressed in civilian clothes, and looked drawn and harassed. General von Witzleben, who was designated by the conspirators to become Commander-in-Chief of the armed forces, arrived even later. This lack of urgency matched Olbricht's and Hoepner's total inaction. Practically nothing, indeed, was done before Stauffenberg himself arrived shortly before five o'clock at the Bendlerstrasse.

Stauffenberg might still have saved the day. But an hour earlier Fromm, on being rather weakly told by Olbricht that Hitler was dead, had telephoned Rastenburg, and learnt from Keitel that this was not the case. Stauffenberg now had to arrest Fromm, and placed Hoepner in command of the Home Army. Several other Army officers and members of the S.S., who were in the building and who remained loyal to Hitler, had to be arrested too.

All this wasted time and the conspirators had none to spare. Now, von Hase, the City Commandant, was alerted and at once gave orders for the Guard Battalion to move into Berlin. Count Helldorf was waiting for the order to bring his Berlin Police into action. Stauffenberg, splendidly active, now telephoned Paris and there Stuelpnagel acted with dispatch, ordering the arrest of all S.S. men in the city and supervising their rounding-up.

Beck next—it was shortly after six o'clock—telephoned Kluge at La Roche Guyon, German Army headquarters in France. Kluge, as usual, could not make up his mind. He promised to ring back in half an hour, and never did. At this moment, in the early evening of a lovely summer's day, all was still not lost for the conspirators. But their plans were moving too slowly.

In Berlin a purely fortuitous event turned the day against them. A member of the Nazi Propaganda Ministry, Dr. Hans Hagen, was giving a lecture that afternoon to the officers of the Guard Battalion, on the mundane subject of 'National Socialist Guidance Questions'. Among those who listened to his lecture was Major Otto Remer, the battalion's commanding officer. Late in the afternoon, and while Hagen was still with him, Remer received the conspirators' instructions to march into the centre of Berlin.

Now, as befitted an active member of the Propaganda Ministry, Hagen had his ear well to the ground and had heard rumours of an impending military *Putsch*. Earlier in the day he had seen what he took to be the retired Commander-in-Chief, ex-Field Marshal von Brauchitsch, driving through the streets of Berlin in a military car. He thought this odd (it was, since Brauchitsch was not in Berlin at all that day!), but the orders given to Remer confirmed his impression that something was afoot. He mounted a bicycle and pedalled to the Propaganda Ministry.

There he managed, after some trouble, to get an interview with Dr. Goebbels. Goebbels first satisfied himself that Hitler was alive, then sent for Remer, who arrived in his office shortly after six o'clock —just when the conspirators in the Bendlerstrasse were at last coming to grips with the situation.

Goebbels had some difficulty in convincing Remer that he was being used as a pawn in a conspiracy against the Nazi regime. In the end he managed to telephone Hitler on his private line, and get Remer to speak to him in person. Hitler's orders to the commander of the Guard Battalion were to crush the revolt immediately, and to take orders only from Goebbels, Himmler or General Reineke, a strong Nazi who was serving in Berlin at the time. Instead of marching to the help of the conspirators, the Guard Battalion now marched to arrest them.

This was the turning-point of July 20, 1944. The rest was tragedy. At 9 p.m. the Radio Deutschlandsender station—which the conspirators had failed to seize—broadcast the news that Hitler would address the German people later that night. The broadcast was actually relayed at 1 a.m. on July 21, when Hitler announced the failure of a plot by 'a very small clique of ambitious officers, devoid of conscience and criminally stupid'. But long before that the conspiracy had been snuffed out in Berlin. Its chief members had been rounded up in the Bendlerstrasse by the S.S., with Remer's backing.

Stauffenberg, Olbricht and others were shot by a firing-squad from the Guard Battalion in the courtyard of the Defence Ministry. Beck was allowed to try to commit suicide—he only wounded himself badly and was finished off by a sergeant. Hoepner and others were arrested, many of them having drifted off to their homes, as Witzleben and Canaris did. Fromm had an adventurous day; he was arrested by Olbricht, then rescued by Remer's men. Finally he gave the orders for the shooting of Stauffenberg and others. He knew that they could incriminate him by telling the Gestapo that he had known about the plot. This the Nazis realized too, and it was they who executed Fromm.

In Paris, Munich and Vienna, where the conspirators had seized power and locked up the S.S., the revolt came to an abrupt end after Hitler's broadcast. A strange inertia descended on the men who, like Stuelpnagel, had executed their orders so promptly and efficiently, in these three cities. Such was the daemonic power of Hitler's name and personality. The S.S. were set loose again, and in Paris they actually sat down to a late-night drinking party with some of their ex-captors.

It has been estimated that around 7,000 arrests were made on and after July 20, 1944, and that nearly 5,000 of Hitler's opponents were killed by shooting, hanging, garrotting and torture. A number of them committed suicide rather than fall into Nazi hands. Among them was Tresckow, who blew himself up with a hand-grenade, and Rommel, who was given the choice of poisoning himself or of standing trial before the People's Court—in which case the Nazis would have taken reprisals against his wife and family. Kluge, too, poisoned himself, when ordered to report to Berlin.

Witzleben was executed by being strangled slowly to death, suspended from a meat-hook. Goerdeler was caught in West Prussia on August 12, but he was not hanged until February 2, 1945. In gaol he continued to wax garrulous and, according to Ritter, conceived the fantastic idea of mentioning the names of dozens of well-known people connected with the Opposition, in the vain hope of dissuading the Nazis from carrying out their mopping-up operations.

Ritter believes that Goerdeler's disclosures, which were not made under torture, helped the Nazis to round up thousands of their enemies. So out of touch had Goerdeler become that he addressed an appeal to Hitler a few days after his arrest, urging him to let his German opponents join him again in forming a truly national front to hold back the foreign foes who were at their gates.

Why did the July 20, 1944, *coup d'état* fail? It could be said that it failed because Colonel Brandt kicked Stauffenberg's brief-case to the wrong side of the oak support of the conference-room table at Rastenburg. But the *coup d'état* could still have succeeded after that. Nor is it enough explanation to say—as Schlabrendorff did to me years later—'History is accurate. If the July 1944 attempt had succeeded, Germany—the real Germany—would have beaten Hitler by a trick. History does not happen that way.'

Schlabrendorff was nearer the mark when he said: 'We were not natural revolutionaries; for our strength lay in the officers and officials who took part. Blood should have run—instead the men of July 20 said to all and sundry: Have a seat.'

'Have a seat' was what Beck, Witzleben and Hoepner did themselves. Although they had clear instructions, Hoepner (and Olbricht) failed to take concrete action during those fateful hours when Stauffenberg was on his way back from the 'Wolf's Lair'. All of these men were chosen for key roles and only one of them, Olbricht, was still on active service. They were out of touch, tired, old and lacking sense of purpose. These men should have had Berlin in their hands by the time Stauffenberg arrived back from Rastenburg. They did nothing; and failed to seize either the radio stations or Gestapo headquarters. Men like Oster and Canaris were never even called to the Bendlerstrasse.

Stauffenberg was called upon to be both the arm and the brain of the conspiracy. Yet he very nearly succeeded, and that is all too often forgotten. Not Hitler alone, but his regime too, were saved by fortuitous circumstances. 'Operation Valkyrie' failed, but it was boldly, brilliantly conceived. Those who took part in it set an example of moral courage which will live on for countless generations of Germans down the ages.

eleven

The German Opposition in Perspective

> 'Praising what is lost
> Makes the remembrance dear.'
>
> WILLIAM SHAKESPEARE, *All's Well That Ends Well*

ONLY a handful of Hitler's opponents survived the atrocious blood-bath which took place after July 20, 1944. Survival was invariably a matter of pure luck. Joseph Mueller and Hjalmar Schacht, for instance, were included in that distinguished band of 'hostages' whom Hitler supposedly intended to use as some kind of pawns in negotiating with the Western Powers, and who were rudely hustled round the Austrian and Bavarian Alps during the closing weeks of the war. Eugen Gerstenmaier argued his case so convincingly in the dock that the People's Court did not sentence him to death. Otto John—who was to serve the West German Government after the war, and be disgraced when he apparently defected to Communist East Germany—flew to Madrid in a Lufthansa plane, established contact with the British Secret Service, and reached England via Lisbon.

Axel von dem Bussche lay badly wounded in hospital from February 1944 onwards and suspicion never fell on him. Life, as he has said since the war, was a sort of serial nightmare to him—relieved only by such comic incidents as his receipt in hospital at Christmas 1944 'from a grateful Fuehrer' of a hamper of food and drink. It was accompanied by the Fuehrer's card, edged in gold—'The sort of thing,' as Bussche put it, 'which I thought was only done by elderly roués sending presents to their mistresses.'

Fabian von Schlabrendorff's survival was nothing short of miraculous. He was brutally tortured by the Gestapo, confronted

250

with the corpse of Tresckow, his dearest friend and mentor, which was burned in front of his eyes. Like so many of the resisters, he resolutely refused to betray a single one of his friends, and only brought his tortures to an end by 'confessing' that he was to have played a part in the replacement of Hitler by a Field Marshal (by then the Gestapo knew all about Witzleben, Rommel and Kluge, but they certainly did not want the German people to know that the two latter had been among Hitler's enemies).

Even so, one must suppose that Schlabrendorff was always certain to be sentenced to death and executed. The documents of his case were, in fact, in the hand of Roland Freisler, the President of the People's Court, when a British plane bombed the court building in Berlin. Freisler was killed, the documents were destroyed, and Schlabrendorf lived on to escape from his gaolers in the last days of the war.

The heroism of the men of the German Opposition to Hitler after capture is an integral part of their epic. Too much has been made by Wheeler-Bennett in his *Nemesis of Power* of the shamefaced appearance of ex-Field Marshal von Witzleben in the dock, and the sheer, fatuous foolishness of ex-General Hoepner under interrogation. Witzleben was a very sick man. In addition, his gaolers deprived him of his braces and his false teeth. In court he clutched at his trousers and mumbled toothlessly, making a perfect target for Freisler's hectoring wit.

Hoepner, indeed, seems to have lost his nerve. He refused to take the chance of suicide offered him by General Fromm, murmuring that he did not think he 'had done anything very bad'. In the dock he cut a wretched figure, although it is possible that he was under the influence of drugs administered by his gaolers. But the cases of Witzleben and Hoepner were exceptional, and in any case both died bravely. So well did other conspirators defend themselves that, according to one eye-witness, the impression was created that the men who were answering accusations were the members of the People's Court, and not the prisoners in the dock.

The Gestapo spared no effort to make their prisoners look silly and contemptible in court. Many were deprived of braces and neckties. Some were not allowed to shave. Some, like Count Marogna-Redwitz, were brought into court shortly after being beaten up, with livid bruises and sticking-plaster on their faces. Yet plenty of them gave at least as good as they got, in face of Freisler's relentless bullying. When Freisler screamed at Joseph Wirmer: 'You will be in Hell soon!' the latter replied with massive irony: 'It will be a pleasure for me to know that you will soon be following me there.'

The youthful Hans von Haeften, when Freisler shouted: 'What is your view of the Fuehrer?' at him, answered: 'I regard him as the personification of evil.' Erich Fellgiebel's retort to Freisler was: 'You must hurry up getting us hanged, Herr President, or you will be hanged before us.' Often, during the court proceedings, the wit of the accused men left Freisler literally foaming at the mouth with rage.

Epic indeed are the last letters of Helmuth James von Moltke, which were smuggled out of prison to his wife and were published in 1950. They radiate the writer's quiet courage and gentle uprightness. In one of them Moltke recounted how Freisler said to him: 'Only in one respect are we Nazis and Christianity the same; we want the whole man.' Moltke found his judges a little shocked by his calmness and good-humour. He reiterated his certain belief that he and his friends had chosen the right path in their search for the renewal of all that was good in Germany and the German people. He believed that the Christian ethic would emerge triumphant in the end, and that right and justice would prevail. The prison pastor, Poelchau, said that Moltke went to his death a happy man. He added: 'He had become a brother to me.'

The stoicism of Moltke and the rest is all the more remarkable when it is remembered that they stood in the dock as traitors to their country and were condemned to a traitor's death. Here was a vast difference between the roles of Hitler's opponents in Germany and of Hitler's enemies in the foreign countries occupied by the Nazis. The resisters of the French Maquis, of Marshal Tito's Partisan Army, of the Dutch, Norwegian and other national resistance movements, were regarded by most of their countrymen as patriots and heroes. How much easier was it for them to be brave and self-sacrificing! They were sure of recognition.

Not so the men of the German Opposition. And, in spite of their courage and steadfastness, pictures of them during the last months of their lives betray a certain apprehensiveness, a sense and foretaste of doom. The furrows on Beck's brow match the drawn lines on

Goerdeler's face. Stauffenberg's repose was exceptional. Part of the heroism of the resisters lay in their doing what they believed they had to do, knowing that the odds were against them and the consequences of failure would be indescribably horrible for them.

The desperately uphill nature of their quest has been underlined, unintentionally, by Field Marshal von Rundstedt's biographer, General Guenther Blumentritt. What a subject for biography—the standardized Prussian automaton which was Rundstedt, the man who refused to think for his country! Blumentritt wrote: 'It is altogether Utopian to imagine that a small Army of 100,000 men could have prevented this [Nazi] movement in a nation of 68,000,000. ... How can an Army, bound by its oath, get rid of a man who at that time had a good 75 per cent of the people behind him.' Blumentritt's view was that 'It is rare in the history of states that generals have overthrown those governments which they did not approve of, and have summoned new ones. In the old Prusso-German Army in particular, the sense of unquestioning allegiance and absolute obedience had been deeply ingrained for centuries.'

Rundstedt was not one of Hitler's favourites and was ready, in private, to make jokes about the 'Bohemian Corporal'. But he never lifted a finger against the Nazi tyranny. He should not necessarily be blamed for this—plenty of good Germans decided that, once war was joined, their first duty was to serve the State. Far more deplorable was Rundstedt's action in reading a valedictory oration at the state funeral of Rommel, his old comrade-in-arms, who had been forced at Hitler's orders to poison himself like a rat. This Blumentritt did not mention in his book.

Aware that the odds were against them, Hitler's opponents recognized the utter ruthlessness of the Nazis. The men of the Social Democratic and Communist undergrounds were soonest aware of this. Their persecution began from the day that the Nazis came to power. The Roman Catholic and Evangelical churchmen who opposed Hitler, too, learnt quickly enough what the true nature of Nazism was. To the conservatives and soldiers realization often came rather more slowly, in that there was a tendency among them—down to the middle of the war—to regard the Nazi regime as still preferable to the obvious alternatives of Weimar-type democracy or Communist dictatorship.

But the conservatives and soldiers learnt one of the bitterest lessons of all—after July 20, 1944, when their wives and children were arrested. Four- and five-year-old Stauffenbergs, Tresckows, Hofackers and others were thrust into the 'Children's Concentration Camp' of Bad Sachsa. There they endured air raids, illness, lice and were given new names—so that their fathers' families should be wiped out. The small Stauffenbergs were to be called 'Meister', the Hofackers 'Franke'. Hitler did not hesitate to visit his wrath on women and children.

There was another factor which made the struggle of Hitler's opponents so desperate—lack of recognition abroad. The Oxford historian, A. L. Rowse, has written bluntly: 'The Generals would certainly have got rid of him [Hitler], if we had not presented him with success after success on a platter.' This was one side of the picture, formed by sensible Germans too, of Western indecision in the years up to the outbreak of war.

The other was the greater interest shown by the West in the Nazis than in their German opponents. Sir John Simon and Lord Hailsham, prominent members of the British Government, received the Nazi racial crank, Rosenberg, in 1933. Two years later Simon and the British Foreign Secretary, Mr. Anthony Eden, called on Hitler. In 1936 it was the turn of the American flying ace and national hero, Charles Lindbergh, to visit him, and in 1937 that of the 'Grand Old Man' of the British Labour Party, George Lansbury.

The former British Prime Minister, Mr. David Lloyd George, came out with a paean of praise for the Nazis. Eden's successor, Lord Halifax, considered military action unjustifiable when Hitler tore up the Treaty of Versailles and marched into the Rhineland, on the grounds that the Germans were 'only walking into their own back-yard'. Both of the London Sunday newspapers, the *Observer* and the *Dispatch*, supported the German entry into the Rhineland, while the London *Times* and *Daily Express* set out to see what was good in Nazism. 'The worst blows suffered by the forces of resistance came,' Rudolf Pechel noted, 'not from Germans but from abroad.'

This continued to happen after July 20, 1944. Winston Churchill made one of his less fortunate remarks about 'Germans killing one another', while the *New York Times* and *Herald Tribune* spared no tear for Hitler's opponents. The latter paper wrote that Americans would not, on the whole, regret that the bomb did not kill Hitler. Among many American leaders there was a curious notion that nothing good could come out of German aristocrats and soldiers—or aristocrats and soldiers anywhere else. Presumably they forgot the parts played in the American Revolution by the Marquis de Lafayette and General George Washington.

The American argument on the subject of the July conspiracy was not entirely irrational. Its essence was that, had the revolt been successful, it would have only meant that the Nazi regime would have been replaced by one which was conservative, even obscurantist and reactionary. Such a regime might have flatly refused to recognize the validity of the Casablanca Declaration or the reality of the Grand Alliance against Germany. It might have sought to play off East against West, and so prolong the war. It might have been undemocratic, unenlightened and inimical to the Western Allies, and it would have sought—on Stauffenberg's and Goerdeler's own showing—to cling on to Austria, the Sudetenland, Posen and the Polish Corridor, and Upper Silesia.

Such a regime, it was argued, would have striven to defeat what was becoming the main Allied war aim, which was that Germany should be deprived of sufficient military and economic power to ensure that she would never again wage aggressive war.

There was some justification for these suspicions, which were shared with the Americans by both the Russians and the British. Hitler's 'secret weapon', for instance, may well have been the diplomatic one—which he never used—of playing off East against West and splitting the Grand Alliance. It was conceivable that some of the conspirators might think along the same lines. The conspirators, at least, would have sought a negotiated peace (which, incidentally, would have left the map of Europe in a somewhat healthier state than is the case today!).

A Beck-Goerdeler regime would equally certainly have tried to keep German-speaking areas within the Reich, although survivors of the Opposition think that major territorial concessions would eventually have had to be made. Thus Albrecht von Kessel, one of the anti-Nazis of the Foreign Office, visualized that a Beck-Goerdeler regime would have had to negotiate with the Grand Alliance as a whole, including the Soviet Union, and that this would have meant enemy occupation of the Reich, the controlled disarmament of Germany, and the cession of Upper Silesia, East Prussia, Austria and the Sudetenland.

'Even so,' Kessel added, 'this would have been a great deal better than what did happen. In particular, the amount of German territory occupied by the Russians would have been restricted. The balance of power in Central Europe would not have been so rudely disturbed.'

A Beck-Goerdeler regime might not have been able to secure orderly internal government at the outset. Some of the conspirators foresaw a civil war between the still powerful remnants of the Nazi Party and the new civil administration. The Russians would no doubt have tried to foment a Communist rising in those parts of Germany which their troops did not occupy, and would have contrived to install a puppet Communist regime in their own 'zone'.

This is, of course, speculation. What is more certain is that the Beck-Goerdeler regime would not have introduced democratic government of the standard Western pattern. Goerdeler visualized a form of 'popular oligarchy', with the population divided into different categories of citizens qualifying to elect and be elected to different representative bodies, on different levels of administration. The 'Kreisauers', indeed, would have opposed Goerdeler's plans, but what would have happened? The Western Allies could only be sure that the introduction of a Western-type democratic system into Germany could not be guaranteed.

The fear that a Beck-Goerdeler regime would have tried to play off East against West was almost certainly overdone. It was partly based on a misreading of the character and aims of Stauffenberg. According to Wheeler-Bennett, for instance, Stauffenberg was 'essentially an "Easterner" by orientation, and before him there shone in all its glittering enticement the vision of a Germany and a Russia liberated from despotism, free and united . . . but for what purpose? For what other purpose than to dominate Europe, if not militarily, at least by an economic hegemony? And thus the dream of the German-Russian collaboration transcends alike the policies of Kaiser, Fuehrer and conspirators in Germany.'

Allen Dulles, too, believed that Stauffenberg was inclined towards seeking agreement with the East and that he was influenced by

Stalin's high-sounding but deceitful phrase: 'Hitlers may come and go, but the German people and State survives.' Dulles thought that Allied saturation-bombing of German cities, while serving one purpose in damaging the morale of the civil population, turned many Germans' thoughts towards a future alliance with Russia. He thought, too, that Stauffenberg would have favoured the establishment of a half-way house in Germany on the road to Communism, by means of a 'revolution of workers, soldiers and farmers'. On the German side Gisevius quotes Stauffenberg as asking rhetorically whether there was 'anything more to be done with the West'.

Opponents of Hitler who are still living mostly reject the views of Wheeler-Bennett, Dulles and Gisevius. 'Stauffenberg was never in favour of a Russo-German *entente*,' Schlabrendorff told me. 'If you consider his background, why should he have been? He was imbued with the traditions of his Catholic, South German family. He was devoted to Western culture. Among Hitler's chief enemies only Fritz von der Schulenburg was a protagonist of the Eastern alliance; and among some of the Prussians there were a few less important people who saw some sense in this. Otherwise—some Social Democrats may have thought about an "understanding" with the Soviet Union, but this did not mean a sell-out to Stalin.'

Von dem Bussche's view of Stauffenberg's alleged 'eastern orientation' was more colloquially caustic—'Goodness me; Claus was much too wise to "get fixed". What interested him was the question: Germany, Bridge or Battleground between East and West? This was a question which we *had* to look at realistically, and I believe that we were right to try to do so.

'Nobody needed a crystal ball to guess that the United States, United Kingdom and Soviet Union (whom *we* Germans, by making war, made bedfellows) would break apart some day. And what was to happen to Germany then? Was it to be split between East and West, or was it simply to become a vacuum? Claus's interest in an *understanding* with Russia might be regarded today as something wicked. But we have to remember that then, as now, Germany had quite a problem to solve—how to settle down on livable, neighbourly terms with the Soviet Union.'

Schlabrendorff and Bussche knew Stauffenberg well. Historians who speculated about his intentions did not. Gisevius disliked him, but probably because Stauffenberg distrusted this ex-Gestapo factotum and refused to take him into his confidence. The Western sympathies of men like Beck and Goerdeler, Leber and Popitz, Leuschner and Tresckow, Oster and Canaris, are beyond all doubt. The vast majority of Germans felt their nation to be an integral part of Western civilization. Had the July 1944 plot succeeded, the odds are that the new Germany would have turned increasingly to the West. A contrary view is simply untenable.

Bussche has drawn attention to another source of foreign misunderstanding of the German Opposition to Hitler. This was the belief, fostered by ignorance of conditions in Germany, that Hitler's enemies were animated by simple, clear-cut motives. In fact, the desire to oppose Hitler was built up out of every sort of instinct, ingrained belief, emotion or even prejudice.

The churchmen opposed Hitler because he was anti-Christian, because he was ruthless and cruel, because he had launched a world war, because his minions were undermining the foundations of the average Christian congregation and the whole Christian community. The Social Democrats opposed Hitler, because to them he represented reaction, the rejection of humanitarianism and political progress, the embodiment of oligarchic principles backed by the bayonet and the jackboot. The young people who revolted against Nazism did so primarily because they regarded it as the antithesis of their ideals of freedom and true comradeship, a Juggernaut which mowed down all those who refused to be regimented.

The motives of Hitler's conservative and military opponents were more complex. They were aware of his loathing for traditions and institutions which were dear to them. They regarded him as a gross and overbearing parvenu, and his brown-shirts largely as louts recruited from the dregs of the population. Some turned against him because of his persecutions of the Jews in Germany; others only after the bigger and more terrible persecutions of the Jews of occupied countries began.

Others, again, were first impelled to question Hitler's policies and purpose because of his conduct of the war. Others had family links with Britain, America or France. Many of the conservatives and soldiers who were, ultimately, sickened by Hitler and all his works still could not bring themselves to oppose his government in time of

war. Such men sometimes took utterly needless risks in battle, pre-
ferring to die fighting rather than commit suicide or conspire against
a regime which was supported by the majority of the German people.

The ignorance of this great majority of the German people was
often as much a hindrance to Hitler's opponents as the ceaseless
activity of the Gestapo or the awesome influence of Hitler's dominating personality. How many Germans shut their eyes to Hitler's
misdeeds and real intentions! In the Munich area alone more than
1,000,000 people knew about Dachau concentration camp, and
charabanc-loads of stolid citizens used to be carried out at the week-
ends on an excursion which was by way of going to the *Dachauer
Moos*—a bleak piece of moorland—but the real purpose of which
was to allow those taking part to gawp through the grim gates of the
camp. But in Munich, Dachau was simply an unsuitable subject for
conversation, and precious few of the citizens of Munich thought it
was a subject about which they had a right and a duty to protest.

A year or two before the outbreak of World War II, I can
remember a Bavarian count—a non-Nazi—refusing even to glance
at a book written about Nazism by an Englishman. I can remember
a German-Jewish school-teacher refusing to discuss the errors of
Hitler's foreign policy, on the grounds that she was the 'servant of
her State'. She went later to the gas-chambers.

How many Germans, when at last learning of one or other of the
myriad atrocities perpetrated by the Nazis, commented: 'If only the
Fuehrer knew about *that*!' And how difficult, even impossible, was
it for such Germans—with their inborn longing to be directed and
regimented—to understand that the Fuehrer not only knew all about
what was going on, but was the fountain-head of Nazi oppression in
all of its most brutal forms! The docility, dumb ignorance and wrong-
mindedness of the mass of the German people between 1933 and 1945
was a perpetual obstacle to coherent planning and positive action by
Hitler's opponents.

What is the place of the Opposition to Hitler in German history?
This is a complex question and one's answer to it is influenced by a
number of factors. Here are some of them.

The story of the Opposition is little understood in Germany and
barely known at all outside Germany. One reason is that the
survivors of the Opposition have shown what seems at first sight a

curious unwillingness to talk about their work, their comrades and associates who died, their former hopes and aims. Both Schlabrendorff and Bussche use the phrase 'my well-known reserve' in connection with many aspects of past history. They seem almost to feel a sense of guilt at still being alive when so many of their friends perished. They are still, in some degree, oppressed by the feeling of failure, in an undertaking so sweeping and so audacious.

A man like Gerstenmaier (of the Evangelical opposition) is unapproachable on the subject of the work of the Opposition, although in his case the main reason may be that he does not want a controversial issue to unsettle the calm, opaque, almost indecently smug atmosphere of the Bonn Republic. General Hans Speidel, Rommel's Chief of Staff, who shared his chief's determination to bring the war to an end and save the German nation from destruction, barely mentioned his own part in the conspiracy in his memoirs.

A second factor at present affecting consideration of the part of the German Opposition is the readiness of bogus 'resisters' to climb on to the band-wagon. All sorts of unknown Germans hid Jews and other people who were being persecuted by Hitler, carried out small acts of kindness to anti-Nazis, spoke their minds whenever they dared about what they believed to be wrong. Such people have often claimed no credit for their actions. But the reverse has often been true of Germans who had no reason or right to claim any credit at all.

A particularly flagrant case was that of Dr. Hans Globke, the Secretary of State in Dr. Adenauer's Chancellery from 1953 to 1963. Dr. Globke wrote the commentary for the atrocious Nuremberg 'Racial Laws' of 1935–6, which were directed against the Jews and were ruthlessly implemented. The Racial Law laid down, for instance, extreme penalties for Jews marrying 'Aryan' Germans or having extra-marital relations with them, and forced German Jews to take 'Jewish-sounding' names. The laws protected 'German Blood and German Honour' and provided an ostensibly 'legal' basis for the frightful persecutions which followed. Dr. Globke, then, as nearly thirty years later, was a tirelessly efficient civil servant punctilious in carrying out his orders without question or delay.

Since the war Globke has on several occasions sought to explain his actions during the Nazi era. His claim that he tried to 'waterdown' the Racial Laws is of dubious value, for the Nazi persecutions of the Jews could not conceivably have been worse. His claim that he gave occasional advice and help to individual Jews may be justified. Indeed, he may have been sorry for them. And who had more reason to be than the man who had played a big part in codifying the precedural side of their persecution?

But in 1963 Globke allowed the story to be circulated that he had really been a member of the Opposition to Hitler all the time, and had only stayed in his office in the Nazi Ministry of the Interior in order to produce information for the Beck-Goerdeler group! The story was at once denied by various associations of former members of resistance groups against Nazism. All that the story succeeded in doing was casting a slur on the genuine Opposition, and a worse slur on Dr. Adenauer's Chancellery.

Only slightly less damaging was the effort in 1962 of General Adolf Heusinger, the Inspector-General of the West German *Bundeswehr* and since then the German delegate to N.A.T.O. headquarters, to identify himself with the Opposition to Hitler. Heusinger was the officer reading his report of the overall military situation in the Rastenburg headquarters when Stauffenberg's bomb exploded. Heusinger was Chief of Operations Branch of the Wehrmacht at the time. He read his report standing immediately next to Hitler. His report, but for a wildly optimistic forecast that the American and British armies could be contained in the Cotentin Peninsula in Normandy, was a gloomy and realistic document.

Heusinger, manifestly, had no knowledge of the bomb-plot—a curious circumstance for a man who eighteen years afterwards claimed to have been a member of the Opposition. Shortly after the war Heusinger wrote a book—in question-and-answer form—which dealt with the problem of resistance to Hitler in Germany. It was a dull, abstract piece of argument, and about the only conclusion that Heusinger reached was that Germans who resisted had as much right to do so as Germans who did not resist had for taking an exactly opposite view and line of action. Heusinger, according to at least one authoritative source, was approached by the conspirators during the war. But he could not see his way to taking an active part in the opposition to Hitler.

General Heinz Guderian, who pledged his unswerving loyalty to Hitler after July 1944, and who was accordingly appointed Chief of the General Staff, has made pointed references to so-called 'resisters' who tried to climb on to the band-wagon after the war and who had done no more than 'whisper in corners'. This is true enough. although his own record was by no means as impeccable as he made out. Several attempts were made to win him over to the conspiracy, and he learnt plenty about it. In one of the two arrogantly offensive books which Guderian wrote after the war, *Memoirs of a Soldier*, he admitted to having heard only on July 18 that Kluge was contemplating a cease-fire on the Western Front. According to his own lights, Guderian betrayed his Fuehrer by not disclosing to him what he knew.

There was a noticeable reluctance on the part of most Germans after the war to accord due credit to the Opposition. At one stage, indeed, it looked as if their manful efforts to overthrow the Nazi regime would be used in order to invent a new 'Stab in the Back' legend. This was especially apparent in Western Germany in the 1950–3 period when, in defiance of the occupying powers and the newly established Federal Government, ex-Nazis once again began to strut the political stage, brazenly unrepentant and spouting the sentiments of Josef Goebbels. Chief among them was Otto Remer, posing as the saviour of Germany in 1944 and claiming that he was 'once again ready to bring the German people to reason'.

Remer demanded the rejection of the men of July 20 and everything that they had stood for. They were mainly traitors to their country, he told large and enthusiastic audiences, and had been in foreign pay. Had they succeeded in overthrowing Hitler, the Russians would have overrun the whole of Germany in no time. Another line of Remer's was that 'ten thousand brave German S.S. men are still sitting in French prisons'. He was violently anti-Western as well as anti-Communist, and produced the ludicrous statement that Dr. Adenauer had signed the Petersberg Agreement with the Western Powers (it was an important step on the road to an independent and sovereign Federal Republic) to ensure that coal would be everlastingly scarce in Germany!

Remer's Socialist Reichs Party never gained much support outside Land Lower Saxony. Even his own followers thought less in terms of propagating a Nazi revival than of their narrow, jingoistic form of nationalism. They wanted an alibi for all Germans who had fought to the end for Hitler. In March 1952 Remer was tried by a Brunswick court for slandering Hitler's opponents. Members of the court received threatening letters, stamped with a Gestapo seal, and *Femegerichte*, secret courts modelled on those of the Middle Ages, sentenced Remer's judges to death (they did nothing to implement their sentences, in contrast to the similarly revived *Femegerichte* of the 1920s). Letters poured in to German newspapers, claiming that men like Oster and Canaris were traitors.

The feeling aroused against the Opposition died down when Remer fled to Egypt. During the next decade there were periodic outbursts of neo-Nazi recrimination and hate, but never again anything so serious. Most Germans, indeed, decided to sit on the fence as far as the Nazi versus anti-Nazi controversy was concerned, and simply try to expunge the past from their minds. Many of them fell back on the opiate of such books as *I was Hitler's Driver* and *With Goebbels to the End*. There was an avalanche of crypto-Nazi literature, and the published letters of Rudolf Hess and Joachim von Ribbentrop sold much better than many books on the German Opposition.

Although this spate of crypto-Nazi literature was beginning to slacken by 1955, there have been dangerous and disturbing books published in Germany since then. Possibly the worst was the so-called *Kaltenbrunner Reports*, published in the summer of 1961. Ernst Kaltenbrunner was the head of the Nazi security services at the time of the July 1944 conspiracy, and his reports were compiled from the 'evidence' extracted from the imprisoned conspirators by torture and threat. This thoroughly unfortunate book was published by the Seewald Verlag of Stuttgart, and edited by K. H. Peter.

In reality, there was no real editing at all; the reports were reproduced as seemingly truthful documents. They contained such 'facts' as that Beck sweated terribly every night for some time before the July 1944 bomb-attempt (denoting a bad conscience or merely weak nerves?), Olbricht had forgotten how to load a pistol, Witzleben read schoolboy-literature, and a certain Major von Leonrod had to ask his Catholic father-confessor whether it was 'right' to oppose a tyrant. The reports contained barbed references to the conspirators' consumption of alcohol, cigarettes and petrol—an obvious effort to smear them.

Peter, the 'editor', stated in a foreword that the 'martyrdom of the rebels on the gallows was no greater and no lesser a sacrifice than the soldier's death of those who were true to their oath'. This would put Stauffenberg on a par with the thugs of the S.S. It is deplorable that, sixteen years after the end of the war, documents like the *Kaltenbrunner Reports* should fall into the wrong hands and be so grievously misused.

Not until July 1959 did the new West German armed forces of the *Bundeswehr* pay official tribute to Hitler's opponents. Then, at long last, General Heusinger published an order of the day on July 20, 1959: 'The act of 20 July 1944—an act directed against wrong and unfreedom—is a shining light in Germany's darkest hour.' At long last, again, a *Bundeswehr* spokesman explained the *Bundeswehr* view of the conspiracy on July 20, 1960. He said that a certain reticence remained advisable, in that it gave the officers and the men of the *Bundeswehr* time to talk things over. This enabled 'a true public opinion to develop in the *Bundeswehr*'.

In 1960, too, the new Inspector General of the *Bundeswehr*, General Foertsch, had this to say: 'The men of July 20 were in the true German military tradition. They understood obedience, loyalty and duty as they should be understood and as we too wish to understand them: as obligations whose meaning rests only on moral and religious ties. . . . They have taught us to think deeply.' In 1961 Dr. Adenauer paid a tribute to the members of the Foreign Office who resisted Hitler, and a plaque was unveiled to them in the Foreign Ministry in Bonn. On it were the names of eleven people executed by the Nazis.

In 1960 General Foertsch admitted that the oath to Hitler had never been valid, after Hitler had forsaken legality. It can safely be adduced from this that the oath was never valid at all. This statement virtually ended an age-old controversy, conducted with German thoroughness and, it must be admitted, with a certain Germanic ponderousness. General von Seeckt had laid down the maxim for the 100,000-strong Reichswehr: 'The oath is to the constitution, and not to the person of the President at the time.' Hitler reversed tradition on August 2, 1934, immediately after Hindenburg's death, when he insisted that the oath should be taken to him personally. The legality of such an ordinance, issued by a dictator, was doubtful.

Hitler, at all events, failed to fulfil his obligations to his own subjects, and could not expect them to go on fulfilling an enforced obligation to him. Nearly twenty years after the war the German people had come in general to the conclusion that the actions of Hitler's opponents were justified, in that they followed the promptings of their individual consciences and their moral judgement. Still regarded as debatable were the warnings given by Oster to Norway and Holland of impending German invasion. Oster, many Germans continued to feel, could have done everything else possible to frustrate Hitler's designs—short of betraying military secrets. Such Germans may forget that Oster's warnings were not given to countries with whom Germany was at war, but to friendly neighbours who had every desire to remain neutral.

The Foertsch statement was one sign that the Opposition should, in time, be accorded its rightful place in German history by the Germans. This will, of course, remain difficult as long as Germany is divided. For the resisters were the last Germans who were able to fight in the true interests of their whole country. At the same time many of them were the best kind of nationalists whom opposition to Hitler turned down the strait and narrow road to humanity, reason and enlightenment. Germans—even if they are notoriously slow to evaluate the lessons of their country's past—must become increasingly aware of the virtues of Hitler's opponents, their defence of morality and tradition, their ready self-sacrifice, their grimly won knowledge of the historical value of their gesture.

Which of the Hohenzollerns laid down their lives in 1918 with such a total lack of hesitation? Which of the Nazi leaders did so in 1945? In 1918 nobody; in 1945 only Josef Goebbels. Himmler swallowed a poison capsule only after capture. Goering committed suicide only after his trial in Nuremberg as a major war-criminal had brought a death-sentence. For the 'big' Nazis there was no genuine ideal for which they could lay down their lives. The 'little' Nazis often died senselessly and uselessly, fighting to the last under orders, glum, insensate automata.

Germans may increasingly tend to remind themselves, in addition, of the immense loss to their country caused by the deaths of so many of Hitler's enemies. For men of outstanding talents and integrity, proven efficiency and ideas, were murdered by the Nazis between July 1944 and May 1945—some of them during the very last days of the war, and with the express purpose of preventing them from serving a non-Nazi, post-war Germany. Surely these twelfth-hour murders were among the worst of the Nazis' crimes, carried out in a mist of *Goetterdaemmerungsgeist*—a crazy compound of a spirit of revenge, a sense of unpardonable guilt, and an unregenerate, suicidal readiness to collaborate in the extinction of the German race!

How valuable would Leber, Haubach, Reichwein have been to the post-war German Social Democratic Party! How useful as administrators would Goerdeler and Popitz have proved, and how much they could have done to perpetuate a solid and decent conservative tradition in a Germany which today has no conservative party! Stauffenberg's vibrant personality, von Hassell's experience and wit, Bonhoeffer's sheer moral worth would surely have found apt expression and employment in the Federal Republic. And there was so much, in the matter of jogging the national conscience, that the 'Kreisauers' could have done.

One historian of the Opposition, Gisevius, had this to say at the end of his book: 'German guilt does exist; it is a reality. It cannot be cast off upon a collective group . . . All of us, and not only the Nazis, strayed into dangerous, evil ways. We were guilty of failure to understand, of wilful blindness, of misguided obedience, of paltry compromising, of exaggerated caution or of persistent shirking of logical conclusions.' This is, in a nutshell, the picture of German failure between 1933 and 1945.

To this moral judgement on the German people as a whole von Kessel had this to add about the men of the German Opposition: 'My friends loved their nation; therefore they wanted to free it from the grip of thieves and murderers. They were pledged to the spirit of the Western world; therefore they wanted to reawaken that spirit, in us and in our neighbours. They worshipped God; therefore they strove in righteous indignation against evil.'

What can one add to this? Perhaps only this, that the resistance of Germans to Hitler must not be allowed to have been in vain. It could not wipe out the horrors of the Nazi regime; nor could it even compensate for those horrors. But it was the example of the exceptional in all mankind, and the special sign of hope for the German people. Much that was best in Germany was lost when Hitler's opponents died. But in their example, if it is truly understood, lies the prospect of the renewal of all that has ever been good in the German way of life. Only, the Germans must themselves understand this.

twelve

The Road Ahead for Germany

'People will not look forward to posterity, who never look backward to their ancestors.'

EDMUND BURKE, *Reflections on the Revolution in France*

NEARLY twenty years after the conspiracy and revolt of July 20, 1944, Dr. Eugen Gerstenmaier, one of the few survivors of the active Opposition to Hitler, gave an address to the Hebrew University of Jerusalem on the subject, 'Are the Germans changing?' Gerstenmaier, who at that stage had served for thirteen years as a member of the West German Bundestag and for more than half that time as President of that assembly, had this to say:

There had been a basic change in German politics. The Germans had modified their old idea of a national, sovereign State, and the free West German Republic had sought to integrate itself as far as possible in the European and Atlantic worlds. The Germans had rejected National Socialism and had accepted a 'liberal, constitutional state'.

Gerstenmaier went on: 'The danger for the Germans is neither the return of National Socialism in any form, nor a turning towards Communism or revenge. The internal danger for Germany is much more a spiritual and mental vacuum and the widespread illusion that this can be overcome by the maximum satisfaction of material needs. The external danger for Germany is the non-acceptance of a morally valid settlement by Soviet Russia.'

The external danger was, in fact, that the Soviet Union would keep Germany divided indefinitely, and so subject the German people to stresses which would prevent them from settling down to the peaceful, neighbourly relations with all nations which most Germans undoubtedly want. In his address Gerstenmaier noted that German

268

reunification must necessarily remain the primary national objective for any and every German government.

As President of the Bundestag and a member of the executive of the Christian Democratic Party which ruled the Federal Republic for the first fifteen years of its existence, Gerstenmaier had necessarily to be guarded in his appraisal and in expressing his worries about the 55,000,000 people of Western Germany and West Berlin. Of the spiritual vacuum he said that 'It arises from inner insecurity and lack of direction, and reveals itself as neglect of responsibility and indecision. The force is missing which gives impetus to personal action.' Indecision, rather than cynicism, was the problem. But, on the credit side, the German people had become quieter, more rational, and far less nationalistic. With some satisfaction, Gerstenmaier noted that the Kreisau Circle, of which he had been a member, had envisaged a close partnership between Germany and her neighbours, and this partnership had become an established fact.

Gerstenmaier is one of the very few survivors of the Opposition to Hitler who has exercised a substantial influence on the development of the West German State and West German democracy. Inevitably he has taken some pride in his achievement and has been inclined to limit criticism which on one side could be healthy, but on the other could have a souring effect. Gerstenmaier is doubtless well aware that the Germans badly need to be reminded of their past, but equally badly need friendship and encouragement.

Others survivors of the German Opposition could often afford to be more outspoken than Gerstenmaier about the shortcomings of the West German State. Here are some of the views which have been expressed to me.

Fritz Erler, of the Social Democratic Party, was worried by present-day materialism in Germany, although he recognized that materialism has not been confined to Germany. He was worried that eighteen years after the war some ex-Nazis were still sitting in high office, and had stubbornly ignored the fact that they were not wanted in public life. But he agreed that ex-Nazis had exercised little influence in post-war Germany. He was worried, too, by what he called 'primitive anti-Communism'; it reminded him sometimes of the hate-campaigns of Dr. Josef Goebbels.

Rather naturally, Erler did not care for the 'identification with the

State' of a single party, the Christian Democratic. Nor did he feel that the patriarchal and authoritarian elements in Dr. Adenauer's fourteen years' Chancellorship had fostered the right kind of democratic thinking. Yet, on the whole, Erler felt that the Federal Republic had made a very fair start and that its citizens were being given a good chance of developing a rational existence and a rational view of life.

Erler's criticisms of West German democracy were those that one might expect. Other survivors of the Opposition felt much as he did. Inge Aicher-Scholl, for instance, equally disliked post-war materialism, violent anti-Communism and the return of ex-Nazis to places of authority. She was disappointed by the partial post-war failure to appreciate the aims of Hitler's enemies. This failure could not be made good by naming streets and youth hostels after them (often people living in such streets have not the faintest idea of the origin of their new names). Most of all, Inge Aicher-Scholl regretted that the liberal spirit which animated her friends of the 'White Rose' movement had not flowered in Germany after 1945.

Looking back at the 'old Germany', Albrecht von Kessel thought that the Federal Republic of today was 'too material, too provincial, too prosperous'. 'We try to bury our heads in the present,' he said, 'and shelve our responsibilities. We should take a more positive view of the community, be ready to do more for it and not wait for someone else to do everything for us.' Von Kessel was irritated by the survival in the older generation of the defeatist attitude of 'What can I do myself about it all?' but he was gratified to find that young Germans were increasingly ready to form their own views and stick up for them.

In general, he too was reasonably optimistic: 'We have a Federal State which is a going concern. Everyone should be grateful for that. Public opinion has become much livelier—look at the way in which both Adenauer and Strauss [Federal Minister of Defence until December 1962] have been forced to relinquish office! And democracy is at last becoming widely accepted and is growing its own roots here, for the first time in German history.'

Von dem Bussche and von Schlabrendorff who, unlike those already mentioned, tried to kill Hitler, have admitted to some feeling of disillusionment. 'We intended to get rid of Hitler, to beat him ourselves', Bussche told me. 'Instead, our job after all had to be left to the countries fighting against Germany.' Schlabrendorff was depressed by human selfishness—'Our people are not yet fully fledged citizens and they are not concerned with the life or well-being of our country. Practically no one is interested any longer in anything but his pocket-book, and his bank-account. Berlin was a focus for all Germans; Bonn is nothing.'

Although he was glad that the West German State had found friends in other countries, and had restored the bases of justice and freedom, Schlabrendorff was inclined to think that it required 'a crisis, at the very least a stern test, to shake Germans out of their lethargy and bring out the best in them'. To him, German reunification looked unattainable—save by the exercise of extreme patience. Humpty-Dumpty could only be put together again if the East German State (and the Communist Block as a whole) should manage to liberalize its political system—in fact, grow up.

Among the few survivors of the Opposition to take a severely critical view of the West German State have been Pastor Martin Niemoeller and Dr. Otto John. The latter clearly believed that there should have been a sweeping 'purge' of ex-Nazis in post-war Germany, conducted by Germans in the interest of the German people. The Germans should have prescribed their own clinical treatment, instead of leaving it to the occupying powers and then trying to wash their hands of it all. John's view was that the unrepentant ex-Nazis who clung on to important posts in Western Germany were a dangerous canker, infecting the otherwise healthy organs of the community.

John's strictures may not have been too wide of the mark. The popular view in Western Germany, ever since 1945, has been that the past should be forgotten and the sufferings of the German people should be held to cancel-out the gross wrongs perpetrated by the Nazis. John was one of a minority of West Germans who rejected this easy equation. In the event, the Federal Government has had to establish a central tracing-service to round up its untried war-criminals, to try and sentence these people, to weed ex-Nazis out of the judiciary, the civil service, the police and the teaching profession. This self-cleansing operation was far from complete by 1963; it might have been better if it had been carried out ten years earlier.

Niemoeller's views of the Federal Republic and of its efforts to seek out a middle road between abjectness and self-satisfaction were bound to be coloured by his distaste for all organized authority. Just after the war he appealed, in Stuttgart, for a nation-wide campaign to propagate the doctrine of corporate guilt and corporate repentance. He rejected West German rearmament and declared that the German people had no God-given right to self-determination and national unity. Niemoeller has perhaps never understood that a mood of repentance must be instilled into a people, but not thrust down its throat. It is a question whether this latter-day Isaiah has encouraged his nation to examine its conscience or, by his sheer bluntness, has induced it to shut its mind to the past.

Of much greater interest to me was the reflective view taken by Pastor Eberhard Bethge. He believed that the constructive purpose of the men of July 20, 1944, was partially obliterated by the code of blinkered anti-Communism adopted after the unsuccessful East German rising of June 17, 1953. The German people found an easy way out of awkward self-examination by fastening on to a new-old enemy, Russian Communism. Yet self-examination remained a stark necessity; otherwise the German people had no hope of working out its own salvation.

'When we sat in prison in 1944,' Bethge told me, 'we told ourselves that Hitler was just an illness to be overcome. Everything, we thought, would be all right as soon as he was gone. Now I know that the German nation has a long process of education ahead of it. We Germans are mightily efficient, but we do not have the necessary human instinct to regulate our efficiency. We have become too important again rather too quickly. For we are still immature. We have a democratic form of government, but democracy does not work in a practical way on the lower levels. Our lives suffer from a total lack of charm; we have still to give them a balance, a self-awareness, a sense of responsibility to our fellow-citizens.'

The survivors of the Opposition to Hitler are united in one thought—that their own German people will not at once appreciate their beliefs and motives. Certainly, they will not do so until they have studied and understood the lessons of the recent past and, preferably, of the last 100 years of German history. In his revealing book *Before and After Hitler*, Harry Pross has listed three distinct and deplorable German attitudes towards the Nazi era. The first is simply to wipe it out of memory, and live in the present. Pross calls this attitude 'the Fascism of the well-filled stomach'.

The second attitude is that 'fate'—in the grim shape of Hitler—was too much for the basically decent German nation. This attitude produces the refrain, '*Hitler war unser Unglueck*' ('Hitler was our misfortune'). Hitler, therefore, was a useful alibi for everything which went wrong.

The third attitude is that the Nazi Reich was 'unique' (in German, '*einmalig*'). This is probably the most damaging of the three, for it deliberately ignores the growth of German nationalism during the last 100 years, and refuses to see in Nazism the final eruption of national pride and appetite for power. Those Germans who adopt this attitude can go on explaining how right it was, for military reasons, that the Kaiser's armies marched into Belgium in 1914.

Pross has himself thrown out one or two reasons why the Nazi era should not be regarded as an isolated incident in German history. The German Empire in 1870 created the new German nation—and not the reverse. The German community was built up from then onwards on force and technical genius, and not on the idea of individual freedom. The Weimar Constitution of 1919 gave, on paper, greater freedom than was enjoyed by the citizens of other European countries; but the German citizen, in his outlook on life, the State and the powers-that-be (*die Obrigkeiten*) remained the least free European of the lot.

In present-day Germany Pross saw plenty of defects which are generally ignored. Democracy is a matter of taking the line of least resistance; government is carried out by technocrats and pressure groups; and even the Press only reflects their views and opinions and has none of its own. The average German, according to Pross, avoids all awkward controversy, so that nobody's feelings should be offended and a dull little utilitarian society can continue to tick-over.

With the obliteration of the political 'far left' and 'radical right', respectability is available for all men; and respectability is all. As for the Opposition to Hitler, its virtual extinction gave it no chance of replacing the Nazi élite with a 'counter-élite'. Instead, there has merely been a shake-down from a Prussian, North German, Protestant outlook to one which is equally traditional, but primarily Catholic, and South and West German. This, Pross thinks, is the Germany which has taken its place gladly in a Europe dominated by bureaucratic, egg-headed organizations—the sort of functional, soulless Europe which men like Moltke and Yorck expressly did *not* want.

This catalogue of defects suggests a depressing overall picture of the West German State to which over 50,000,000 Germans belong and which more than 70,000,000 Germans pin their hopes. It is, indeed, not at all hard to pick out defects in the West Germans. One ex-German who returned to his old homeland in 1962 was disturbed chiefly by the uneasy dissatisfaction which he found everywhere. People were complaining incessantly—about the Government ('What are they doing in Bonn with all our money?'), about the slowing-down of the economic miracle, about their personal troubles. This perpetual grumbling was interlaced with a peculiar, ventriloquist dummy's sort of talk—in which 'saying the right thing' was much more important than saying anything with a real meaning. This ex-German found all too many people completely bound up with their own selfish interests; to him modern Germany seemed to be without a soul. He was disturbed.

German youth, because it is moderate, modest and unassuming, usually receives more favourable mentions and opinions than any other section of German society. But youth too is tinctured with escapism and frustration. It is all very well to manage without ideals, but it is difficult to do without some feeling of trust and respect for the older generation. In millions of German homes there has been, post-war, an unbridged gap between the father who supported or tolerated the Nazi regime and the son who believes that the whole older generation contributed to the Nazi catastrophe.

German youth, at least, is proving that the old adage, 'The leopard cannot change his spots', can never be applied to the history of a nation. Even if lacking in sparkle and self-reliance, present-day West German youth has become more rational, slower to form opinions and more careful in expressing them, more conscious of the lives and interests of people living outside their own country, more concerned with a common-sense view of life than with slogans, mottoes and dreams of national might and glory. As for the leopard and his spots, who would have prophesied the metamorphoses, in the last two centuries, of the French and Spanish peoples—to mention only two? Or the changes, in this century, in China and Black Africa?

Nevertheless, the twelve years of the Nazi era will cast a long shadow far into the future and over the lives of many generations of Germans. Even when they have freed themselves from all sense of guilt—and the thirty-five-year-olds of 1963 could already do that with a clear conscience—Germans will continue to be aware of the outside world's attitude of accusation towards their country. The monstrousness of the Nazi régime will not grow less in men's minds.

Its practical consequences may still be painfully apparent in fifty years' time. The division of Germany may easily last as long as that; and as long as it lasts it will be a threat to world peace. For the division of a great nation in the heart of Europe will never offer a firm basis for peaceful coexistence. It will merely maintain East-West tension, and it may eventually induce Germans to forget that they can only redeem their country's good name by working their passage, by seeking peaceful relations with all nations, by asking little for themselves and offering friendship and co-operation to others. The strain of remaining patient is going to be very heavy for Germans of both East and West in the years ahead.

One would like, perhaps, to see a more positive democracy develop in Western Germany in the meantime. Professor Theodor Eschenburg, the Rector of Tuebingen University, has talked about the prevalence of *Gefaelligkeitsdemokratie*—meaning the acceptance of democracy as the line of least resistance. This has been accompanied by what German writers call the 'inner emigration'—the avoidance by anyone who reached years of discretion before 1945 of identifying himself with the Nazi era in any way. This attitude of mind was especially evident during the Eichmann trial in 1962. These two negative characteristics, according to one young German writer, Gudrun Tempel, go hand in hand with a third: 'Politics exist on a thin surface above a mass of non-political people who still, as of old, want to be told what to do.'

Here, then, dominated and irked by these three characteristics, is what one might call the German 'uncitizen'—a decent enough chap in his way, but someone whose mind is shuttered against a clear understanding of the past or hope for the future. 'The Germans', Gudrun Tempel wrote, 'are dangerous not because they are worse than other nations, but because within themselves they do not carry a deterrent against being bad. . . . The great danger of the Germans in a world so much in the balance is not the presence of anything, but the absence of almost everything definite, except faith in the god of efficiency.'

The picture of the part of the German people leading a free life may not be as bleak as these words suggest. Democracy was handed to the West Germans on a plate after 1945, they did not have to struggle to gain their political freedom. It would hardly be surprising if German democracy were a punier growth than is actually the case. In fact, it is putting out new roots continually, and the complacency and indifference of many West Germans cannot prevent custom and usage from strengthening the democratic system all the time. And a knowledge of the German past is being spread all the time, by newspaper articles and books, by films and television documentaries, by the frequent appeals of statesmen, churchmen and sociologists. A new start really is being made.

Even the most chronic sufferer from the current German disease of *Ueberbeschaeftigung*—the over-mobilization of time and energy in order to banish every uncomfortable thought and memory—cannot fail to be affected by an appeal like that of Bishop Dibelius of Berlin in April 1963: 'With us it has always been a case of: the Nazis were to blame! The neutrals were to blame! It was the Pope's fault! Naturally, our own Evangelical churches were to blame! And then, in the merest whisper, from a very few voices; perhaps, perhaps, all of us were to blame.'

A true understanding of the nature of the Opposition to Hitler is vitally important for all Germans who want to learn the lessons of their country's past, and what really went wrong in German history. For the Opposition represented that 'other Germany' which could not redeem, but has at least offset the German people's failure to play its proper part in Western civilization. It may well seem unbecoming and presumptuous for a foreigner to write this. Yet that too is necessary, for so many Germans seem still to be both ignorant of the Opposition and lacking gratitude to its members.

This is sad. To a nation which must continue to strive for self-fulfilment, the contribution of a Stauffenberg or a Tresckow may in time come to loom larger than that of a Seeckt or a Stresemann, perhaps even than that of an Adenauer or a Bismarck. For it was Hitler's German enemies who put the German nation, so brilliantly efficient, so talented and so lacking in the power of self-examination, on the right road to finding its own soul.

bibliography

Where American editions of foreign books have appeared, they and not the original or English editions are listed here. Books dealing in detail with the Opposition to Hitler are marked with asterisks.

Abshagen, Karl Heinz: *Canaris* (Stuttgart, 1949).

Andreas-Friedrich, Ruth: *Berlin Underground 1939–1945* (New York, 1947).

Assmann, Kaepitan zur See Kurt: *Deutsche Schicksals-Jahre* (Wiesbaden, 1950).

Best, Captain S. Payne: *The Venlo Incident* (London, 1950).

Birdsall, Paul: *Versailles, Twenty-five Years After* (New York, 1942).

Bluecher von Wahlstatt, Count Kurt: *Know Your Germans* (London, 1952).

Blumentritt, General Guenther: *Von Rundstedt* (London, 1952).

Bonhoeffer, Dietrich: *Prisoner for God: Letters and Papers from Prison* (New York, 1954).

Brandt, Willy: *My Road to Berlin* (New York, 1960).

Bruedigan, Heinz: *Wahrheit und Faelschung* (Frankfurt, 1959).

Bullock, Alan: *Hitler; a Study in Tyranny* (New York, 1953).

Choltitz, General Dietrich von: *Brennt Paris?* (Mannheim, 1960).

Colvin, Ian: *Master Spy* (New York, 1951).

D.D.R. Ministry of National Defense: *Die Geschichte der deutschen Antifaschistischen Widerstandsbewegung* (Berlin, 1958).

Dahrendorf, Gustav: *Julius Leber, ein Mann geht seinen Weg* (Frankfurt, 1952).

Dibelius, Bishop Otto: *Reden an eine gespaltene Stadt* (Stuttgart, 1961).

Donahoe, James: *Hitler's Conservative Opponents in Bavaria* (Leiden, 1961).

*Dulles, Allen W.: *Germany's Underground* (New York, 1947).

*Duncan-Jones, A. S.: *The Struggle for Religious Freedom in Germany* (London, 1948).

Einsiedel, Count Heinrich von: *I Joined the Russians* (New Haven, 1953).

*Fitzgibbon, Constantine: *The Shirt of Nessus* (New York, 1956).

Flicke, W.: *Rote Kapelle* (Duesseldorf, 1949).

Friedman, Philip: *Das Andere Deutschland* (Munich, 1960).

Frischauer, Willi: *Goering* (Boston, 1951).

Frischauer, Willi: *The Man Who Came Back* (London, 1958).

Gisevius, Hans Bernd: *To the Bitter End* (Boston, 1947).

Goerlitz, Walter: *The German General Staff* (New York, 1953).

Gollwitzer, Helmut: *Dying We Live* (New York, 1956).

Guderian, General Heinz: *Panzer Leader* (New York, 1952).

Guderian, General Heinz: *So geht es nicht!* (Heidelberg, 1952).

Hammer, Walter: *Theodor Haubach* (Frankfurt, 1955).

*Hassell, Ulrich von: *Diaries* (New York, 1947).

Henderson, Sir Nevile: *Failure of a Mission, Berlin 1937-1939* (New York, 1940).

Henk, Emil: *Die Tragoedie des 20 Juli* (Heidelberg, 1946).

*Herder Verlag: *Collected Reports and Documents* (Freiburg, 1961).

*Hermelink, Heinrich: *Kirche im Kampf* (Tuebingen, 1950).

Heusinger, General Adolf: *Befehl im Widerstreit* (Stuttgart, 1950).

Hitler, Adolf: *Mein Kampf* (Boston, 1940).

Hofer, Walther: *Die Diktatur Hitlers* (Konstanz, 1960).

Jonas, Klaus: *Life of Crown Prince William* (Pittsburgh, 1961).

Kennan, George F.: *Russia and the West Under Lenin and Stalin* (Boston, 1961).

Kogon, Eugen: *Theory and Practice of Hell* (New York, 1950).

Kohn, Hans: *The Mind of Germany* (New York, 1960).

Kordt, Erich: *Nicht aus den Akten* (Stuttgart, 1950).

Kordt, Erich: *Wahn und Wirklichkeit* (Stuttgart, 1947).

*Leber, Annedore: *Conscience in Revolt* (London, 1957).

*Leber, Annedore: *Das Gewissen Entscheidet* (Berlin, 1957).

Leber, Annedore: *Den Toten, immer lebendigen Freuden* (Berlin, 1946).

*Leber, Annedore and Freya, Countess Moltke: *Fuer und Wider* (Berlin, 1961).

Liddell Hart. Captain B. H.: *German Generals Talk* (New York, 1948).

Lilje, Bishop Hans: *The Valley of the Shadow* (Philadelphia, 1950).

Metzner Verlag: *Vollmacht des Gewissens* (Frankfurt, 1960).

*Moltke, Count Helmuth James graf von: *A German of the Resistance* (New York, 1946).

Morgan, Brigadier-General J. H.: *Assize of Arms* (New York, 1946).

Namier, Sir Lewis: *In the Nazi Era* (New York, 1952).

Olden, Rudolf: *Hitler* (New York, 1936).

Papen, Franz von: *Memoirs* (New York, 1952).

*Pechel, Rudolf: *Deutscher Widerstand* (Zurich, 1947).

Persecution of the Catholic Church in the Third Reich (London, 1942).

Prittie, Terence: *Germany Divided* (Boston, 1961).

Pross, Harry: *Vor und nach Hitler* (Freiburg, 1962).

Riess, Curt: *Josef Goebbels* (New York, 1948).

*Ritter, Gerhard: *German Resistance* (New York, 1959).

*Rothfels, Hans: *The German Opposition to Hitler* (New York, 1962).

Rowse, A. L.: *Appeasement* (New York, 1961).

Royce, Hans: *20 Juli 1944* (Bonn, 1952).

Salomon, Ernst von: *Fragebogen* (New York, 1954).

Schacht, Hjalmar: *Account Settled* (London, 1949).

Schellenberg, Walter: *Labyrinth* (New York, 1956).

*Schlabrendorff, Fabian von: *They Almost Killed Hitler* (New York, 1947).

Schmedemann, Walter: *Hamburgs Schicksal* (Hamburg, 1960).

Schneider, Reinhold: *Gedenkwort zum 20 Juli* (Freiburg, 1947).

*Scholl, Inge (Mrs. Otl Aicher): *Six Against Tyranny* (London, 1955).

Shirer, William L.: *Berlin Diary* (New York, 1941).

Shirer, William L.: *The Rise and Fall of the Third Reich* (New York, 1960).

Speidel, General Hans: *We Defeated Normandy* (London, 1951).

Steltzer, Theodor: *Von deutscher Politik* (Frankfurt, 1949).

Stroelin, Karl: *Verraeter oder Patrioten?* (Stuttgart, 1952).

Taylor, A. J. P.: *The Origins of the Second World War* (New York, 1962).

Thompson, Dorothy: *Listen, Hans* (Boston, 1942).

Trevor-Roper, Hugh: *The Last Days of Hitler* (New York, 1947).

Vogel, Heinrich: *Der Prediger von Buchenwald* (Berlin, 1953).

Vossler, Dr. K.: *Gedenkrede fuer Opfer der Universitaet Muenchen* (Munich, 1947).

*Weisenborn, Guenther: *Der Lautlose Aufstand* (Hamburg, 1954).

Weizsaecker, Ernst von: *Memoirs* (New York, 1951).

Wheeler-Bennett, Sir John: *Munich: Prologue to Tragedy* (New York, 1948).

Wheeler-Bennett, Sir John: *The Nemesis of Power* (New York, 1954).

Young, Brigadier Desmond: *Rommel the Desert Fox* (New York, 1950).

Zahn, Gordon: *German Catholics and Hitler's Wars* (New York, 1962).

*Zeller, Eberhard: *Geist der Freiheit* (Munich, 1954).

index

290